COOKS
INCORPORATED

Published by Miami Valley Health Foundation

Dayton, Ohio

Published by Miami Valley Health Foundation, 31 Wyoming Street, Dayton, Ohio 45409-2753

Proceeds from the sale of this book will benefit the Emergency and Trauma Center of Miami Valley Hospital,
serving the greater Miami Valley region.

Printed in the USA by Hammer Graphics, Inc., Piqua, Ohio
Typographical design by Graphic Impact, Kettering, Ohio. Cover and section art by Amy Duchesneau
City feature copy by the Jack Raymond Company, Inc., Edward F. McDougal, New York, New York
Direction and production by Maureen McDougal Willits, Kettering, Ohio

Library of Congress Catalog Card Number: 92-61200

ISBN: 0-9633527-0-9

First printing: September, 1992   15,000 copies

Cooks Incorporated

TABLE OF CONTENTS

Each chapter in Cooks Incorporated begins with a vignette about one of the many unique Miami Valley communities served by Miami Valley Hospital. We hope you enjoy reading about the area we call "home."

Cooks Incorporated

FOREWORD

Hospitality is a high point of the Miami Valley. We love to be with family and friends for birthdays and weddings, for festivals and sporting events, and for no reason at all. Food is a vital ingredient of all these occasions.

Cooks Incorporated showcases the talents of the Miami Valley region's outstanding cooks. Their recipes bring to mind thoughts of good times and good food shared with friends.

By purchasing this book, you are supporting Miami Valley Hospital's Emergency and Trauma Center, which offers the most comprehensive emergency care available in our region. The high quality services of this center, extended by our CareFlight air ambulance service, benefit people throughout the Miami Valley from St. Mary's south to Monroe and from Washington Courthouse to Richmond, Indiana.

Thank you for contributing to the enhancement of this healing and life-giving resource for all.

Let the cooking begin!

Thomas G. Breitenbach
President and Chief Executive Officer
Miami Valley Hospital, Dayton, Ohio

Dayton, Ohio

Dayton's reputation from its very inception in 1796 is one of meeting seemingly impossible challenges. When George Newcom set forth from Cincinnati, traveling the Great Miami River, it was in the face of dangerous flood warnings. With two other families, the Newcoms settled the area, and by the turn of the century the community boasted a school and a church. By 1810, the census recorded over 7,000 inhabitants in Montgomery County, nearly 400 residing in Dayton Township.

The convergence of three rivers – the Mad, the Miami and the Stillwater – was a major reason for settlement of the region, but learning to live peacefully with the Indians proved a far easier task than learning to live with rivers that continually overflowed their banks.

In 1913, torrential rains caused a flood with waters reaching second-story levels. Dayton's spirit of cooperation prevailed with a citizenry response that was immediate, heroic, and effective. Led by John Patterson, the Miami Conservancy District was formed, and the work of reconstruction began. Arthur Morgan was hired to design what became the nation's first comprehensive flood control project by constructing a series of "dry" dams. Dayton's project became the prototype for a number of other flood control projects, including that of the Tennessee Valley Authority.

One cannot talk about Dayton without acknowledging the creative genius of its inventors and scientists. The brilliance of people like Orville and Wilbur Wright, Charles "Boss" Kettering, Colonel Edward A. Deeds, and John H. Patterson fostered wholly new industries and spawned economic growth and prosperity.

Patterson's genius was founded in organization, the ability to see potential in the otherwise unremarkable, and a keen insight to salesmanship. In 1884 he obtained the rights to a machine with no apparent practical use. By 1911, the cash register had become one of the most essential tools of retailing with NCR, fondly referred to as "The Cash," recording the sale of its millionth machine.

The Wright brothers' first successful powered flight in 1903 and their development of the world's first practical airplane – the Wright Flyer III – earned Dayton the sobriquet "Birthplace of Aviation." Then in 1919, Floyd Smith helped men jump out of airplanes with his invention of the modern parachute!

Although Charles Kettering is noted for his invention of the self-starter, he is also responsible for the automobile ignition system and the development of leaded gasoline. His inventions revolutionized forever the auto industry. Kettering and Edward A. Deeds founded DELCO, now a division of General Motors.

The spirit of invention spread like a smile across the Dayton horizon. Unique ideas turned into valuable products. When Barrett Green invented microencapsulation, it opened the door to carbonless paper as well as timed-release medication. Some of Dayton's inventions added new capabilities to existing products, such as the ice cube tray and the frost proof refrigerator. Others have helped us enjoy the frivolous such as the ice cream cone and the mood ring, while some revolutionized whole industries. Picnickers can thank Ermal Fraze for the pull top found today on nearly every pop can in America. Handymen and women can remember Dayton every time they climb a step ladder!

Dayton's reputation for innovation extends to government. Dayton was the first major city to adopt the commissioner/manager form of municipal government. Its priority boards amplify the voice of the citizenry as a direct channel to city hall.

Dayton's neighborhoods are rich with ethnic, artistic, and cultural assets. Renovation programs are restoring many of the city's historical treasures, while community garden projects punctuate the city landscape. The *Festival of Neighborhoods* is proclaimed each year with colorful banners hung high above city streets. Dayton proudly acknowledges its three-time designation as an "All-American City," the latest in 1991.

A symbiotic relationship exists between Dayton and cities in the region. Together... they form partnerships for mutual benefit. Together... they promote a rich heritage of innovation, creativity, invention, and cultural diversity. Together... they provide an environment that accommodates the needs and dreams of all those who seek their own lifestyle. Together... they walk proudly with those they call neighbor.

Cooks Incorporated

SHRIMP RÉMOULADE

Preparation time: 10 minutes   *Serves: 16*

4 pounds large shrimp, cooked,
   peeled, deveined
2 Tablespoons celery, chopped
2 Tablespoons parsley, chopped
8 ounces Thousand Island dressing

1 teaspoon paprika
1 Tablespoon vinegar
1 Tablespoon lemon juice
1 Tablespoon horseradish
1 Tablespoon Worcestershire

1. Mix ingredients for sauce.

2. Place in a 9x12-inch dish.

3. Add shrimp.

4. Cover. Chill overnight.

5. Insert toothpicks in shrimps before serving.

SHRIMP-BACON BITES

Preparation time: 10 minutes   *Yield: 8*

1 cup shrimp, cleaned, cooked,
   deveined
½ clove garlic, slivered

½ cup chili sauce
8 to 10 slices bacon, cut into halves

1. Mix shrimp, garlic; pour chili sauce on mixture.

2. Cover; refrigerate several hours, stirring occasionally.

3. Fry bacon until partially cooked; drain.

4. Wrap each shrimp in bacon piece; secure with a toothpick. Place on a cookie
   sheet.

5. Broil 2-3 inches from heat for 3 minutes until bacon is crisp.

6. Serve immediately.

Also a good accompaniment for a soup and salad supper.

SHRIMP TOAST

Preparation time: 30 minutes   *Yield: 32*
Baking time: 10-15 minutes

2 green onions
1 clove garlic
1 thin slice fresh ginger root
1 egg white
1½ teaspoons cornstarch
1½ teaspoons dry sherry

1½ teaspoons salt
½ cup water chestnuts
½ pound raw shrimp, shelled,
     deveined
8 thin slices firm white bread
¼ cup butter or margarine

1. With a food processor, process first 3 ingredients until coarsely chopped
    (or mince by hand).

2. In processor, add egg white, cornstarch, sherry, salt; process a few seconds
    (or mix in by hand).

3. Add water chestnuts, shrimp; process with on and off bursts until finely
    chopped (or mince by hand and stir together).

4. Cut crusts from bread; butter both sides. Spread shrimp mixture on one side.

5. Cut each slice on the diagonal twice to make 4 triangles. Place on a baking sheet.

6. Bake, uncovered, at 375° for 10-15 minutes until bread is toasted.

May be made up to 8 hours ahead and refrigerated before baking.

CRABMEAT CANAPÉS

Preparation time: 10 minutes   *Yield: 36*

1 6½-ounce can crabmeat, flaked
¼ teaspoon prepared mustard
⅛ teaspoon cayenne pepper
¼ teaspoon lemon juice
1 Tablespoon prepared horseradish

2 Tablespoons chili sauce
     (Del Monte suggested)
Toasted bread, cut into
     small rounds
Parsley or chives

1. Mix all ingredients. Chill.

2. Serve on toasted bread rounds.

3. Garnish with parsley or chives.

CLAM CASINO MIX

Preparation time: 30 minutes   *Yield: 24*

¼ cup margarine
½ pound bacon, finely diced
1 green pepper, finely diced
1 red pepper, finely diced
½ large onion, finely diced
1 Tablespoon shallot, finely diced
½ teaspoon fresh garlic, chopped

Juice from ½ lemon
Dash Worcestershire sauce
½ cup bread crumbs
Pepper to taste (optional)
Salt to taste (optional)
24 clams
Margarine

1. Melt margarine over medium heat.
2. Add bacon; cook until almost done, not crisp.
3. Add peppers, onion, shallot; cook 5 minutes until onions are translucent.
4. Add garlic. Cook 2 more minutes; add lemon juice, Worcestershire.
5. Slowly add bread crumbs until desired consistency is obtained.
6. Season with pepper, salt, if desired.
7. Preheat broiler.
8. Cover clams on the half shell. Place on a cookie sheet.
9. Dot with margarine.
10. Broil on the lower oven rack until stuffing begins to brown.

Di Paolo's Restaurant
Oxford, Ohio

Prepare clams by washing thoroughly. Steam, covered, in 2 inches of water just until clams can be opened with a knife blade. Drain clams before covering with casino mix.

BRAUNSCHWEIGER BALL

Preparation time: 15 minutes + chilling   *Serves: 20*

1   pound braunschweiger
3   ounces cream cheese
1   teaspoon onion, grated
1   teaspoon Worcestershire sauce
1   teaspoon prepared mustard

1   teaspoon mayonnaise
3   ounces cream cheese
1   Tablespoon milk
Parsley, chopped
Paprika

1.   Mix first 6 ingredients until smooth.

2.   Place in a bowl lined with plastic wrap. Chill overnight.

3.   Remove from bowl. Shape into a ball.

4.   Mix cream cheese with milk. Spread over ball.

5.   Dust with parsley, paprika; serve with crackers.

Surround with holly leaves for the holidays.

GLAZED SAUSAGE BITES

Preparation time: 20 minutes   *Yield: 40-50*
Baking time: 15-20 minutes

1   pound sausage (Bob Evans Hot
    suggested)
1   egg
½   cup saltine cracker crumbs (about
    14 crackers)
⅓   cup milk

½   teaspoon sage
½   cup water
¼   cup catsup
2   Tablespoons brown sugar
1   Tablespoon vinegar
1   Tablespoon soy sauce

1.   Mix first 5 ingredients thoroughly.

2.   Shape into bite-size balls.

3.   Place on a jelly roll pan.

4.   Bake at 350° for 15-20 minutes until thoroughly cooked.

5.   Mix remaining ingredients for sauce.

6.   Add sausage balls to sauce; simmer 10 minutes.

A nice change from the usual meatballs. These freeze well.

TUXEDO TENDERLOIN APPETIZER

Preparation time: 10 minutes + marinating　　　　　　　　*Serves: 10*
Roasting time: 35-50 minutes

5 to 8 pounds tenderloin of beef
Black pepper, coarsely ground
2 cloves fresh garlic, crushed

1½ to 2 cups soy sauce
3 to 4 strips bacon
1 medium onion, sliced
Leaf lettuce

1. Place roast in plastic bag; sprinkle with pepper. Mix garlic, soy sauce. Pour over roast.

2. Marinate in refrigerator overnight. Turn bag over 1 or 2 times.

3. Allow roast to come to room temperature.

4. Place strips of bacon on top.

5. Place meat on rack.

6. Pour marinade over meat.

7. Top with onion slices.

8. Preheat oven to 450°. Immediately reduce to 400°. Roast meat on the center oven rack for 35-50 minutes. Internal temperature of roast should be 135° for rare roast.

9. Cool.

10. Slice thin.

11. Garnish with red or green leafy lettuce.

12. Serve chilled with tiny rolls or party rye.

Save the marinade to use as a base for stir-fry with vegetables, or add sherry and use as a sauce to serve over beef.

Also good as an entrée sliced 2 inches thick.

PIROGI (LATVIAN MEAT PASTRY)

Preparation time: 3 ½hours   *Serves: 20-30*
Baking time: 30 minutes

5 cups flour	4 eggs, slightly beaten
¾ cup sugar	2 pounds bacon, uncooked, diced
1 teaspoon salt	1 pound ham, cooked, diced
2 packages dry yeast	1 large onion, diced
¼ cup warm water	1 Tablespoon ground black pepper
¾ cup warm milk	¼ cup Dijon mustard
1 cup butter	2 eggs, beaten with water

1. Mix flour, sugar, salt together.

2. Dissolve yeast in water; add to dry mixture.

3. Dissolve butter in warm milk; add to flour mixture. Mix well.

4 Add eggs to flour-butter mixture. Mix well.

5. Let dough rise until double.

6. Combine bacon, ham, onion for filling.

7. Break off from dough 50-60 pieces (cherry tomato size) for individual pirogis.

8. Flatten each dough piece to 3-4 inches in diameter. (Dough will be thin). Place on a cookie sheet.

9. Spread mustard on dough.

10. Place 1 heaping teaspoon filling mixture in center of each. Fold bottoms together.

11. Brush with egg wash.

12. Bake at 250° for 30 minutes.

Freezes well. Reheat frozen pastries at 250° for 30 minutes.
Great for a pre-Octoberfest party.
Also good for lunch with a cup of bouillon.

PISTACHIO CHICKEN APPETIZER

Preparation time: 20 minutes   *Yield: 30*
Baking time: 10-15 minute

1 whole chicken breast, skinned, boned
⅓ cup flour
¼ teaspoon salt
⅛ teaspoon pepper
1 egg, beaten

1 Tablespoon milk
⅔ cup shelled pistachios, finely chopped
3 Tablespoons butter or margarine
1 Tablespoon lime juice
French bread rounds

1. Cut chicken into 1-inch squares.
2. Combine flour, salt, pepper; shake chicken in seasoned flour.
3. Combine egg, milk; dip floured chicken into egg mixture.
4. Roll in pistachios. Chill 1 hour.
5. Melt butter with lime juice in a shallow baking pan.
6. Place chicken bits in pan; turn once to coat with butter.
7. Bake at 350° for 10-15 minutes until tender, lightly brown.
8. To serve, place one piece of chicken on each round of bread.

GOLDEN CHICKEN NUGGETS

Preparation time: 25 minutes   *Yield: 48*
Baking time: 10 minutes

4 whole chicken breasts, skinned, boned
½ cup unseasoned fine dry bread crumbs
¼ cup grated Parmesan cheese

1 teaspoon salt
1 teaspoon thyme
1 teaspoon basil
½ cup butter or margarine, melted

1. Cut each breast into 12 nuggets, about 1½-inches square.
2. Combine bread crumbs, cheese, seasonings, herbs.
3. Dip chicken nuggets into melted butter, then into crumb mixture.
4. Place in single layer on ungreased baking sheets lined with foil.
5. Bake at 400° for 10 minutes.

May be served hot or cold.

TOASTED MUSHROOM ROLLS

Preparation time: 30 minutes   *Yield: 42*

½ pound mushrooms, minced
¼ cup butter, melted
3 Tablespoons flour
¾ teaspoon salt

1 cup light cream
2 teaspoons chives, minced
1 teaspoon lemon juice
21 slices white bread

1. Sauté mushrooms 5 minutes in melted butter.

2. Blend in flour, salt.

3. Stir in cream; cook until thick.

4. Add chives, lemon juice. Cool.

5. Remove bread crusts. Thin slices by rolling with a rolling pin.

6. Spread with mushroom mixture. Roll up.

7. Cut each roll in half. Place on baking sheets.

8. Toast on all sides at 400°.

May be frozen before cutting and toasting.

NUTRIENT ANALYSIS (Per Serving)

Carbohydrate .... 6 grams
Protein .... 1 gram
Fat .... 3 grams
Calories .... 50 (54% from fat)
Cholesterol .... 7 milligrams
Sodium .... 90 milligrams

Cooks Incorporated

TOASTED MUSHROOM ROLLS - LIGHT OPTION

Preparation time: 30 minutes   *Yield: 42*

½ **pound mushrooms, minced**
2 **Tablespoons margarine, melted**
3 **Tablespoons flour**
1 **cup evaporated skim milk**

2 **teaspoons chives, minced**
1 **teaspoon lemon juice**
2 **Tablespoons sherry**
  (for moisture)
21 **slices white bread**

1. Sauté mushrooms in melted margarine 5 minutes.

2. Blend in flour.

3. Stir in milk; cook until thick.

4. Add chives, lemon juice, sherry. Cool.

5. Remove bread crusts. Thin slices by rolling with a rolling pin.

6. Spread slices with prepared mixture. Roll up.

7. Cut each roll in half. Place on baking sheets.

8. Toast on all sides in a 400° oven.

NUTRIENT ANALYSIS (Per Serving)

Carbohydrate .... 6 grams
Protein .... 2 grams
Fat .... 1 gram
Calories .... 39 (23% from fat)
Cholesterol .... 0.2 milligram
Sodium .... 48 milligrams

MUSHROOM PUFFS OR ROLL-UPS

Preparation time: 15 minutes   *Serves: 6-8*

½ pound mushrooms, finely
   chopped
8 ounces cream cheese
1 Tablespoon onion, grated

2 egg yolks
Garlic salt
½ teaspoon baking powder
1¼ teaspoons beau monde seasoning
Toast rounds or thinly sliced bread

Puffs on Toast

1. Sauté mushrooms, onions.

2. Mix with remaining ingredients.

3. Place on toast rounds on a baking sheet.

4. Broil until lightly browned.

Mushroom Roll-ups

1. Remove crust from thinly sliced bread.

2. Spread mixture on bread.

3. Roll as a jelly roll. Freeze.

4. Cut each roll into 3 or 4 pieces.

5. Melt 1 cup butter or margarine.

6. Dip rolls into melted butter. Place on a cookie sheet.

7. Bake at 350° for 25 minutes.

REUBEN DIP

Preparation time: 15 minutes
Baking time: 20 minutes

Serves: 20

12 ounces chipped corned beef
   (deli or Carl Buddig suggested)
8 ounces shredded Swiss cheese
8 ounces shredded Cheddar cheese
1 16-ounce can sauerkraut, drained

¾ cup mayonnaise (Hellman's
   suggested)
2 Tablespoons horseradish
2 Tablespoons Thousand Island
   dressing

1.   Chop, mix first 4 ingredients.

2.   Mix remaining ingredients; add to corned beef mixture.

3.   Place in a flat 9 or 10-inch quiche dish.

4.   Bake at 325° on the center oven rack for 20 minutes until cheese melts.

5.   Serve with rye crackers or party rye bread.

A great dip or spread for pre-game parties.

SAUERKRAUT BALLS

Preparation time: 30 minutes

Yield: 36

8 ounces sausage, crumbled
¼ cup onion, chopped
1 14-ounce can sauerkraut, drained,
   chopped
2 Tablespoons bread crumbs
1 3-ounce package cream cheese
2 Tablespoons parsley, chopped

1 teaspoon prepared mustard
¼ teaspoon garlic salt
Dash pepper
1 egg
3 Tablespoons milk
⅓ cup flour
1¼ cups bread crumbs
Cooking oil for frying

1.   Brown sausage, onion. Drain.

2.   Add next 7 ingredients; blend well. Chill for firmness.

3.   Beat egg, milk; set aside.

4.   Shape chilled mixture into small balls. Coat with flour.

5.   Dip into egg mixture, then bread crumbs.

6.   Deep fry at 400° until golden brown.

SPINACH SPIRALS

Preparation time: 30 minutes   *Yield: 50*

2 10-ounce packages frozen
   chopped spinach
6 scallions or green onions, chopped
1 package dry ranch dressing
   (Hidden Valley suggested)

1 cup sour cream
1 cup mayonnaise
1 18-ounce package 9-inch flour
   tortillas.

1. Cook spinach according to package directions. Drain.

2. Squeeze excess moisture from spinach; pat dry with paper towels.

3. Mix spinach with remaining ingredients.

4. Spread mixture on tortillas. Roll tortillas.

5. Cover. Refrigerate overnight or at least 8 hours.

6. Cut into 1-inch rolls.

NUTRIENT ANALYSIS (Per Serving)

Carbohydrate .... 4 grams
Protein .... 1 gram
Fat .... 6 grams
Calories .... 63 (89% from fat)
Cholesterol .... 5 milligrams
Sodium .... 121 milligrams

SPINACH SPIRALS - LIGHT OPTION

Preparation time: 30 minutes   *Yield: 50*

2 **10-ounce packages frozen chopped spinach**
6 **scallions or green onions, chopped**
1 **package light ranch dressing mix (Good Seasons suggested)**

1 **cup light sour cream**
1 **cup fat-free mayonnaise (Kraft suggested)**
1 **18-ounce package 9-inch corn tortillas**

1. Cook spinach according to package directions. Drain.

2. Squeeze excess moisture from spinach; pat dry with paper towels.

3. Mix spinach with remaining ingredients.

4. Spread mixture on tortillas. Roll tortillas.

5. Cover. Refrigerate overnight or at least 8 hours.

6. Cut into 1-inch rolls.

NUTRIENT ANALYSIS (Per Serving)

Carbohydrate .... 5 grams
Protein .... 1 gram
Fat .... 1 gram
Calories .... 28 (30% from fat)
Cholesterol .... 1 milligram
Sodium .... 144 milligrams

CAVIAR BULLSEYE

Preparation time: 30 minutes   *Serves: 12*

8 ounces whipped cream cheese
3 Tablespoons sour cream
¼ teaspoon garlic salt
2 Tablespoons mayonnaise
4 hard-boiled eggs

4 to 5 scallions, green and white,
   chopped
½ cup parsley, finely chopped
2 ounces black caviar
4 ounces red caviar

1. Mix first four ingredients until smooth; sprinkle evenly in a 9 or 10-inch tart dish with sides.

2. Cut eggs in half. Remove yolks; chop fine. Chop whites separately.

3. Put a mound of black caviar in center of tart dish.

4. Make a circle of each ingredient around the caviar in this order: egg yolks, scallions, red cavier, egg whites, parsley.

A beautiful presentation.

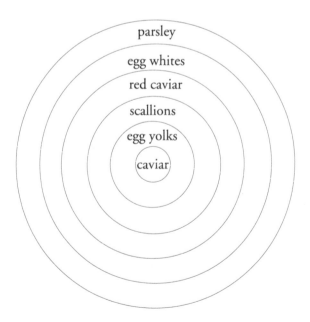

COWBOY CAVIAR

Preparation time: 20 minutes   *Serves: 12*

1 15-ounce can black beans, rinsed, drained
1 4-ounce can ripe olives, drained, chopped
¼ cup small onion, finely chopped
1 clove garlic, minced
2 Tablespoons canola oil
2 Tablespoons lime juice
¼ teaspoon salt
¼ teaspoon red pepper flakes, crushed
¼ teaspoon ground cumin
⅛ teaspoon pepper
1 8-ounce package cream cheese, softened
2 hard boiled eggs, peeled, separated, chopped
1 green onion, including stem, sliced

1. Combine first 10 ingredients. Refrigerate 4 hours or overnight.

2. When ready to serve, drain bean mixture.

3. Mix 2 Tablespoons marinade with cream cheese until blended.

4. Spread cream cheese mixture on serving plate.

5. Spoon bean mixture over cream cheese evenly.

6. Arrange eggs on bean mixture in a ring around edge of plate.

7. Sprinkle with green onion.

8. Serve with tortilla chips or crackers.

PROSCIUTTO-TOPPED BRIE WITH DRIED TOMATOES

Preparation time: 20 minutes
Baking time: 12-18 minutes

Serves: 4

1 8-ounce Brie round or wedge, chilled

3 Tablespoons sun-dried tomatoes packed in oil, drained, finely chopped

1 ounce prosciutto, thinly sliced, finely chopped

1 Tablespoon oil from tomatoes

1. Cut Brie in half horizontally. Set 1 half, cut side up, in a buttered shallow baking dish slightly larger than cheese.

2. Evenly distribute chopped tomatoes over cut cheese. Place other half of cheese on top, cut side down.

3. Mix prosciutto with oil; spread on top of cheese. Cover. Chill.

4. Bake uncovered at 350° for 12-18 minutes. Serve hot with crackers.

WARM BRIE WITH WINTER FRUIT

Preparation time: 30 minutes
Baking time: 25-30 minutes

Serves: 16-20

¾ cup dates, pitted, chopped
1 apple, peeled, cored, diced
1 small ripe pear, peeled, cored, diced
½ cup currants

½ cup pecans, chopped
½ cup rosé wine
1 wheel (2 pounds) ripe Brie, chilled
Toasted baguette slices, melba rounds or crackers

1. Mix fruits, pecans in a small bowl.

2. Pour wine over; allow fruit to soften approximately 2 hours.

3. Cut Brie in half to make 2 round layers. Place 1 layer, cut side up, in a shallow rimmed baking dish (quiche dish). Spread with 2¼ cups fruit mix.

4. Place remaining layer, cut side down, on fruit.

5. Spoon remaining fruit on top in center of cheese round.

6. Bake uncovered at 350° for 25-30 minutes. Spread on baguettes or crackers.

If made ahead, cover and chill filled cheese up to 2 days.

FOUR-CHEESE FOCACCIA

Preparation time: 30 minutes mixing; 2½ hours rising   *Yield: 35 squares*
Baking time: 35-45 minutes

2½ teaspoons active dry yeast
½ teaspoon sugar
1 cup warm water
3½ cups unbleached all-purpose flour
1 teaspoon salt
5 Tablespoons olive oil, divided
¾ cup freshly grated Parmesan cheese, divided

1 cup grated whole milk mozzarella
½ cup Gorgonzola, finely crumbled
1 cup fontina, grated
1 small onion, thinly sliced, separated into rings
Pepper to taste
1 teaspoon coarse salt

1. In the bowl of an electric mixer fitted with the paddle attachment, proof yeast with sugar in water 5 minutes until mixture is foamy.

2. Add flour, salt, 3 Tablespoons oil, ½ cup Parmesan cheese. Mix well.

3. Change to the dough hook. Knead dough 2 minutes until softened, slightly sticky.

4. Form dough into a ball. Place in an oiled bowl; turn to coat with oil. Cover with plastic wrap.

5. Let dough rise in a warm place for 1½ hours.

6. Punch dough down.

7. Press dough evenly into an oiled jelly roll pan. Cover loosely; set in a warm place for 1 hour.

8. In a bowl, stir together remaining Parmesan cheese, mozzarella, Gorgonzola, fontina, onion, pepper. Sprinkle mixture evenly over dough.

9. Drizzle remaining oil over surface; sprinkle with salt.

10. Bake at 400° for 35-45 minutes.

11. Cool in pan on a rack. Cut into squares; serve warm or at room temperature.

Dough may be prepared ahead through step 4. Cover, chill overnight. Let dough return to room temperature before proceeding with the recipe.

Dorothy Lane Market
Dayton, Ohio

ROQUEFORT CHEESE BALL

Preparation time: 15 minutes　　　　　　　　　　　*Yield: 2 1-pound balls*

2　8-ounce packages cream cheese, softened
1　3-ounce package cream cheese, softened
1　8-ounce package Old English cheese, softened

1　4-ounce package Roquefort cheese, softened
1　small onion, grated
¼　teaspoon garlic salt
1　cup pecans, crushed

1. Blend together all three cheeses.

2. Add onion, garlic salt.

3. Shape into 2 balls. Refrigerate.

4. When firm, roll in crushed pecans.

Creamy, easy to manage.

CREAMY ORIENTAL SPREAD

Preparation time: 90 minutes　　　　　　　　　　　*Serves: 12*

1　8-ounce package cream cheese
Soy sauce

Up to 3 dashes Tabasco sauce
2　Tablespoons margarine
1　Tablespoon sesame seeds

1. In a small dish, put enough soy sauce to cover half of cream cheese. Carefully stir in Tabasco sauce.

2. Soak cream cheese at least 45 minutes. Turn over; soak other side 45 minutes.

3. Melt margarine in a pie tin; put enough sesame seeds in tin to cover bottom.

4. Brown at 325-350° for a few minutes. Watch carefully.

5. Spread toasted seeds over cream cheese.

6. Serve with crackers.

Keeps well for weeks in the refrigerator or may be frozen. Wrap in foil after seeds cool.

CHEDDAR CHEESE SPREAD

Preparation time: 10-15 minutes   *Serves: 24*

¾ pound Cheddar cheese, grated
½ teaspoon dry mustard
2 Tablespoons parsley, chopped
2 Tablespoons onion, minced
1 Tablespoon butter, softened
⅛ teaspoon Tabasco sauce

⅛ teaspoon Worcestershire sauce
3 to 4 Tablespoons cocktail sauce
    (Del Monte suggested)
3 Tablespoons sherry
⅓ cup mayonnaise
Garnishes

1. Blend all ingredients. Chill.

2. Cut out shapes.

3. Cover cut-outs with foil; mound cheese spread to shape.

4. Decorate with olives, green pepper, corn chips, etc.

5. Place shaped cheese on crackers to serve.

Use your imagination to enhance the presentation. Shapes might include wreaths for Christmas, a bird for Thanksgiving, or musical notes for a recital.

TWO-WAY HORSERADISH CHEESE SPREAD

Preparation time: 11 minutes   *Serves: 20-30*

1 pound processed cheese (Velveeta
    suggested)
1 cup mayonnaise

4 ounces horseradish, well drained
Chips or crackers

1. Melt cheese over low heat, stirring in mayonnaise and horseradish.

2. Serve hot with chips for dipping, or let cool in serving container and serve with crackers.

Keeps refrigerated for several days. Reheat to serve as dip.

QUESADILLAS

Preparation time: 1½ hours   *Yield: 40 wedges*

1 **package ranch dressing mix**   ⅓ **cup chunky salsa**
   (Hidden Valley Original suggested)   3 **cups Monterey Jack cheese,**
¾ **cup mayonnaise**   **shredded**
⅓ **cup milk**   10 **10-inch flour tortillas**
                                              Vegetable oil

1. Blend together first 5 ingredients. Refrigerate 1 hour.

2. Spread mixture over 5 tortillas. Cover with remaining tortillas.

3. Brush tops with oil.

4. Place on a baking sheet.

5. Broil until golden; turn; repeat process.

6. Broil until cheese melts.

7. Cut into 8 wedges.

8. Serve with sour cream, salsa, guacamole.

For entrée, add cooked chicken pieces to fillings.

GUACAMOLE DIP

Preparation time: 20 minutes   *Serves: 6-8*

2 **ripe avocados, peeled, mashed**   1 **Tablespoon lemon juice**
1 **tomato, peeled, seeded**   1 **Tablespoon cider vinegar**
1 **small red onion, finely diced**   2 **Tablespoons salad oil**
1 **Tablespoon jalapeño pepper,**   1 **teaspoon salt**
   finely diced   **Dash ground coriander**

1. Mix all together.

2. Put avocado seed in to keep dip green if made ahead of time.

3. Serve with corn chips.

MEXICAN CHEESE DIP

Preparation time: 20 minutes   *Serves: 10*

8 ounces cream cheese, at room
   temperature
½ teaspoon seasoned salt
¼ cup mayonnaise

⅓ cup fresh or canned tomatoes,
   drained, chopped
4 ounces chilies, drained, chopped
3 Tablespoons sweet onion, minced

1. Beat together first 3 ingredients.
2. Stir in remaining ingredients; chill to thicken.
3. Serve with tortilla chips.

May be made a day ahead of time.

UNKIE JOE'S HOMEMADE PICANTE SAUCE

Preparation time: 20 minutes   *Serves: 4-6*

2 8-ounce cans tomato sauce
1 small onion, finely chopped
1 medium green pepper, finely
   chopped
2 teaspoons chili powder
½ teaspoon cumin
½ teaspoon black pepper

½ teaspoon garlic powder
1 Tablespoon catsup
8 to 10 drops Tabasco sauce
½ teaspoon lime juice
2 Tablespoons fresh cilantro,
   minced, or ½ teaspoon dried
   cilantro

1. Combine all ingredients except lime juice, cilantro in a medium sauce pan.
2. Bring to a boil; reduce heat; simmer 15 minutes.
3. Remove from heat. Stir in lime juice, cilantro.
4. Cool to room temperature.
5. Serve with tortilla chips.

May be prepared 5-7 days in advance.

WEST COAST DIP

Preparation time: 30 minutes
Baking time: 25-30 minutes

Serves: 10-12+

1 medium green pepper, chopped
1 Tablespoon vegetable oil
2 14-ounce cans artichoke hearts, drained, finely chopped
1½ cups mayonnaise (Hellman's Light suggested)
½ cup green onion, finely chopped
½ cup pimento, drained, chopped
1 cup freshly grated Parmesan cheese

1 Tablespoon fresh lemon juice
1 Tablespoon Worcestershire sauce
3 pickled jalapeño peppers, seeded, minced
1 teaspoon celery salt
¾ pound crabmeat or imitation crabmeat, finely chopped
⅓ cup almonds, sliced

1. In a small frying pan over moderate heat, cook green pepper in oil until just softened. Cool.

2. In a large bowl, combine green pepper with remaining ingredients, except almonds.

3. Transfer mixture to a 10-inch deep-dish pie plate. Sprinkle with almonds.

4. Bake at 375° for 25-30 minutes. Serve warm with pita triangles.

SALSA, THE REAL THING

Preparation time: 30-45 minutes

Yield: ½ gallon

8 large ripe tomatoes, diced
1 medium green pepper, diced
1 medium onion, diced
1 large tomatillo, diced
4 cloves garlic, diced

2 to 4 jalapeño peppers
½ large bunch cilantro, large stems trimmed
¼ cup olive oil
¼ cup red wine vinegar
Salt to taste

1. Mix all ingredients together in a large bowl.

2. Process in small batches in food processor with pulse or on/off method to chop very small, not to liquify.

3. Serve with taco chips, sour cream.

Use the freshest, nicest tomatoes. May be stored in refrigerator for 1 week.

Tastes like salsa from Mexico. Also good with eggs or as a salad topper.

HOLLY'S BREAD BOWL

Preparation time: 130 minutes
Baking time: 45 minutes

Serves: 6-12

24 ounces round French, Hawaiian, or sourdough bread
¼ cup butter, softened
2 teaspoons Dijon mustard
1 10-ounce package frozen chopped spinach, thawed
8 ounces Monterey Jack cheese, cut into ½-inch cubes

1 pound lean ground beef, browned
1 large onion, chopped
2 cloves garlic, minced or pressed
1 teaspoon salt
¼ teaspoon pepper
1 Tablespoon Italian herb seasonings

1. Cut down through the top of bread, forming a lid about 4 inches in diameter.

2. Pull out soft bread from inside, leaving a bowl-shaped shell about 1 inch thick.

3. Cut enough of the soft bread into ½-inch cubes to make 3 cups. Set aside.

4. In a bowl, stir together butter, mustard. Spread over inside surfaces of bread shell.

5. Add onion, garlic to skillet with browned ground beef. Cook until onion is limp. Drain excess fat.

6. Stir in seasonings.

7. Squeeze liquid from spinach; add to meat, bread cubes, cheese. Stir until blended well.

8. Spoon filling to fit inside bread bowl. Set lid in place; wrap loosely in aluminum foil.

9. Bake at 400° for 45 minutes.

10. Wrap loaf in additional foil or newspaper to keep warm up to 2 hours.

11. Serve on bread or crackers.

Terrific for picnics, tailgates, cross-country ski parties.

CELERY SEED BREAD

Preparation time: 20 minutes
Baking time: 20 minutes

Serves: 8-12

½ cup butter or margarine, softened
⅓ teaspoon salt
Dash cayenne

¼ teaspoon paprika
½ teaspoon celery seed
1 loaf unsliced white or Italian bread

1. Blend first 5 ingredients.
2. Slice all crusts from bread.
3. Cut down middle of loaf lengthwise almost through to bottom.
4. Cut at 2-inch intervals crosswise from top almost through to bottom.
5. Spread butter mixture over all surfaces except bottom.
6. Bake at 350° for 20 minutes.
7. Cut apart. Serve warm.

May be refrigerated 24 hours before baking. Also freezes well for 1 month.

BLEU CHEESE AND VIDALIA SANDWICHES

Preparation time: 20 minutes

Serves: 8

¾ cup vegetable oil
3 Tablespoons fresh lemon juice
1½ teaspoons salt
¾ teaspoon sugar
⅛ teaspoon ground black pepper

4 ounces bleu cheese, crumbled
1 large Vidalia or sweet onion, very thinly sliced
Sweet butter
Danish pumpernickel bread or miniature rye bread slices

1. Mix first 5 ingredients together in a bowl.
2. Add bleu cheese, onion slices to oil mixture. Mix gently until coated.
3. Cover; refrigerate overnight.
4. Drain liquid from mixture.
5. Place in a serving bowl.
6. Serve with buttered bread.

BEAU MONDE BREAD

Preparation time: 20 minutes　　　　　　　　　　　　　　*Serves: 10*
Baking time: 30 minutes

1　loaf sandwich bread, unsliced
½　pound butter or margarine, softened
2　Tablespoons onion, grated
1　Tablespoon prepared mustard

½　teaspoon beau monde seasoning
2　Tablespoons lemon juice
1　Tablespoon poppy seeds
8　ounces Swiss cheese, sliced

1. Cut all crusts from bread. Slice bread on the diagonal ¾ way through the bread. Repeat in the opposite direction, making criss-cross pattern.

2. Place Swiss cheese slices in the criss-crosses.

3. Blend butter with seasonings. Spread seasoning mixture evenly on loaf.

4. Place loaf on aluminum foil rolled loosely ¾ way up the sides of the loaf.

5. Bake at 350° for 30 minutes.

May be frozen before baking.

PARMESAN BREAD STICKS

Preparation time: 5 minutes　　　　　　　　　　　　　　*Yield: 24-32*

**6 to 8 hot dog buns, quartered
　lengthwise**

**¼　cup butter, melted
Parmesan cheese**

1. Dip 2 cut-up sides in butter; sprinkle with Parmesan cheese.

2. Bake at 400° for 8 minutes until golden brown.

Also good served with soup.

JIM'S POPCORN

Preparation time: 20 minutes　　　　　　　　　　　　　　*Serves: 4*
Baking time: 8-10 minutes

2　quarts popcorn (⅓ cup unpopped)
1　cup nuts
¼　cup butter, melted
2　teaspoons dried dill weed

1　teaspoon Worcestershire sauce
¼　teaspoon garlic powder
¼　teaspoon onion powder
Salt to taste

1. Mix all ingredients together; bake at 325° for 8-10 minutes.

Store popcorn kernals in freezer for freshness and to eliminate kernels which won't pop.

BACON-WRAPPED WATER CHESTNUTS

Preparation time: 20 minutes
Baking time: 1 hour, 20 minutes

Yield: 30

1   8-ounce can whole water chestnuts
1   16-ounce package sliced bacon,
    halved

½ cup catsup
¼ cup dark brown sugar
2   dashes Tabasco sauce

1. Drain water chestnuts,. Cut large ones in half.

2. Wrap ½ slice bacon around each water chestnut.

3. Secure with a toothpick

4. Place in 13x9x2-inch baking dish.

5. Bake at 300° for 1 hour until bacon is crisp. Drain.

6. Place in another baking dish.

7. Combine catsup, brown sugar, Tabasco. Pour over bacon and water chestnuts.

8. Bake at 300° for 20 minutes.

SWEDISH NUTS

Preparation time: 45 minutes
Baking time: 30 minutes

Serves: 20

½ cup butter or margarine
2   egg whites, beaten until stiff

1   cup sugar
Dash salt
3   cups pecans

1. Preheat oven to 325°.

2. Melt butter or margarine in an 8½ x13-inch pan.

3. Slowly add sugar, salt to stiffly beaten egg whites. Beat again until stiff.

4. Fold in nuts.

5. Spread mixture over melted butter or margarine.

6. Bake for 30 minutes, stirring every 10 minutes; turn as mixture cooks.

Bake until butter is absorbed, nuts broken.
Very rich, buttery, and addictive!

Lebanon, Ohio

There is a flavor about Lebanon that encourages residents and touring visitors alike to establish a pace that suits both their moods and their interests.

Galleries and museums are extraordinarily well organized and documented and thus of significant value to students, researchers, and historians. One of the collections in the Warren County Historical Society Museum, located in Lebanon, includes artifacts stemming from prehistoric times on through the Victorian period and extensive displays of paleontological and archeological artifacts.

Students of Americana make pilgrimages to Lebanon to feast on Shaker collections. The Robert and Virginia Jones Gallery is cited as one of the finest examples of Shaker craftsman handiwork in the U.S. And the story of the lifestyle of a 19th Century Shaker community is told at The Union Village. At one time there were 19 Shaker communities in the United States. The Jones collection is held to be the most complete of any in the Midwest.

Latter-day craftsmen have developed a knowledge of Shaker techniques and now offer very fine reproductions of furniture and decorative pieces which are available in Lebanon. The Village Green of Lebanon features vintage toys, guns, and clothing in a number of shops.

Lebanon is the home of Ohio's oldest inn and restaurant - the Golden Lamb. Known for it hearty fare in stagecoach days, today the Golden Lamb features gourmet meals together with an historic atmosphere. Deluxe rooms are available for overnight guests. Each room is furnished with period antiques, but modernized for the contemporary traveler with telephone, air conditioning, television, and bath.

Soups & Sandwiches

PEASANT VEGETABLE SOUP

Preparation time: 1½ hours + soaking   *Yield: 2 gallons*

2 cups dried white beans
¼ cup bacon fat
1 cup onion, chopped
2 carrots, chopped
3 leeks, white part only, sliced
4 cups celery, chopped
1 teaspoon thyme

1 bay leaf
½ gallon chicken stock
½ gallon beef stock
1 ham hock
2 cups cabbage, shredded
½ Tablespoon garlic, chopped
½ cup parsley, chopped
Dash salt, pepper to taste

1. Soak beans overnight.

2. Melt fat in stock pot.

3. Add onion, carrots, leeks, celery; cook until tender.

4. Stir in seasonings, stock, ham hock, beans. Bring to a boil. Simmer 40 minutes until beans are tender.

5. Remove ham hock; cut off meat. Return to pan.

6. Add cabbage, garlic, parsley; simmer 5-10 minutes. Season to taste.

Edgewick's Catering
Springfield, Ohio

Variations: Add horseradish for a spicier taste. Eliminate bacon fat for a healthier option.

Accompaniments: Crusty French bread, sharp Cheddar cheese.

MAIN DISH MINESTRONE

Preparation time: 1 hour   *Serves: 6-8*

2   Tablespoons olive oil
2   Tablespoons butter
½   pound Italian sausage, sliced or crumbled
1   large onion, chopped
1   clove garlic, minced
½   cup celery, chopped
½   cup green pepper, chopped
½   cup carrots, chopped
2   Tablespoons parsley, chopped

½   teaspoon dried basil
Pinch thyme
2   cups (19-ounces) canned tomatoes, chopped
4   cups chicken stock
2   cups cabbage, shredded
1   cup kidney beans
½   cup elbow macaroni or other pasta
Salt, pepper to taste
Grated Parmesan cheese (optional)

1.   In a large heavy sauce pan, heat oil, butter. Add sausage; brown.

2.   Add onion, garlic, celery, green pepper, carrots, parsley. Cook until softened.

3.   Stir in spices.

4.   Stir in tomatoes, stock. Bring to a boil; reduce heat. Cover; simmer 10 minutes.

5.   Add cabbage, beans, macaroni. Cover; simmer 30 minutes.

6   If too thick, dilute with water to correct consistency.

7.   Season to taste.

8.   Top with Parmesan cheese if desired.

Seasonal vegetables may also be added.

Accompaniment: Sourdough or French bread rolls.

Cooks Incorporated

SALUTE TO ASPARAGUS

Preparation time: 30 minutes   *Serves: 6-8*

¾ **pound fresh asparagus, cleaned,**   **Salt to taste**
   trimmed, cut into 1-inch pieces   6 **ounces cream cheese, cut into**
4 **cups regular-strength chicken broth**   **½-inch cubes**

1. Combine cut asparagus with broth in a sauce pan. Bring to a boil. Do not cover. Simmer gently 4-5 minutes until asparagus is tender, crisp.

2. Add salt to taste if needed.

3. Drop cubes of cream cheese into the bottom of a soup tureen. Add asparagus, broth.

4. Serve immediately.

If desired, use a spoonful of sour cream on individual servings instead of cream cheese.

ASPARAGUS SOUP

Preparation time: 30 minutes   *Serves: 4*

1 **pound asparagus, cut into quarters**   3 **slices white bread, cubed**
½ **cup onion, chopped**   1 **Tablespoon butter, melted**
1 **teaspoon chicken base**   **Garlic salt**
1 **cup milk**   2 **asparagus tips, finely chopped**
¼ **teaspoon nutmeg**   **Pimento (optional)**

1. Combine asparagus spears, onion, chicken base in a pot. Cover with water. Cook until soft. Cool slightly.

2. Place in a blender. Blend until smooth. Return to pot.

3. Add milk, nutmeg. Heat to serve.

4. Toast bread cubes in a skillet with melted butter. Sprinkle with garlic salt. Place on top of soup.

5. Sprinkle chopped asparagus tips over soup just before serving.

6. Garnish with pimento for color.

DAYTON'S BEST BLACK BEAN SOUP

Preparation time: 2½-3½ hours + soaking   *Serves: 8*

1   pound black beans
¼ cup olive oil
3   yellow onions (1½ cups), diced
4   cloves garlic, minced
1   ham hock or meaty ham bone
1½ teaspoons dried oregano
1   bay leaf
¼ teaspoon curry powder
1½ teaspoons cumin
1½ teaspoons salt
½ teaspoon Tabasco

¾ teaspoon freshly ground pepper
3   Tablespoons parsley, chopped, divided
10 cups (2½ quarts) water or ½ water, ½ beef bouillon
1   small red or green bell pepper, diced
1½ teaspoons lime juice
1½ teaspoons brown sugar
3   Tablespoons sherry
Onion, cheese, sour cream, or cilantro for garnish (optional)

1. Wash beans; soak overnight in water.

2. Drain beans.

3. Combine beans with next 11 ingredients and 1 Tablespoon parsley in a large pot.

4. Add the 2½ quarts liquid. Simmer uncovered 2-3 hours until tender.

5. Purée 2 cups of beans; return to pot.

6. Remove ham bone; cut up meat; return to pot.

7. Stir in remaining parsley, red or green pepper, lime juice, brown sugar, sherry.

8. Cook an additional 30 minutes, stirring frequently.

9. Correct seasonings as desired.

10. Remove bay leaf before serving.

11. Garnish as desired.

CREAM OF BROCCOLI SOUP

Preparation time: 30 minutes   *Yield: 6 cups*

3 cups broccoli, chopped
¼ cup butter, melted
2 Tablespoons onion, chopped
3 ribs of celery, minced
¼ cup flour

4 cups chicken broth
2 cups milk or cream
Pinch nutmeg
1½ teaspoons salt
⅛ teaspoon pepper

1. Blanch broccoli. Drain, reserving water.
2. Sauté onion, celery in melted butter until tender.
3. Stir in flour.
4. Stir in chicken stock slowly, bringing to a boil.
5. Add broccoli, milk, reserved broccoli water, seasonings.

WILD RICE SOUP

Preparation time: 30 minutes   *Serves: 4*

¼ cup wild rice
4 cups homemade or canned
    chicken stock
¼ cup butter, melted
½ cup celery, diced
¼ cup onion, diced
2 Tablespoons fresh mushrooms,
    sliced

½ cup green pepper, diced
1 cup half and half
½ cup flour
½ teaspoon white pepper
2 Tablespoons almonds, sliced
1 Tablespoon pimento, chopped

1. Cook rice in stock until tender; set aside.
2. Sauté celery, onion, mushrooms, green pepper in melted butter until tender.
3. Add flour; cook 2 minutes, adding rice, salt, pepper.
4. Stir in half and half.
5. Garnish with almonds, pimentos.

Wild rice gives an interesting flavor.

CABBAGE SOUP

Preparation time: 2½ - 3 hours   *Serves: 10*

1 medium cabbage, cut into strips
Melted butter
2 medium onions, sliced
1 clove garlic, minced

1 pound lean stew meat
3 8-ounce cans tomato sauce
1 14½-ounce can stewed tomatoes
Salt, pepper to taste
Juice from 3 to 4 lemons

1. Rub strips of cabbage with salt. Brown onions, garlic in a small amount of butter in a 6 to 8-quart pot.

2. Add beef, cabbage, enough water to cover. Bring to a boil.

3. Add tomato sauce, stewed tomatoes, salt, pepper to taste; return to a boil.

4. Add lemon juice. Cover; simmer 30 minutes.

5. Taste. If too sour, add sugar; if too sweet, add more lemon juice.

6. Simmer 1-1½ hours until meat is very tender.

Best when made a day ahead.

CARROT AND ORANGE SOUP

Preparation time: 20 minutes   *Serves: 6*

1 teaspoon butter, melted
3 cups carrots, chopped
1 onion, chopped
3¾ cups chicken stock

1 teaspoon salt
1 teaspoon sugar
Juice of 4 oranges, strained
¼ pint heavy cream, whipped
Chives

1. Add carrots, onion to melted butter in a sauce pan.

2. Sauté until slightly soft.

3. Pour in stock, salt, sugar; simmer 1 hour.

4. Purée vegetables; add strained orange juice.

5. Garnish with whipped cream, chopped chives.

Middfest International
Middletown, Ohio

This was a tasters' favorite at the festival.

Cooks Incorporated

CURRIED CARROT - PEANUT SOUP

Preparation time: 1 hour   *Serves: 6*

1   pound carrots, sliced
6   cups regular-strength chicken
    broth, divided
½   cup onion, finely chopped

¼   cup creamy-style peanut butter
1   clove garlic, minced or pressed
2   Tablespoons curry powder
¼   cup white or brown rice
2   cups small broccoli florets

1. Cook carrots in 3 cups chicken broth until very tender.

2. In a blender, purée in batches with liquid until smooth.

3. Return to pan; add remaining broth and other ingredients, except broccoli.

4. Cook 30-40 minutes until rice is tender, stirring occasionally.

5. Add broccoli; cook 5 minutes until just tender.

An unusual, spicy soup.

SKINNY VICHYSSOISE

Preparation time: 1 hour   *Serves: 6-8*

3   medium leeks, whites only, minced
1   medium onion, minced
4 to 5 cups chicken stock or broth,
    divided

4   medium potatoes, peeled, sliced
2   teaspoons chervil
2   cups non-fat yogurt
1   Tablespoon lemon juice

1. Combine leeks, onion with ⅓ cup chicken stock or broth.

2. Steam mixture in a large sauce pan 8 minutes.

3. Add potatoes to leek mixture.

4. Add 3½-4 cups chicken stock. Simmer 15-20 minutes until tender.

5. Purée in blender, adding remaining ingredients.

A rich, creamy soup. May be served either cold or hot.

Accompaniments: Melba, sesame toast or French bread and a very dry white
Burgundy or Chardonnay.

GARLIC SOUP

Preparation time: 1 hour   *Serves: 6*

35 cloves garlic, unpeeled
2 Tablespoons olive oil
1 small onion, chopped
1 small green pepper, chopped
1 28-ounce can plum tomatoes,
   undrained, chopped
¼ teaspoon allspice

⅛ teaspoon ground cloves
¼ teaspoon tarragon
Salt, freshly ground pepper to taste
4 cups chicken broth
1 egg yolk, beaten
6 slices French bread, toasted

1. Boil garlic cloves 3 minutes in enough water to cover. Drain; peel.

2. Heat oil in a deep pot. Cook onion, green pepper, garlic 8-10 minutes until soft, not browned. Stir frequently.

3. Add tomatoes, spices, broth; bring to boil. Reduce heat; simmer uncovered 20 minutes.

4. Pour soup through a sieve into a bowl.

5. With a wooden spoon or spatula, press down very hard on solids to extract all juices. Reserve solids. Return strained soup to the pot.

6. With a whisk, gradually beat ½ cup soup into egg yolk in a small bowl.

7. Gradually add yolk mixture to soup, beating constantly.

8. Cook gently 1-2 minutes. Do not boil or the soup will curdle.

9. Spread reserved vegetable solids on toasted French bread slices.

10. Arrange on a dish; serve with soup.

A very special combination of flavors and textures.

CREAM OF ONION SOUP

Preparation time: 2 hours   *Serves: 4*

2 large Spanish onions, thinly sliced   Salt, pepper to taste
¼ cup butter, melted   Sliced pumpernickel bread, cubed
1 tomato, peeled, sliced, chopped   Grated Parmesan cheese
4 cups chicken stock or broth

1. Sauté onions in melted butter until soft.

2. Add tomato. Cook 5 minutes.

3. Add chicken broth. Simmer over low heat 1½ hours.

4. Purée mixture in a blender in 2 batches until smooth.

5. Reheat. Add salt, pepper.

6. In a small skillet, sauté bread until crisp.

7. Divide soup among 4 flameproof bowls.

8. Top with bread cubes, Parmesan cheese.

9. Broil 3-4 minutes until brown, bubbly.

GOURMET POTATO SOUP

Preparation time: 30 minutes   *Serves: 4*

3 cups potatoes, diced
½ cup celery, diced
½ cup onion, diced
Salt to taste
1½ cups water

2 cups milk, divided
1 Tablespoon chicken-flavored
   gravy base
8 ounces sour cream
2 Tablespoons chives
1 to 2 Tablespoons flour

1. Combine first 4 ingredients in a large sauce pan.

2. Cover with water. Simmer 20 minutes. Add 1 cup milk.

3. In a medium bowl, blend gravy base, sour cream, chives, flour; gradually stir in remaining milk.

4. Pour ⅓ hot potato mixture into sour cream mix. Return to saucepan.

5. Cook, stir until thickened. Add remaining potato mixture.

A very hearty soup.

CREAM OF POTATO SOUP

Preparation time: 45 minutes   *Serves: 4*

2 Tablespoons margarine, melted
½ cup onion, chopped
¼ cup celery, chopped
1½ cups potatoes, peeled, diced
1 cup chicken broth

¼ cup fresh parsley, chopped
¼ teaspoon thyme, crushed
¼ teaspoon celery seed
¼ teaspoon salt
½ teaspoon pepper
1½ cups milk

1. In a sauce pan, cook onion, celery in melted margarine 4 minutes, stirring frequently until soft.

2. Add remaining ingredients, except milk. Simmer 15 minutes until potatoes are almost tender.

3. Add milk. Simmer 15 minutes, stirring occasionally.

4. In a blender at medium speed, blend ¼ of mixture until smooth.

5. Return to sauce pan. Heat 1 minute.

Cooks Incorporated

GET-WELL SOUP

Preparation time: 1½ hours   *Serves: 8-10*

10 cups water
4 chicken breasts, skinned
1 cup onions, chopped
1 bunch green onion, chopped
2 cups carrots, cut up
2 cups celery, cut up
3 bay leaves

2 to 3 cloves garlic, cooked whole,
    mashed after cooking
2 teaspoons salt
½ teaspoon pepper
½ teaspoon thyme
4 ounces egg noodles
¼ cup parsley, chopped

1. Put all ingredients, except noodles, parsley, in a large pot. Cook 1 hour.

2. Remove chicken; discard bones; cut chicken into bite-size pieces.

3. Add noodles; cook 15-20 minutes.

4. Stir in parsley, chicken.

5. Remove bay leaves before serving.

BUTTERNUT SQUASH SOUP

Preparation time: 45 minutes   *Serves: 6*

1 quart de-fatted chicken broth,
    divided
1 small clove garlic
1 medium onion, coarsely chopped
¼ to ½ teaspoon curry powder

⅛ teaspoon dried red pepper
2½ pounds butternut squash, peeled,
    seeded, cut into 1½-inch cubes
1 cup water
1 Tablespoon creamy peanut butter
1 cup non-fat milk powder

1. Pour ½ cup chicken broth into a large sauce pan.

2. Add garlic, onion, curry powder, red pepper; cook until onion wilts.

3. Add squash to sauce pan along with remaining chicken broth, water. Boil gently, covered, 20-30 minutes until squash is tender.

4. Remove from heat. Stir in peanut butter, powdered milk.

5. Whirl in electric blender ½ at a time until smooth.

6. Reheat to serve.

SPINACH COCONUT SOUP (CRÉME ANTILLAISE)

Preparation time: 1 hour *Serves: 4-6*

14 ounces fresh spinach, washed, drained
2 Tablespoons butter, melted
2 medium white onions, thinly sliced
1½ quarts hot beef stock
⅓ cup short grain rice, rinsed

3 Tablespoons coconut, freshly grated
Nutmeg, freshly grated
Coarse salt
6 Tablespoons créme fraîche or ⅔ cup heavy cream
White pepper, freshly ground

1. Sauté onions 15 minutes in melted butter over medium heat in a 4-quart casserole until soft, golden, not brown.

2. Pour hot beef stock over onions; bring to a boil.

4. Add rice, coconut. Reduce heat to medium. Simmer uncovered 20 minutes until rice is tender.

5. Add spinach. Return to boil; cook 5 minutes.

6. Add generous grating of nutmeg. Season to taste.

7. Purée the soup in a food processor. Complete the purée by pressing through a fine sieve. Stir créme fraîche into soup; bring to simmer. Add 5-6 turns of pepper.

8. Serve hot.

May be prepared 2 days in advance. Freezes well after completion of purée.

Accompaniments: Pork or chicken which is prepared with a sauce containing tomatoes, onions, garlic, cinnamon and fruit; Alsatian wine (Gewurtztraminer or Reisling suggested).

CORN CHOWDER

Preparation time: 20-30 minutes

Serves: 4-6

2 cups water
2 cups potatoes, diced
½ cup onion, chopped
½ cup celery, diced
2 Tablespoons margarine
½ teaspoon dried basil
1 large bay leaf

1 17-ounce can cream-style corn
1 can evaporated milk
1 16-ounce can tomatoes, crushed, or
  chopped
2 teaspoons salt
⅛ teaspoon pepper
½ cup shredded Cheddar cheese
1 Tablespoon fresh parsley, minced

1. Combine first 7 ingredients in a large pot or Dutch oven. Bring to a boil.

2. Reduce heat; simmer 10 minutes until potatoes are tender.

3. Discard bay leaf. Stir in corn, milk, tomatoes, salt, pepper; heat thoroughly.

4. Add cheese. Cook over low heat, stirring constantly until cheese is melted.

5. Sprinkle parsley over chowder.

TORTELLINI SOUP

Preparation time: 30 minutes

Serves: 10-12

12 ounces fresh spinach, chopped
4½ quarts regular-strength chicken
  broth
8 ounces fresh cheese-filled plain or
  spinach tortellini
1 1-pound chicken breast skinned,
  boned, cut into ½-inch chunks

½ pound mushrooms, sliced
1 red bell pepper, stemmed, seeded,
  diced
1 cup rice, cooked
2 teaspoons dry tarragon leaves
Freshly ground pepper to taste
Salt
Freshly grated Parmesan cheese

1. Bring broth to boil.

2. Add tortellini; boil gently 6-8 minutes until tender.

3. Add spinach, chicken, mushrooms, bell pepper, rice, tarragon; simmer 5 minutes until chicken is no longer pink.

4. Add pepper, salt.

5. Ladle into bowls. Offer Parmesan cheese.

CHEDDAR CHEESE CHOWDER

Preparation time: 50 minutes   *Serves: 8-10*

3 cups water
3 chicken bouillon cubes
4 medium baking potatoes, peeled, diced
1 medium onion, sliced
1 cup carrots, sliced
½ cup green pepper, diced

½ to 1½ heads broccoli, cut up
⅓ cup margarine, melted
⅓ cup flour
3½ cups milk
4 cups (1 pound) shredded Cheddar cheese
Tabasco sauce to taste
Freshly ground pepper to taste

1. Combine water with bouillon cubes in a 5 to 6-quart sauce pan; bring to a boil.
2. Add vegetables; cover; simmer 5-10 minutes.
3. Blend flour into melted margarine; cook 1 minute.
4. Gradually add milk.
5. Cook over medium heat until thick, stirring constantly.
6. Add cheese; stir until melted.
7. Combine cheese sauce with Tabasco.
8. Season with fresh pepper.
9. Cook over low heat until ready to serve. Do not boil.
10. Serve in small bowls.

A great winter soup.

Accompaniment: French bread or sandwiches.

BASQUE SEAFOOD SOUP

Preparation time: 45 minutes   *Serves: 4-6*

1 **large onion, chopped**
½ **cup celery with leaves, chopped**
1 **large clove garlic, minced**
2 **Tablespoons butter or olive oil**
2 **16-ounce cans tomatoes, cut up**
½ **cup dry white wine**
½ **cup parsley, minced**
1 **teaspoon salt**

¼ **teaspoon pepper**
¼ **teaspoon dried thyme**
1 **pound fresh tilapia, halibut or other firm white fish, cut into 1-inch chunks**
⅔ **pound fresh shrimp, shelled, deveined**
1 **green onion, chopped (optional)**

1. In a large sauce pan, sauté onion, celery, garlic in butter until tender.

2. Add tomatoes, wine, parsley, salt, pepper, thyme. Cover; simmer 30 minutes.

3. Add fish, stirring gently to avoid breaking; simmer 4 minutes.

4. Add shrimp; continue cooking 1 minute.

5. Turn off heat; let rest 1 minute.

6. Sprinkle green onion over each serving if desired.

May be refrigerated or frozen after tomato mixture simmers. Simmer again before adding fish.

Accompaniments: Crusty bread, mixed green salad, dry white wine.

OYSTER BISQUE

Preparation time: 20-25 minutes   *Serves: 4*

1 pint large raw oysters, drained
4 cups milk
1 onion, halved
2 stalks celery
1 sprig parsley
1 bay leaf

¼ cup butter, melted
¼ cup flour
1¾ teaspoons salt
⅜ teaspoon pepper
⅜ teaspoon celery salt
½ teaspoon Worcestershire sauce

1. Slowly bring oysters just to a boil in a small saucepan. (Enough liquid will remain on oysters to cook without adding additional liquid.)

2. Cook until oysters curl around the edges. Remove immediately.

3. Chop oysters. Set aside.

4. Scald milk with onion, celery, parsley, bay leaf.

5. Remove seasonings from milk.

6. Blend remaining ingredients, except Worcestershire, in a large pan.

7. Slowly stir in milk. Stir over low heat until thickened.

8. Add chopped oysters, Worcestershire.

NUTRIENT ANALYSIS (Per Serving)

Carbohydrate .... 26 grams
Protein .... 18 grams
Fat .... 23 grams
Calories .... 384 (54% from fat)
Cholesterol .... 129 milligrams
Sodium .... 1464 milligrams

Cooks Incorporated

OYSTER STEW-LIGHT OPTION

Preparation time: 20-25 minutes   *Serves: 3-4*

1 **pint large raw oysters, drained**	¼ **cup flour**
1 **onion, halved**	½ **teaspoon salt**
2 **stalks celery**	⅛ **teaspoon pepper**
2 **sprigs parsley**	⅛ **teaspoon celery salt**
4 **Tablespoons butter-flavor sprinkles**	4 **cups skim milk**
(Molly McButter suggested)	3 **dashes Tabasco**

1. Slowly bring oysters to a boil in small saucepan. (Enough liquid will remain on oysters to cook without adding additional liquid.)

2 Cook until oysters curl around edges. Remove immediately.

3. Chop oysters. Set aside.

4. Sauté onion, celery, parsley until limp in butter buds.

5. Add flour, salt, pepper, celery salt.

4. Stir in milk.

5. Add chopped oysters, Tabasco.

NUTRIENT ANALYSIS (Per Serving)

Carbohydrate .... 30 grams
Protein .... 18 grams
Fat .... 3 grams
Calories .... 223 (12% from fat)
Cholesterol .... 66 milligrams
Sodium .... 762 milligrams

PEKING HOT AND SOUR SOUP

Preparation time: 1½ hours

¼ cup cooked pork tenderloin, shredded
1 teaspoon dry sherry
3 Tablespoons cornstarch, divided
¼ cup dried wood ears
¼ cup dried golden needles
2 cups boiling water
1½ cups cold water, divided

2 Tablespoons cider vinegar
¼ teaspoon white ground pepper
1 10¾-ounce can chicken broth
½ teaspoon salt
1 Tablespoon soy sauce
½ cup bean curd (tofu), diced
1 egg, beaten
1 teaspoon sesame seed oil
1 Tablespoon scallions, thinly sliced

1. Mix shredded pork, sherry, and 1 teaspoon corn starch.

2. In separate bowls cover wood ears, golden needles with boiling water. Cover; soak 20 minutes. Snap off wood pieces from wood ears and hard stems from golden needles. Wash, drain, squeeze out water.

3. Mix remaining cornstarch with ½ cup cold water.

4. Combine vinegar, pepper in a soup tureen.

5. Pour chicken broth with remaining cold water, salt, soy sauce into medium sauce pan. Bring to a boil.

6. Stir in pork mixture; boil 1 minute.

7. Add wood ears, golden needles; boil 1 minute longer.

8. Add bean curd. When soup returns to boiling, stir in well-stirred cornstarch mixture until thickened.

9. Mix in beaten egg. Remove from heat immediately.

10. Combine soup with vinegar and pepper mixture in tureen.

11. Garnish with sesame seed oil, scallions.

12. Serve hot.

Wood ears (mushrooms) and golden needles (lily flowers) are available at oriental food markets.

Accompaniment: Chinese food.

Cooks Incorporated

MINESTRONE SOUP MIX/SOUP

Preparation time: 2 hours, 15 minutes + soaking   *Serves: 8*

Mix

½ cup dried light red kidney beans
½ cup dried lentils
½ cup dried chick-peas
½ cup dried pinto beans

½ cup dried yellow split peas
½ cup dried green peas
½ cup great northern beans
½ cup dried black turtle beans

1. Combine beans, peas in a large bowl.
2. Store in jars with tight-fitting lids or plastic bags.

Soup

2 cups (1 pound) Minestrone Soup Mix
6 cups water, divided
¾ pound boneless smoked pork chops, cut into bite-size pieces
1 cup onion, chopped
2 cloves garlic, crushed
6 carrots, pared, sliced
4 stalks celery, sliced

1 teaspoon leaf marjoram, crumbled
1 teaspoon leaf basil, crumbled
½ teaspoon leaf oregano, crumbled
1 bay leaf
1 teaspoon salt
½ teaspoon pepper
1 35-ounce can Italian plum tomatoes
Parmesan cheese

1. Pick over soup mix; wash.
2. Combine mix with 4 cups water in a kettle or Dutch oven; let stand overnight.
3. Brown diced pork, onion, garlic in a medium-sized skillet.
4. Add to soup mix and soaking liquid.
5. Add remaining ingredients, except cheese. Stir to mix.
6. Bring to a boil. Lower heat; simmer 2 hours until beans are tender. If soup is too thick, add all or part of remaining water.
7. Pass Parmesan cheese to sprinkle on top when served.

Accompaniment: Bread sticks or crusty Italian bread.

BEAN SOUP MIX/SOUP

Preparation time: 3½ hours + soaking   *Serves: 4*

Mix

2 ounces dried pinto beans
2 ounces dried navy beans
1 ounce dried large lima beans
1 ounce dried small lima beans

1 ounce dried split peas
1 ounce dried lentils
1 ounce dried kidney beans

1. Combine beans; mix.
2. Store in plastic bags or suitable containers.

Soup

Bean Soup Mix
2 teaspoons salt for soaking
Water
Ham bone or ham hocks
1 large onion, chopped
1 28-ounce can tomatoes (optional)

1 pod red pepper or 1 teaspoon chili
   powder
Juice of 1 lemon
Salt, pepper to taste
1 cup carrots, sliced

1. Wash beans thoroughly; place in a large kettle. Cover with water mixed with 2 teaspoons salt; soak overnight.
2. Drain; add 2 quarts water, ham bone or ham hocks.
3. Bring slowly to a boil; simmer slowly 2½-3 hours.
4. Add remaining ingredients. Simmer another 30 minutes.

Pack mix attractively in glass jars or plastic bags for gift giving. Include the soup recipe.

Accompaniments: Cornbread, green salad.

REAL CHILI

Preparation time: 2 hours + marinating   *Serves: 6*

1 pound flank steak
1 can beer
1 teaspoon coarse black pepper
½ cup sweet onion, chopped
⅓ cup green bell pepper, chopped
½ cup cayenne pepper sauce (Durkee
   suggested)
1 teaspoon chili powder
1 14-ounce can stewed tomatoes,
   drained

1 15-ounce can navy beans, drained
1 30-ounce can dark red kidney
   beans, undrained
½ teaspoon cumin
⅓ cup pickled jalapeño pepper slices
   with liquid
1½ cups water
Sour cream to taste

1. Marinate flank steak in beer 4 hours. Refrigerate. Drain. Cube to ¼-inch
    thickness.

2. Sauté beef in a large skillet preheated to medium-high heat. After 5 minutes,
    drain liquid. Return to heat.

3. Add black pepper; continue to brown, stirring often. Do not cover.

4. When brown, lower heat to lowest setting.

5. Stir in onion, green pepper, cayenne sauce, chili powder. Cover; let simmer 20
    minutes, stirring often.

6. Add stewed tomatoes, beans, cumin, jalapeño peppers, water. Simmer 1 hour,
    stirring often.

7. Serve with dollop of sour cream.

Make a day ahead to enhance the flavor.

FIREHOUSE CHILI

Preparation time: 4 hours   *Yield: 2-3 quarts*

1½ pounds ground chuck
1 cup onion, chopped
1 whole garlic bulb, peeled, chopped
2 15-ounce cans tomato sauce
2 15-ounce cans whole tomatoes, broken up
2 to 3 Tablespoons chili powder
1 teaspoon black pepper
½ teaspoon cayenne
1 Tablespoon ground cumin
½ teaspoon crushed red pepper

½ teaspoon onion powder
2 teaspoons Tabasco sauce
½ teaspoon garlic powder
½ teaspoon Italian seasoning
1 to 2 Tablespoons sugar
2 teaspoons salt
1 teaspoon Worcestershire sauce
2 bay leaves
5 to 10 hot pepper rings (Vlasic suggested)
Red kidney beans (optional)
Tomato juice (optional)

1. Brown ground chuck with 1 cup onion, garlic.

2. Add tomato sauce, whole tomatoes. Simmer.

3. While simmering, add spices. (Amounts in recipe may be adjusted to taste.) Add kidney beans, if desired.

4. Simmer 4 hours, thinning with tomato juice if necessary.

A very hot chili.

Middletown Fire Fighters
Middletown, Ohio

Accompaniments: Shredded Cheddar cheese, chopped onion, oyster crackers.

TEXAS CHILI

Preparation time: 30 minutes

Serves: 6-8

2 pounds ground beef
1 cup green pepper, chopped
1½ cups onion, chopped
1 clove garlic, minced
1 16-ounce can kidney beans, drained
24 ounces tomato sauce
1 16-ounce can tomatoes, chopped
12 ounces green chilies, fresh or
   canned, seeded, chopped

2 Tablespoons plus 1 teaspoon
   chili powder
3 Tablespoons ground cumin
½ teaspoon dried basil
½ teaspoon salt
½ teaspoon pepper
½ to 1 teaspoon hot sauce (optional)
Shredded cheese
Onion, finely chopped
Cooked rice or pasta (optional)

1. Combine first 4 ingredients in a Dutch oven. Cook over medium heat until meat browns, stirring occasionally. Drain well.

2. Add next 10 ingredients. Cover; reduce heat. Simmer 30 minutes, stirring occasionally.

3. Garnish with cheese, onion.

4. Serve over rice or pasta, if desired.

Accompaniments: Cornbread, salad.

COLD CUCUMBER SOUP

Preparation time: 45 minutes   *Serves: 10*

3 Tablespoons butter, melted
2 leeks
1 small onion, chopped
2½ cups cucumber, unpeeled, diced
1 cup watercress leaves
1 cup raw potatoes, finely diced

2 Tablespoons parsley
3 cups chicken broth
½ teaspoon dry mustard
Salt, pepper
1 cup heavy cream
Fresh dill weed, chopped

1. Cook leeks, onion in melted butter until transparent.

2. Add all ingredients except cream, dill.

3. Bring to a boil; reduce heat. Simmer 30 minutes until potatoes are tender.

4. Purée in a blender. Season; chill.

5. Before serving, blend in cream, garnish with dill.

Rich, creamy. Refreshing for summer.

TOMATO BASIL SOUP

Preparation time: 2½ hours   *Serves: 8*

6 pounds very ripe fresh tomatoes,
    cored, cut into chunks
½ Tablespoon sugar
2 to 3 teaspoons salt

Juice and rind of 1½ lemons
1 Tablespoon onion, finely grated
½ cup fresh basil, finely chopped
Heavy cream
Parsley

1. Purée tomatoes in a food processor. Pass through a food mill or sieve to remove skins, seeds.

2. Season with remaining ingredients, except cream; chill.

3. Place 1 Tablespoon heavy cream in bottom of each 8-ounce soup bowl.

4. Ladle in soup.

5. Swirl cream. Sprinkle with parsley. Serve chilled.

Lemon and basil flavors are distinctive.

Mary Jo's Cuisine
Oxford, Ohio

GAZPACHO SOUP

Preparation time: 25 minutes + chilling   *Serves: 4-6*

6 to 8 large ripe tomatoes, skinned, quartered
1 **cucumber, peeled, chopped**
2 **garlic cloves**
½ **teaspoon paprika**
½ **teaspoon sugar**
1 **teaspoon salt**
1 **small onion, chopped**

½ **cup green pepper, chopped (optional)**
¼ **cup olive oil**
2 **to 3 Tablespoons wine vinegar**
½ **to ¾ teaspoon Tabasco sauce**
¼ **teaspoon oregano**
1 **to 2 cups clear chicken broth**
Vegetable garnishes

1. Blend first 8 ingredients in a food processor.

2. Add next 5 ingredients; blend 1 minute.

3. Chill overnight.

4. Serve with garnishes of chopped scallions, green peppers, cucumbers, fresh ripe or canned whole tomatoes.

Variation: Sprinkle top with a finely chopped unpeeled lime or freshly grated Parmesan cheese.

CHILLED FRESH STRAWBERRY SOUP

Preparation time: 30 minutes + chilling　　　　　　　　　*Yield: 4-6*

1 **quart strawberries, washed, hulled**
¼ **cup water**
½ **cup sugar**
1 **Tablespoon cornstarch**

⅔ **cup heavy cream**
⅛ **teaspoon salt**
Dash cinnamon
½ **cup sour cream or vanilla yogurt**
　　(optional)

1. Combine strawberries, water, sugar in a 3-quart sauce pan. Cover; bring to boil. Lower heat; uncover. Simmer 15 minutes until berries are soft.

2. Purée mixture in a blender or food processor. Strain to eliminate seeds, if desired.

3. Combine cornstarch, cream, salt, cinnamon.

4. Add to soup. Heat until soup begins to simmer. Simmer 1-2 minutes until thick.

5. Remove from heat; chill 2 hours.

6. Serve in small bowls or demitasse cups topped with sour cream or yogurt.

Very sweet. Also a good dessert.

Accompaniment: Chicken salad.

BLACK RASPBERRY SOUP

Preparation time: 30 minutes   *Serves: 2*

1   pint black raspberries
½ cup heavy cream
¼ cup sugar
2   Tablespoons black
    raspberry liqueur

8 ounces plain unsweetened yogurt
½ cup sour cream
6 ounces raspberry sorbet
2 mint leaves

1.   Purée black raspberries; strain to eliminate seeds. Set aside.

2.   Whip heavy cream until soft peaks form. Set aside.

3.   Combine sugar, black raspberry liqueur.

4.   Whip mixture into yogurt.

5.   Add raspberries, sour cream. Mix well.

6.   Fold in whipped cream; refrigerate.

7.   At service time, place 3 individual 1-ounce scoops of raspberry sorbet in each 8-ounce soup bowl.

8.   Garnish each with a mint leaf.

A beautiful presentation with a refreshing taste. A perfect sweet to finish an elegant meal.

Dayton Racquet Club
Dayton, Ohio

Accompaniment: Sauterne Sudiraut wine

MEXICAN-STYLE SANDWICH SQUARES

Preparation time: 20 minutes   *Yield: 6*

2 cups cornbread mix (Hodgson Mill
   Jalapeño Cornbread Mix suggested)
1 25-ounce can cream style corn
2 large eggs
½ cup 2% milk

2 Tablespoons oil
¾ cup Monterey Jack cheese, grated
1 15-ounce can black beans, rinsed,
   well drained
8 ounces mild thick and chunky salsa

Sauce

¼ cup cold water
1 Tablespoon cornstarch
1 16-ounce can Italian style stewed
   tomatoes, cut up

1 teaspoon Worcestershire sauce
2 dashes Tabasco sauce
1 red onion, finely chopped

1. Combine first 6 ingredients, stirring until blended.
2. Spread ½ mixture in a well-greased 8x8x2-inch baking dish.
3. Combine beans, salsa; spread over batter.
4. Top with remaining batter.
5. Bake at 350° for 35 minutes.
6. Let stand 5 minutes before cutting into squares.
7. In a sauce pan, combine water, cornstarch.
8. Stir in tomatoes, Worcestershire sauce, Tabasco.
9. Cook, stirring until mixture thickens.
10. Serve over cornbread squares.
11. Top with onion.

A great warm sandwich.

GRILLED ONION-CHEESE SANDWICH

Preparation time: 20 minutes   *Serves: 2*

1   Tablespoon olive oil
1   medium white onion, thinly sliced
Dash salt
4 to 6 slices provolone cheese

2   14-ounce cans artichoke hearts,
    drained, sliced
4   slices round loaf sourdough bread
2   Tablespoons butter, melted
Sprouts

1. Sauté onions in olive oil until soft, brown. Add salt to taste.

2. Place provolone cheese on bread slices.

3. Add thinly sliced artichokes, followed by sautéed onions.

4. Brush outer parts of bread with butter

5. Grill in skillet or on griddle until cheese melts, bread browns.

6. Open sandwich. Place sprouts inside.

7. Cut; serve.

TIPS ON SOUPS

(From Our Good Cooks!)

Use puréed potatoes or other vegetables to thicken soups and stews as a healthier alternative. In cream soups, use nonfat dry milk or evaporated skim milk.

Refrigerate soups and stews until fat congeals on top to make removal easy before reheating. Place a piece of waxed paper on top; the paper and the fat will peel right off. If time does not allow for refrigeration, use a paper towel to absorb surface oil or a skimmer to pour it off. A gravy separator is also a great gadget for removing excess fat.

Use ice cubes to eliminate fat from soup and stew. Drop a few into the pot; stir. Fat will cling to cubes. Discard cubes before they melt.

Drop a lettuce leaf into a pot of homemade soup to absorb excess grease from the top.

Add cut raw potatoes to soup which is too salty. Discard after they have cooked and absorbed the salt.

Add a teaspoon each of cider vinegar and sugar to remedy a too-salty soup or vegetable.

Always remove bay leaves before serving soup.

Greenville, Ohio

Greenville, the Darke County Seat, is a thriving metropolis in the heart of the leading agricultural county in Ohio. Often referred to as the "Treaty City," Greenville was the site for the signing of the Treaty of Greenville by General Anthony Wayne in 1795. This treaty brought an end to 40 years of war with the Northwestern Indians and, after ratification by the United States Senate, cleared the way for area settlement.

Greenville represents a happy union of agriculture, industry, and a quality of life that embraces cultural development and a relaxed informal lifestyle. Saturdays find the downtown streets, cafes, restaurants, and mercantile stores full of people. Neighbors greet neighbors from all parts of the County, and sidewalk tete-a-tetes are common-place. Later in the evening "cruising" replaces strolling as cars move slowly up and down Broadway. Friends wave to friends, and those lucky enough to find curb-side parking engage in bantering salutes.

Darke County is home to some nationally known idols. Lowell Thomas, the well-known journalist, explorer, and pioneer newscaster, spent many years in Darke County and frequently contributed his time to Greenville's causes.

Annie Oakley, who learned to use her father's Kentucky rifle, won a match against Frank Butler, a professional marksman who shortly became her husband. They joined "Buffalo Bill" Cody's Wild West Show. Annie and Frank performed throughout the U.S. and Europe, which included an appearance before Britain's Queen Victoria. Greenville's Garth Museum, located just outside the downtown district, features the lives of Annie Oakley and Lowell Thomas in separate galleries.

Darke County's fair, in Greenville, was founded in 1852 and hailed as the "Largest County Fair on Earth." It still carries that billing today – albeit without an audit.

Salads & Dressings

Cooks Incorporated

SPINACH-PINE NUT SALAD

Preparation time: 30 minutes   *Serves: 10*

1   large package spinach, washed,   ¼   teaspoon salt
    drained   2   shallots
5   navel oranges, sectioned, or 1 small   2   Tablespoons red wine vinegar
    can mandarins, drained   2   teaspoons salt
1   small red onion, thinly sliced   1   teaspoon white pepper
1   Tablespoon butter or margarine,   2   teaspoons Dijon mustard
    melted   2   Tablespoons honey
⅓   cup raw pine nuts, divided   ½   cup oil

1.   In a large bowl, toss spinach, oranges, onion. Set aside.

2.   Place pine nuts in a skillet with melted butter. Toast, stirring constantly.

3.   Sprinkle salt over toasted nuts; set aside.

4.   In processor, drop in shallots. Add remaining ingredients, except oil.

5.   Slowly drizzle in oil with processor running.

6.   Add 3-4 Tablespoons toasted pine nuts; process to puree.

7.   Drizzle dressing over salad; sprinkle with remaining pine nuts.

Watch pine nuts carefully while toasting to avoid burning.

HEARTS OF PALM SALAD

Preparation time: 15 minutes   *Serves: 6*

6 cups fresh spinach, washed, torn
1 small carrot, shredded
½ cup oil and vinegar salad dressing

1 14-ounce can hearts of palm,
   drained, sliced, chilled
¼ teaspoon dried oregano, crushed
Fresh summer savory sprigs (optional)

1. Toss together spinach, carrot.
2. Cover; chill.
3. Place salad dressing, oregano in a screw-top jar.
4. Cover; shake to combine.
5. Chill.
6. Before serving, mound spinach onto 6 salad plates.
7. Top with hearts of palm.
8. Drizzle dressing mixture over salads.
9. Garnish with oregano, savory sprigs if desired.
10. Serve immediately.

Cooks Incorporated

DAVID'S SALAD WITH "MY MOM'S SPECIAL VINAIGRETTE"

Preparation time: 20 minutes   *Serves: 6-8*

Salad

4 tomatoes, cored, roughly chopped
1 small red onion, thinly sliced

3 ounces bleu cheese, crumbled
Greens, torn into bite-sized pieces
Alfalfa sprouts

Dressing

¾ cup olive oil
2 ounces red wine vinegar
1½ ounces balsamic vinegar
1 Tablespoon Dijon mustard
1½ Tablespoons catsup

1 Tablespoon garlic powder
1½ Tablespoons brown sugar
1 Tablespoon salt
2½ Tablespoons cracked
   black pepper

1. Mix tomatoes, onion, bleu cheese. Set aside.

2. Combine all dressing ingredients. Mix well.

3. Place greens on salad plates.

4. Toss tomato mixture with desired amount of dressing.

5. Top greens with tossed tomato mixture.

6. Top with fresh alfalfa sprouts.

Peasant Stock Restaurant
Kettering, Ohio

An attractive, interesting salad. Any fresh greens may be used.

NICK'S GREEK SALAD SUPREME

Preparation time: 30 minutes   *Serves: 4*

Salad

⅓ head lettuce, broken into bite-size
   pieces
3 sprigs parsley leaves, snipped, or
   1 teaspoon dry parsley
½ sweet white, red, or 3 green onions,
   thinly sliced
½ carrot, thinly sliced
½ stalk celery, thinly sliced

½ green pepper, thinly sliced
1 tomato, diced
⅓ cucumber, seeded, diced
4 ounces feta cheese, crumbled
   or cubed
4 radishes, sliced
12 calamata olives, seeds left
   in (optional)
4 anchovies (optional)

Dressing

½ cup olive oil
¼ cup wine vinegar
⅓ teaspoon salt
⅓ teaspoon ground pepper

⅓ teaspoon oregano
⅓ teaspoon thyme
1 teaspoon garlic powder or 2 cloves,
   pressed

1. Refrigerate all salad ingredients to crisp before serving.
2. Refrigerate salad bowls.
3. Place dressing ingredients in a container; shake well; refrigerate.
4. Shake dressing again.
5. Place vegetables in large bowl; combine with dressing; toss well.
6. Garnish with olives, anchovies, if desired.

A real gourmet salad!

BAKED GOAT CHEESE AND SALAD

Preparation time: 45 minutes + marinating   *Serves: 4*

4 to 6 cups assorted greens - arugula, romaine, bibb, oak leaf, ruby lettuce
1 log goat cheese, 3¼ x 1½ inches
½ cup olive oil
4 sprigs fresh thyme or dried thyme
¾ cup fine white bread crumbs

1 teaspoon fresh or dried thyme leaves
3 Tablespoons balsamic vinegar
¼ teaspoon salt (optional)
⅛ teaspoon black pepper, freshly ground

1. Crisp greens for 24 hours.
2. Cut cheese into 8 ¾-inch thick rounds.
3. Arrange in a shallow dish.
4. Combine oil, sprigs of thyme. Pour over cheese; marinate several hours or overnight.
5. Preheat oven to 350° degrees.
6. Combine bread crumbs, thyme, salt, pepper.
7. Roll rounds of goat cheese in mixture.
8. Place in a shallow baking dish.
9. Bake for 10 minutes until cheese is softened, crumbs are golden.
10. Combine oil from the marinade with vinegar, salt, pepper.
11. Pour over greens; toss well.
12. Serve immediately on individual plates with 2 slices of warm goat cheese on the side.

BLEU CHEESE SALAD

Preparation time: 1 hour *Serves: 8*

Salad

1 cup croutons
1 Tablespoon butter, melted
2 cups romaine lettuce, washed, torn
2 cups bibb lettuce, washed, torn
2 cups Boston lettuce, washed, torn

1 cup cherry tomatoes, split
1 avocado, sliced
2 hard boiled eggs, diced
1 can artichoke hearts, drained, split

1. Toast croutons lightly in melted butter in a skillet.
2. Combine remaining ingredients in a salad bowl.

Dressing

½ cup bleu cheese, crumbled
3 Tablespoons cream
½ teaspoon prepared mustard

⅛ teaspoon Worcestershire sauce
Salt, pepper to taste
2 Tablespoons wine vinegar
6 Tablespoons olive oil

1. Whisk together all ingredients except olive oil.
2. Add olive oil slowly.
3. Mash in bleu cheese. Blend.
4. Add dressing to salad ingredients. Toss well.

A delicious, colorful salad with crunch and flavor.

Cooks Incorporated

SMOKED MOZZARELLA AND TOMATO SALAD

Preparation time: 15 minutes   *Serves: 6*

6 ounces smoked mozzarella, diced
    into ½-inch chunks
1½ pints (about 1½ pounds) cherry
    tomatoes, halved

¼ cup packed fresh basil leaves,
    shredded
2 Tablespoons white wine vinegar
Salt, pepper to taste
⅓ cup virgin olive oil

1. Combine mozzarella, tomatoes, basil in a bowl.

2. In a small bowl whisk together vinegar, salt, pepper. Add oil in a stream, whisking until dressing is emulsified.

3. Pour dressing over salad; toss well. Chill, covered, for at least 15 minutes and up to 6 hours.

Accompaniment: Lemon and basil poached chicken breasts.

BROCCOLI SALAD

Preparation time: 30 minutes   *Serves: 8-10*

1 to 2 bunches broccoli
1 cup sour cream
1 cup mayonnaise

Scant ⅓ cup lime juice
½ teaspoon white horseradish
½ teaspoon Dijon mustard
½ teaspoon salt

1. Cook broccoli briefly. Plunge into ice water to preserve bright green color. (Broccoli should be crunchy but chewable.)

2. Divide broccoli into serving size pieces; chill.

3. One-half hour or more before serving, combine remaining ingredients.

4. Just before serving, pour sauce over broccoli.

Crisp, clean, tart taste for summer dinner.

BROCCOLI SALAD WITH RAISINS AND PINE NUTS

Preparation time: 20 minutes   *Serves: 4-6 luncheon salad; 10-12 side salad*

Salad

2 bunches broccoli, cut into very small florets

1 16-ounce can red beans, rinsed
1 cup raisins
½ cup pine nuts, slightly toasted

Dressing

¼ cup honey
2 Tablespoons Dijon mustard
3 Tablespoons seasoned gourmet rice vinegar

1 Tablespoon oil
¼ teaspoon garlic salt
1 Tablespoon catsup (optional – for color)

1.   Place all salad ingredients in bowl.
2.   Mix dressing ingredients; pour over salad. Chill 1-2 hours.

A nice broccoli salad variation. May be used as a full meal.

BROCCOLI SALAD WITH APPLES AND CHEESE

Preparation time: 30 minutes   *Serves: 6*

1 bunch fresh broccoli, washed, drained, cut into bite-sized pieces
2 fresh unpeeled red apples, washed, drained, cut into bite-sized pieces

½ cup Swiss cheese, cubed
½ cup Cheddar cheese, cubed
¾ cup slaw dressing (Marzetti or homemade suggested)
½ cup walnut or pecan pieces

1.   Mix broccoli, apples, cheeses in a large bowl.
2.   Add slaw dressing; stir well.
3.   Stir in nuts.
4.   Cover; store in refrigerator.

Discard tough, outer parts of broccoli.
Keeps fresh 2-3 days in refrigerator.
Vary amount of dressing according to size of broccoli bunch.

Cooks Incorporated

CAULIFLOWER SALAD

Preparation time: 20-30 minutes　　　　　　　　　　　　　　　*Serves: 8*

4　cups cauliflower florets
½　pound bacon, cooked, drained,
　　chopped
8　cups lettuce, torn
1　bunch green onions, chopped

⅓　cup grated Parmesan cheese
⅓　cup sugar
⅔　cup salad dressing (regular or low
　　calorie Miracle Whip suggested)
2　Tablespoons wine vinegar

1.　Mix vegetables, bacon in a salad bowl.

2.　Top with Parmesan cheese.

3.　Combine remaining ingredients for dressing; refrigerate until ready to use.

4.　Toss salad with dressing just before serving.

Do not add all dressing at once; recipe makes more than most people want.

GREEN BEAN SALAD

Preparation time: 20 minutes　　　　　　　　　　　　　　　*Serves: 4-6*

½　pound fresh green beans, cleaned,
　　ends cut off, strings removed
1　onion, sliced into 1-inch pieces

¾　cup vinaigrette or oil and vinegar
　　dressing
½　cup pine nuts or walnuts, toasted
Lettuce

1.　Steam whole beans 6 minutes; drain.

2.　Combine beans, onions.

3.　Add dressing; stir to coat. Chill several hours.

4.　Serve on a small bed of lettuce.

COUSCOUS VEGETABLE SALAD

Preparation time: 1 hour   *Serves: 6*

1½ cups cooked couscous
¾ cup very hot water
¼ cup oil
2 medium tomatoes, diced
1 cup cucumber, diced
6 green onions, chopped
1½ cups canned garbanzo beans,
     drained

1 cup parsley, chopped
¼ teaspoon ground black pepper
½ cup olive oil
¾ cup fresh lemon juice, strained
½ teaspoon garlic powder
1 teaspoon Dijon mustard
1 teaspoon dry mint
½ teaspoon salt

1. Cook couscous in hot water and oil. Cover. Let sit 20 minutes. Fluff with a fork.

2. Combine remaining ingredients. Add to couscous.

3. Let sit one hour. Serve cold.

Current Cuisine
Yellow Springs, Ohio

Accompaniment: Roast lamb or grilled meats.

FUMI SALAD (CHINESE COLE SLAW)

Preparation time: 15 minutes   *Serves: 10-12*

1   head cabbage (1½ pounds), chopped
8   green onions, chopped
8   Tablespoons almonds, chopped or slivered
8   Tablespoons sesame seeds
2   packages ramen noodles with seasoning

4   Tablespoons sugar
1   cup salad oil
6   Tablespoons gourmet seasoned rice vinegar
1   teaspoon pepper
1   teaspoon salt

1. Combine cabbage, onions in a bowl.

2. Brown almonds, sesame seeds in a dry skillet.

3. Crush noodles.

4. Make dressing by blending packages of ramen seasoning with remaining ingredients.

5. Add dressing just before serving.

Accompaniment: Chinese meal

CASHEW AND GREEN PEA SALAD

Preparation time: 30 minutes   *Serves: 6-8*

1   10-ounce package frozen peas, thawed, not cooked
½   pound bacon, cooked, crumbled

½   cup celery, chopped
½   cup onion, choppped
1   cup cashew nuts, chopped
½   cup sour cream

1. Combine all ingredients except sour cream, nuts.

2. Mix; chill.

3. Add sour cream, nuts.

4. Mix well before serving on lettuce leaves.

If dressing is added too soon, celery will bleed and cashews soften.

Accompaniments: Meat, poultry, or fish, rolls.

Salads & Dressings

SESAME PEPPERS

Preparation time: 30 minutes + marinating   *Serves: 12*

1   green bell pepper, thinly sliced
1   red bell pepper, thinly sliced
1   yellow bell pepper, thinly sliced
1   bunch green onions or 1 shallot,
    thinly sliced

¼   cup sesame tempura oil (KA-ME
    suggested)
3   Tablespoons rice wine vinegar
    (KA-ME suggested)
3   Tablespoons sugar
1   teaspoon sesame seeds

1. Arrange vegetables in a container suitable for marinating.

2. Place remaining ingredients in a shaker; shake briskly until sugar dissolves.

3. Pour mixture over vegetables.

4. Cover tightly; turn upside down and back to coat evenly.

5. Marinate overnight.

6. Serve chilled over greens.

A colorful, tasty salad.

Accompaniment: Beef, chicken or mett sausage.

CARROT AND GRAPE SALAD

Preparation time: 10-15 minutes   *Serves: 4*

½ cup nonfat plain yogurt
1½ Tablespoons light or fat-free
    mayonnaise
1½ cup carrots, shredded

⅓ cup raisins (optional)
¾ cup seedless grapes
½ teaspoon celery seed
1   Tablespoon dried parsley flakes

1. Mix yogurt, mayonnaise.

2. Combine remaining ingredients.

3. Add yogurt mixture.

Low in fat.

MANDARIN SALAD

Preparation time: 10-15 minutes   *Serves: 4-6*

½ teaspoon salt
Dash pepper
¼ cup salad oil
1 Tablespoon parsley, chopped
2 Tablespoons sugar
2 Tablespoons vinegar
Dash Tabasco sauce
½ cup almonds, sliced

3 Tablespoons sugar
½ head iceberg lettuce, chopped
½ head romaine lettuce, chopped
1 cup celery, chopped
2 green onions, chopped
1 11-ounce can mandarin oranges,
   drained

1. Combine first 7 ingredients; mix well. Chill.

2. In a small sauce pan over medium heat, cook almonds and sugar, stirring until sugar liquifies, nuts are coated.

3. Cool on wax paper or foil.

4. Combine lettuce, celery, green onions in salad bowl.

5. Top with mandarin oranges.

6. Just before serving, toss with chilled dressing; top with sugar coated almonds.

BALSAMIC FRUIT AND AVOCADO SALAD

Preparation time: 25 minutes   *Serves: 8-10*

4 whole navel oranges, peeled, cut crosswise into ½-inch slices
3 pints fresh strawberries, hulled, halved or quartered
3 Tablespoons balsamic vinegar
¼ cup corn or vegetable oil

1 teaspoon fresh black pepper, cracked
4 ripe avocados, peeled, sliced lengthwise
3 Tablespoons fresh lemon juice
Fresh mint leaves

1. Cut orange slices into quarters or smaller. Combine with strawberries.
2. Add vinegar, oil, pepper; toss.
3. Brush avocado slices with lemon juice.
4. Arrange avocado slices around edge of a platter. Pile fruit mixture in center.
5. Garnish with mint leaves.

Ingredients may be prepared 3 hours ahead, refrigerated, and tossed together just before serving.

RED RASPBERRY RING

Preparation time: 20 minutes   *Serves: 8-10*

1 10-ounce package frozen red raspberries, thawed
2 3-ounce packages red raspberry flavored gelatin
2 cups boiling water

1 pint vanilla ice cream
1 6-ounce can frozen pink lemonade concentrate, thawed
½ cup pecans, chopped

1. Drain raspberries, reserving syrup.
2. Dissolve gelatin in boiling water; add ice cream by spoonfuls; stir until melted.
3. Stir in lemonade concentrate, raspberry syrup.
4. Chill until partially set; add raspberries, pecans.
5. Turn into a 6-cup ring mold; chill until firm.

Refreshing, pretty, nice for the holidays.

Accompaniment: Poultry or chicken salad.

ELEGANTE CHICKEN LUNCHEON SALAD

Preparation time: 40 minutes   *Serves: 4*

4   large chicken breast halves, skinned, boned

1   13¾-ounce can chicken broth or stock

Dressing

1½ ounces cream cheese
2   Tablespoons mayonnaise
1   teaspoon lemon juice

¼   teaspoon grated lemon peel
⅛   teaspoon salt
1   Tablespoon fresh dill, snipped, or 1½ teaspoons dried dill weed

Salad Ingredients to Layer

4   large romaine, bibb, or iceberg lettuce leaves
2   tomatoes, cut into 4 thick slices
Seasoned salt

¼   cup slivered almonds, toasted
1   Tablespoon fresh or 1½ teaspoons dried dill weed
1   avocado, peeled, sliced into eighths

1. Cover and simmer chicken breasts in broth 30 minutes.
2. Refrigerate in broth.
3. About 30 minutes before serving salads, remove chicken from broth onto paper towels.
4. Mix dressing ingredients.
5. Coat rounded side of each breast with dressing.
6. Arrange each salad plate with large lettuce leaf, thick slice of tomato; sprinkle with seasoned salt.
7. Top with the chicken breast.
8. Sprinkle with almonds, dill.
9. Garnish with avocado.

Dip avocado slices in lemon juice to prevent turning brown.
A delicious luncheon salad.

Accompaniments: Muffins, bread sticks, or sticky rolls, and a light dessert such as lemon chiffon pie.

COBB SALAD

Preparation time: 80 minutes

Serves: 8

Salad

1 large head iceberg lettuce, chopped
3 cups chicken breast, cooked, cooled, chopped
3 tomatoes, peeled, chopped
8 slices bacon, fried crisp, crumbled

1 cup cauliflower, chopped
1 large avocado, sliced
1 14-ounce can artichoke hearts, chopped
3 hard-cooked eggs, chopped

Dressing

2 ounces bleu cheese, crumbled
1 cup mayonnaise
½ cup sour cream

1 teaspoon lemon juice
1 Tablespoon onion, chopped
1 Tablespoon parsley, chopped
1 Tablespoon vinegar

1. Combine all salad ingredients in a large bowl. Refrigerate.
2. Combine all dressing ingredients. Refrigerate.
3. Toss salad with dressing 1 hour before serving.

NUTRIENT ANALYSIS (Per Serving)

Carbohydrate .... 9 grams
Protein .... 26 grams
Fat .... 39 grams
Calories .... 487 (72% from fat)
Cholesterol .... 156 milligrams
Sodium .... 504 milligrams

Cooks Incorporated

COBB SALAD - LIGHT OPTION

Preparation time: 80 minutes *Serves: 8*

Salad

1 large head iceberg lettuce, chopped
2 cups chicken breast, cooked, cooled, chopped
3 tomatoes, peeled, chopped
3 Tablespoons bacon flavored chips (Bac-O suggested)

1 cup cauliflower, chopped
½ avocado, sliced
1 14-ounce can artichoke hearts, chopped
3 hard-cooked egg whites, chopped

Dressing

1 cup fat-free bleu cheese dressing
1 package dry creamy Italian dressing (Good Seasons suggested)
1 Tablespoon lemon juice

1 Tablespoon onion, chopped
1 Tablespoon parsley, chopped
2 Tablespoons vinegar
Pepper to taste

1. Combine all salad ingredients in a large bowl. Refrigerate.
2. Combine all dressing ingredients. Refrigerate.
3. Combine salad with dressing just before serving.

NUTRIENT ANALYSIS (Per Serving)

Carbohydrate .... 18 grams
Protein .... 21 grams
Fat .... 5 grams
Calories .... 197 (23% from fat)
Cholesterol .... 44 milligrams
Sodium .... 640 milligrams

CHICKEN SALAD MEDITERRANEAN

Preparation time: 30 minutes + marinating   *Serves: 4-6*

3 whole chicken breasts, cooked, skinned, boned, coarsely broken
⅓ cup olive oil
1½ teaspoons oregano
Juice of 1 lemon

¾ cup calamata olives, halved, seeded
2 Tablespoons capers
8 cherry tomatoes, halved
¼ pound green beans, cooked
Salt, pepper to taste

1. Combine olive oil, oregano, lemon juice for marinade.
2. Cover chicken with marinade; let stand one hour.
3. Mix with remaining ingredients; chill.

Use a glass bowl to show the colors.

CURRIED CHICKEN SALAD

Preparation time: 15 minutes   *Serves: 4*

1 cup cooked chicken breast per person
(1 chicken breast equals 1 ½-2 cups cooked)
¼ cup mayonnaise per cup meat (Hellman's suggested)
¼ cup cole slaw dressing per cup meat (Marzetti suggested)

1 teaspoon curry powder per cup dressing
4 to 5 mandarin orange sections per cup meat
8 to 10 seedless grapes per cup meat
Toasted almonds
Bacon bits, coconut (optional)

1. Poach chicken breasts in celery and onion seasoned water until done.
2. Cool; bone; cut into chunks. Chill.
3. Combine all ingredients; top with almonds.
4. Add bacon bits and/or coconut if desired.

Chicken may be poached ahead and frozen in stock.

Recipe may also be baked, served warm.

Cooks Incorporated

CHICKEN SALAD ORIENTAL

Preparation time: 40 minutes   *Serves: 4*

1 to 2 boneless, skinless chicken
   breasts
1 head of lettuce, torn
2 to 3 green onions, diced
1 to 2 carrots, diced
¼ cup sesame seeds

½ cup almonds
¼ cup pine nuts (optional)
4 Tablespoons sugar
2 teaspoons salt
½ teaspoon black pepper
4 Tablespoons red wine vinegar
½ cup salad oil

1.   Cook chicken breasts thoroughly 20-25 minutes at 375°. Cool. Chop into bite-sized pieces.

2.   Place lettuce, onions, carrots in a large bowl. Set aside.

3.   Toast sesame seeds in a dry skillet over medium heat, stirring constantly until lightly browned.

4.   Pour sesame seeds onto lettuce mixture.

5.   Combine sugar, salt, pepper, vinegar in a saucepan over medium heat until liquefied; stir; turn down to simmer.

6.   Toast almonds, pine nuts at 400° for 5 minutes. Watch carefully to avoid burning.

7.   Add chicken, nuts to salad.

8.   Add oil to sauce; pour over salad.

9.   Toss; serve immediately.

Chicken and sauce may be prepared ahead. Refrigerate in separate containers. Reheat sauce in microwave until sugar liquefies.

TURKEY TORTELLINI SALAD

Preparation time: 15 minutes   *Serves: 4*

1 9-ounce package refrigerated
   tortellini stuffed with cheese
½ cup green onion, chopped
¼ cup red bell pepper, diced
2 cups turkey breast, diced

½ cup gourmet rice wine vinegar
½ teaspoon ground basil
1 Tablespoon dried parsley flakes
1 Tablespoon dried chives
Dash garlic powder

1. Cook tortellini per package directions. Drain. Cool.

2. Mix remaining ingredients well.

3. Add tortellini, tossing lightly.

4. Cover; refrigerate 2-4 hours, tossing lightly every hour.

SHRIMP TOMATO VINAIGRETTE

Preparation time: 30 minutes   *Serves: 4*

2 cups shrimp, cooked, deveined
6 ounces frozen pea pods, thawed,
   drained
2 Tablespoons green onions with tops,
   sliced
½ cup salad oil
¼ cup dry sherry
¼ cup wine vinegar

1 envelope Italian dressing mix
   (Good Seasons suggested)
1 to 2 Tablespoons capers,
   well drained
Dash freshly ground pepper
4 tomatoes, cut partially through
   into wedges with stem end down

1. In a bowl, combine shrimp, pea pods, onion.

2. Combine remaining ingredients. Pour over shrimp mixture.

3. Chill several hours.

4. Just before serving, drain shrimp mixture; reserve marinade.

5. Spoon shrimp mixture into tomato shells on a serving platter lined with lettuce.

6. Pass remaining marinade.

Cooks Incorporated

SHRIMP SALAD

Preparation time: 45 minutes   *Serves: 8*

Salad

Lettuce, fresh spinach, torn
¾ to 1 pound shrimp, cleaned,
   deveined

1 pound bacon, fried crisp, crumbled
1 to 2 large avocados

Dressing

⅓ cup sugar
1 teaspoon dry mustard
1¼ teaspoons salt

⅓ cup vinegar
1 cup oil
¼ cup onion, grated
Cayenne to taste

1. Combine greens, shrimp, bacon, avocados in a large bowl.

2. Combine all ingredients for dressing. Mix well.

3. Pour dressing over salad. Toss.

Dressing delicious on other salads.

OLD-FASHIONED POTATO SALAD

Preparation time: 20 minutes   *Serves: 8-10*

2½ pounds white potatoes, pared,
   cooked, diced
3 hard cooked eggs, diced
1 small onion, finely chopped
1 8-ounce jar sweet gherkins, diced
2 Tablespoons sweet gherkin juice

4 ounces pimento, diced
¼ cup sugar
½ teaspoon salt
1¼ teaspoons celery seed
1½ cups mayonnaise
Lettuce

1. Place potatoes in a large bowl.

2. Add remaining ingredients. Mix carefully to blend.

3. Chill at least 1 hour.

4. Serve on a dark green lettuce leaf.

GERMAN POTATO SALAD

Preparation time: 20 minutes *Serves: 6-8*

6 medium-sized potatoes, boiled in skins, peeled, sliced

6 to 8 slices bacon, crisp-cooked, crumbled

⅓ cup bacon drippings

½ cup onions, chopped

2 Tablespoons flour

2 Tablespoons sugar

1 teaspoon salt

½ teaspoon celery seed

Dash black pepper

½ cup cider vinegar

¾ cup water

Dash sherry (optional)

1. Cook onions in bacon drippings until tender.

2. Add flour, sugar, salt, celery seed, pepper.

3. Gradually stir in water, vinegar.

4. Cook until mixture boils, stirring constantly.

5. Boil 1 minute; pour over potatoes.

6. Add crumbled bacon and dash of sherry, if desired.

7. Serve hot.

Also an excellent sauce for cooked green beans or cabbage.

Accompaniment: Barbecued pork chops or ribs.

ITALIAN SPINACH PASTA SALAD

Preparation time: 1 hour   *Serves: 4*

Dressing

1 medium clove garlic, finely minced
½ cup red wine vinegar
6 Tablespoons virgin or extra virgin
   olive oil
¾ teaspoon salt

Freshly ground pepper
½ cup fresh parsley sprigs, chopped
½ teaspoon dried oregano or 1
   teaspoon fresh oregano leaves,
   minced
1 teaspoon fresh basil, minced, or
   ½ teaspoon dried basil

Salad

8 ounces linguine, cooked al dente,
   cooled to room temperature
6 ounces provolone cheese, julienned
5 ounces pepperoni, thinly sliced
1 red onion, thinly sliced

1 red bell pepper, julienned
1 medium zucchini, sliced
   or julienned
Calamata olives
2½ ounces fresh spinach, washed,
   patted dry

1. In a small bowl or the work bowl of a food processor, combine minced garlic, vinegar.

2. Add oils, salt, pepper, herbs; combine.

3. In a large bowl, combine salad ingredients.

4. Add dressing; toss gently to coat.

5. Taste and correct seasoning.

6. Serve immediately.

Salad ingredients may be prepared in advance and tossed with dressing just before serving.

Put dressing over warm linguine so it absorbs olive oil to give more olive taste. Add other ingredients; add spinach last before serving to keep it crisp.

Dorothy Lane Market
Dayton, Ohio

An excellent entrée.
Accompaniments: Crusty bread, wine.

ORZO SALAD

Preparation time: 30 minutes   *Serves: 8-10*

1 cup orzo (rice shaped pasta),   1 large tomato, chopped
   cooked, rinsed, drained   ⅓ cup olive oil or salad oil
1 cup feta cheese, diced   ¼ cup fresh lemon juice
3 Tablespoons fresh parsley   1 clove garlic, pressed or finely
3 Tablespoons fresh or ½ Tablespoon   minced
   dried dill weed or basil   Salt, pepper to taste

1. Mix orzo with feta cheese, parsley, dill (or basil), tomato.

2. Combine oil, lemon juice, garlic.

3. Add to orzo mixture.

4. Refrigerate until ready to serve.

Accompaniment: Seafood or meat.

WILD RICE SALAD

Preparation time: 30 minutes   *Serves: 8*

1 cup brown rice, cooked   1 small red onion, sliced
1 cup wild rice, cooked   ½ cup toasted walnuts, chopped
2 medium tomatoes, cooked   ¼ cup raspberry vinegar
1 bunch kale, cleaned, chopped   ½ cup olive oil
1 medium carrot, grated   Salt, pepper to taste

1. Fluff cooked rice with a fork. Chill.

2. Combine chilled rice with vegetables, walnuts.

3. Combine vinegar oil, seasonings for dressing.

4. Mix dressing with rice mixture.

5. Serve chilled or at room temperature.

May be prepared 8 hours before serving.

Current Cuisine
Yellow Springs, Ohio

POPPY SEED DRESSING

Preparation time: 10 minutes   *Yield: 1½ cups*

8   ounces honey
1   Tablespoon dry mustard
3   Tablespoons vinegar

1   teaspoon poppy seeds
⅔   cup salad oil

1.   Place first 4 ingredients into blender; mix well.

2.   Turn blender on high; stream in oil very slowly until thickened.

3.   Chill before serving.

THOUSAND ISLAND DRESSING

Preparation time: 15 minutes   *Yield: 1½ cups*

¾   cup low calorie mayonnaise
½   cup spicy vegetable juice
    (V-8 suggested)
1   teaspoon dried minced onion

1   Tablespoon green pepper, minced,
    (optional)
3   Tablespoons dill pickle, minced,
    or relish
2   packets artificial sweetner
    (Equal suggested)

1.   Blend all ingredients with a fork or wire whisk.

2.   Cover; store in refrigerator.

Best when used within 2 weeks.

A tasty, low calorie dressing.

DIJON DRESSING

Preparation time: 5-10 minutes   *Yield: 16 ounces*

1 Tablespoon Dijon mustard
2 Tablespoons egg substitute
   (Egg Beaters suggested)
1 Tablespoon dill weed

1 clove garlic, pressed
Ground fresh pepper to taste
1⅓ cups corn oil
Scant ½ cup vinegar, any flavor
Grated Parmesan cheese

1. Mix together mustard, egg substitute.

2. Add remaining ingredients, except Parmesan

3. Shake together in a bottle.

4. Before tossing, sprinkle salad with grated Parmesan cheese.

5. Add dressing; toss salad before serving.

HONEY LIME DRESSING

Preparation time: 15 minutes   *Yield: 16 ounces*

1 cup salad oil
½ cup fresh lime juice
½ cup honey

1 Tablespoon lime peel, grated
1½ teaspoon celery seed
1 teaspoon salt
¼ teaspoon pepper

1. Combine all ingredients.

2. Mix well.

May be prepared 1 week ahead.

HELEN'S VINEGAR AND OIL DRESSING

Preparation time: 5 minutes   *Serves: 6-8*

⅓ cup sugar
1 teaspoon salt
1 teaspoon dry mustard
¼ teaspoon ground thyme

¼ teaspoon ground pepper
1 garlic bud, cut in half
½ cup vinegar
½ cup salad oil

1. Mix all dry ingredients.

2. Mix well in shaker.

3. Add garlic bud.

4. Refrigerate.

5. When ready to use, add vinegar, salad oil. Shake or whip.

6. Remove garlic bud before serving.

Refrigerates indefinitely.

Mustard and thyme give an unusual flavor.

For a sweeter dressing, increase sugar to ½ cup.

TIPS ON SALADS

(From Our Good Cooks!)

Toss a salad with your hands. Use disposable plastic gloves to mix it thoroughly without coating hands with dressing.

Toss salad for a large group in a large white plastic bag.

Perk up soggy lettuce by adding lemon juice to a bowl of cold water; soak lettuce in the refrigerator for an hour.

Keep lettuce and celery longer by storing in paper bags instead of plastic.

Stand limp celery in a pitcher of water in the refrigerator to re-crisp.

Remove the core from a head of lettuce by hitting the core end once sharply against the counter. The core will loosen and pull out easily.

Spray gelatin molds with cooking spray for easy removal.

Dampen the dish on which gelatin is to be unmolded. It can then be easily moved for centering.

Add herbs to salad dressings several hours before serving. Refrigerate.

Dilute creamy salad dressing with low or no-fat plain yogurt to reduce calories.

Take advantage of reduced and no fat salad dressings and mayonnaises, but learn to use smaller amounts because of sodium content.

Lighten salad dressing recipes by substituting fruit juice for half the oil, or try 1 part oil to 1 part vinegar. Balsamic vinegar is nice because it is mild.

Yellow Springs, Ohio

A place to live, a place to work, a place to study, a place to play, a place to paint, a place to write, a place to teach, a place to learn, a place to listen, a place to speak, a place to pray, a place to think, a place to sing, a place to dance. And just where is there such a place? It can be found nestled in the countryside just east of Dayton.

In 1853, Horace Mann put down roots in the small Village of Yellow Springs at a college called Antioch. He and his faculty formed a family of scholars free to explore the lore of knowledge unencumbered by established, parochial methods. Antioch's reputation for innovative education remains its hallmark.

Today, Yellow Springs is home to 5,000 persons – an eclectic combination of artisans, scientists, businessmen, and educators. Almost as testimony to the ideals of education and democracy, 95 percent of Yellow Springs voters cast ballots on election day!

This community, with its yellow springs, with its schools and churches, with its farms and its factories, thrives as a center of the arts and sciences. A walk through the village, tantalizes the senses as the aroma of home-baked bread wafts from one of the many fine cafes or restaurants. Shops with handcrafted jewelry, clothing and textiles, pottery, and fine art invite long leisurely afternoons exploring Yellow Springs' treasures. A trip to Yellow Springs would not be complete without a stop at Young's Dairy where rich, homemade ice cream tempts the palate and augments the waist.

John Bryan State Park beckons as a place for picnics, hiking, and camping at its 1,000-acre facility, while Glen Helen offers a 1,000-acre preserve with cliffs, valleys, cascades, and the spring from which the village got its name.

Alas, Yellow Springs is also a place to visit!

Bread

OLD WORLD BREAD

Preparation time: 15 minutes + rising   *Yield: 2 loaves*
Baking time: 30 minutes

½ cup warm water
1 package dry yeast
2¼ cups rye flour (Hodgson Mill suggested)
1 cup whole wheat flour (Hodgson Mill suggested)

¼ cup dark brown sugar
½ cup powdered milk
1 Tablespoon salt
2 cups very warm tap water
3 cups unbleached flour

1. Proof yeast in a cup in warm water.
2. Combine all dry ingredients except unbleached flour by hand or with a mixer. Add to yeast.
3. Add warm water; mix thoroughly.
4. Add unbleached flour; mix well.
5. Remove from mixing bowl onto a well-floured surface; knead until smooth, elastic.
6. Place in a greased bowl; oil top.
7. Cover with waxed paper; allow to rise until double.
8. Pound down; remove to floured surface.
9. Divide dough into 2 parts. Round each; place each in a greased 8 or 9-inch cake pan.
10. Allow to rise until almost double.
11. Bake at 375° for 30 minutes. (Cover with foil during baking if bread becomes too brown.)
12. Remove from pans immediately; cool on wire racks.

An easy rapid yeast recipe.

HONEY OF A WHOLE WHEAT BREAD

Preparation time: 15 minutes + rising　　　　　　　　　　*Yield: 2 loaves*
Baking time: 35-40 minutes

3½ to 4 cups all-purpose flour,
 divided (Better for
 Bread suggested)
2½ cups whole wheat flour, divided
 (Robin Hood Stone Ground
 suggested)
2 packages dry yeast

2 teaspoons salt
1 cup milk or skim milk
1 cup water
⅓ cup honey
3 Tablespoons shortening (solid,
 butter, or oil)
1 egg (2 egg whites or egg substitute
 also acceptable)

1. Combine 2 cups all-purpose flour with 1 cup wheat flour, yeast, salt in a large mixer bowl; mix well.

2. Heat milk, water, honey, shortening in a saucepan until warm (120-130°; shortening need not melt).

3. Add to flour mixture.

4. Add egg. Blend at low speed until moistened. Beat 3 minutes at medium speed.

5. Gradually stir in by hand the remaining wheat flour and enough all-purpose flour to make a firm dough.

6. Knead on a floured surface 5-8 minutes (125-150 strokes).

7. Place in a greased bowl, turning to grease top. Cover.

8. Let rise in a warm place about 1 hour until double. (Preheat oven for 1 minute; turn off; place bread in closed oven to rise.)

9. Punch down dough. Divide into 2 parts.

10. Roll or pat out each into a 14x7-inch rectangle.

11. Starting with the shorter side, roll up tightly, pressing dough into roll with each turn. Pinch edges to seal.

12. Place in 2 greased 8 or 9-inch loaf pans.

13. Cover; let rise in a warm place about 35-40 minutes until almost double.

(Continued on facing page)

14. Preheat oven to 375° while bread is rising.

15. Bake on the center oven rack for 35-40 minutes until loaf sounds hollow when tapped with finger.

16. Remove from pans immediately; cool on racks.

17. When lukewarm, brush lightly with margarine to ensure soft crust.

OATMEAL BREAD

Preparation time: 20 minutes + rising   *Yield: 2 loaves*
Baking time: 40-50 minutes

1   **package dry yeast**
½   **cup warm water**
2   **cups milk**
2   **cups uncooked oatmeal (Quaker Oats suggested)**
¼   **cup brown sugar**

1   **Tablespoon salt**
2   **Tablespoons shortening**
5   **cups unbleached all-purpose flour, divided**
1   **egg white with water**
    Oatmeal

1. Proof yeast in warm water.

2. Scald milk. Add oats, sugar, salt, shortening.

3. Add yeast to mixture.

4. Add 2 cups flour. Beat 2 minutes with an electric mixer at medium speed.

5. Add enough additional flour to make a soft dough. Knead.

6. Place in a greased bowl; cover with plastic wrap; let rise until double.

7. Turn out onto a floured surface.

8. Cut in half; shape into 2 loaves; place in 2 greased 8-inch loaf pans.

9. Let rise.

10. Brush with egg white and water. Sprinkle with oatmeal.

11. Bake at 375° on the center oven rack for 40-50 minutes.

Freezes well after baking.
An easy, healthy bread. Makes great toast and sandwiches.

DILL - RYE BREAD

Preparation time: 10 minutes + rising　　　　　　　　　*Yield: 1 large loaf*
Baking time: 35-45minutes

¼ cup warm water
2 packages dry yeast
3 to 3½ cups all-purpose flour, divided
½ cup dry milk
2 Tablespoons shortening

2 Tablespoons sugar
2 teaspoons salt
1 teaspoon dill seeds
1 teaspoon dill weed
1 teaspoon caraway seeds
1½ cups warm water
1½ cups rye flour

1. Proof yeast in a cup with ¼ cup warm water.

2. Measure 2 cups all-purpose flour into a mixer bowl.

3. Add dry milk, shortening, sugar, salt, dill seeds, dill weed, caraway seeds.

4. Add 1½ cups warm water. Mix 2-3 minutes.

5. Add rye flour, yeast mixture; mix 2 minutes.

6. Add enough all-purpose flour to make a rough mass; knead.

7. Shape into a ball; place into a greased bowl. Cover with plastic wrap. Let rise until double.

8. Divide into smaller loaves, using 2 or 3 greased 3½x5-inch pans, or make one large loaf in a greased 5x8-inch pan.

9. Cover shaped loaves with plastic; let rise until double.

10. Bake at 375° on the center oven rack for 35-45 minutes.

May be frozen after baking. Also works well when formed into rolls.

Great for ham and cheese sandwiches and canapes.

For a very aromatic, tasty bread, eliminate all the dill herbs and substitute 2 teaspoons rosemary.

POLISH RAISIN BREAD

Preparation time: 30 minutes + rising　　　　　　　　*Yield: 2 loaves*
Baking time: 40 minutes

1 cup warm water	½ cup butter
1 package yeast	4½ cups flour
¾ cup sugar	1 teaspoon vanilla
2 eggs	1 cup raisins
1 teaspoon salt	2 eggs, well beaten
1 cup evaporated milk	

1. Dissolve yeast in warm water (110°). Set aside.

2. Mix sugar, eggs, salt.

3. Heat milk; melt butter with warm milk. Add to sugar mixture.

4. Add flour, yeast alternately.

5. Add vanilla, raisins.

6. Knead 10 minutes. Keep sprinkling flour on dough; knead until no longer sticky.

7. Place in a warm place in a greased bowl; cover with a towel; let rise about 2 hours until double in size.

8. Separate into 2 parts; place into 2 greased 9x5½x2½-inch loaf pans.

9. Let rise again until double in size.

10. Brush tops with beaten eggs.

11. Bake at 375° for 10 minutes; reduce heat to 325°; bake for 30 minutes.

Very important to have the water warm enough for the yeast.
Excellent toasted.

POPPY SEED BREAD

Preparation time: 10-15 minutes
Baking time: 1 hour

Yield: 2 loaves

Bread

3 cups all-purpose flour
2 cups sugar
3 eggs
1½ teaspoons baking powder
1½ teaspoons salt

1½ Tablespoons poppy seeds
1½ cups milk
¾ cup vegetable oil
1½ teaspoons vanilla
1½ teaspoons almond extract

Glaze

1 cup powdered sugar, sifted
2 Tablespoons orange juice

¼ teaspoon vanilla
¼ teaspoon almond extract

1. Combine all bread ingredients in a large bowl.
2. Beat 2 minutes at medium speed of an electric mixer.
3. Spoon batter into 2 greased and floured 8x4x3-inch loaf pans.
4. Bake at 350° on the center oven rack for 1 hour or until a wooden toothpick inserted in the center comes out clean.
5. Cool in pans 10 minutes; remove; cool completely on wire racks.
6. Combine all ingredients for glaze; mix well.
7. Drizzle orange glaze over bread.

May be frozen after baking with or without the glaze.

Wonderful for luncheons, coffees, or with salad.

ONION DILL BREAD

Preparation time: 15 minutes
Processing time: 4 hours, 10 minutes

Yield: 1 loaf
For automatic bread machine

¼ cup water
1 large egg, unbeaten, at room
   temperature
¾ cup vanilla yogurt
¾ cup small curd cottage cheese
1½ Tablespoons butter
2 cups all-purpose flour

1⅓ cups whole wheat flour
¼ teaspoon baking soda
1½ teaspoons salt
3 Tablespoons minced dried onion
2½ Tablespoons whole dill seed
1 package dry yeast

1. Place ingredients in bread machine in order listed.

2. Process.

Check instructions for your bread machine for hints and particular instructions.

BEER BREAD

Preparation time: 5 minutes
Baking time: 35 minutes

Yield: 1 loaf

3 cups self-rising flour
3 Tablespoons sugar

1 12-ounce can beer, at room
   temperature

1. Combine all ingredients in a bowl.

2. Spread mixture in a greased and floured 8-inch loaf pan.

4. Bake at 375° on the center oven rack for 35 minutes or more.

Best when served warm; also toasts well.
Use immediately, as this bread does not store well.

CARDAMOM BREAD

Preparation time: 30-45 minutes + rising   *Yield: 2 loaves or 1 crown*
Baking time: 25-30 minutes

Bread

4½ to 5 cups all-purpose flour,
   divided
½ cup sugar
1 teaspoon salt
1 teaspoon whole cardamom seed,
   crushed, or 1 teaspoon
   ground cardamom

2 packages dry yeast
½ cup warm water
½ cup milk
2 eggs
½ cup butter, at room
   temperature

Filling

½ cup sugar
1 teaspoon whole cardamom seed,
   crushed, or 1 teaspoon
   ground cardamom

1 egg, beaten

1. Combine 2 cups flour with other dry ingredients in a mixing bowl.

2. Add water, milk; mix well.

3. Add eggs, butter; combine thoroughly.

4. Add remaining flour until a workable dough forms.

5. Knead until smooth. Round into a ball.

6. Place in a greased bowl; oil top; cover with waxed paper. Let rise until double.

7. Punch down raised dough.

8. Combine ingredients for filling in a small bowl.

(Continued on facing page)

9. To make 2 loaves
   - Divide dough into 2 portions.
   - Roll each into an 18x9-inch rectangle.
   - Cut each into 3 18-inch strips.
   - Place 1 Tablespoon filling down the center of each strip.
   - Pinch edges of strips together to seal in filling.
   - Braid each of the 3 strips.
   - Place braids into 2 well-greased 8-inch loaf pans.
10. To make a wreath or crown
   - Roll all dough into a 12x24-inch rectangle.
   - Cut into 3 strips.
   - Place 2 Tablespoons filling down center of each; pinch edges.
   - Braid strips.
   - Place braid in the shape of a crown or wreath on a baking sheet covered with baking paper (microwave wrap).
11. Allow formed loaves or crown to rise until almost double.
12. Brush tops with beaten egg.
13. Sprinkle with remaining filling mixture.
14. Bake at 350° for 25-30 minutes.
15. Remove immediately from pans; cool on wire rack.

Whole cardamom crushed in a mortar or with an ice crusher holds the flavor best. Wonderful with cream cheese for a special brunch or coffee.

LUNCHEON DINNER ROLLS

Preparation time: 10-15 minutes + rising
Baking time: 20 minutes

Yield: 16 dinner size or
32 luncheon size

1 package yeast
2 Tablespoons lukewarm water
½ cup milk
2½ Tablespoons sugar

½ teaspoon salt
2 Tablespoons butter
1 egg
2½ cups flour

1. Proof yeast in water.

2. Scald milk; add sugar, salt, butter. Cool.

3. Add yeast mixture to liquid. Gradually add egg, flour.

4. Knead until smooth, elastic.

5. Place into a greased bowl. Cover with plastic. Let rise until double.

6. Punch down dough.

7. Shape into rolls. Place 16 dough balls into a greased round glass oven dish. If making small rolls, place 16 in each of 2 dishes.

8. Let rise.

9. Bake at 375° for 10 minutes; reduce heat to 350°; bake 10 additional minutes until brown.

To freeze, wrap in foil; reheat in oven.
Great on a buffet table. Sweet taste compliments meat, poultry, or ham.

BUSY DAY BISCUITS

Preparation time: 10 minutes
Baking time: 15 minutes

Yield: 6

1 cup self-rising flour
1 Tablespoon mayonnaise

½ cup 2% milk

1. Mix all ingredients until well blended.

2. Drop by Tablespoons onto a greased cookie sheet.

3. Bake at 400° for 15 minutes.

So easy and so tasty! Freeze well after baking.

BRIOCHE

Preparation time: 20 minutes + rising
Baking time: 10-12 minutes

½ cup lukewarm whole milk
1 package dry yeast
½ cup butter, melted
2 large eggs, at room temperature

¼ cup sugar
¼ teaspoon salt
2½ cups flour, divided
Melted butter

1. Place milk, yeast in a mixing bowl. Let stand 5 minutes. Stir well.

2. Add butter, eggs, sugar, salt, 1 cup flour. Beat well.

3. Add remaining flour to make a soft dough. Beat until smooth.

4. Cover with plastic wrap; let rise until double.

5. Punch dough down.

6. Let rise again. Punch down.

7. Knead lightly to form a smooth ball.

8. Reserve a piece of dough the size of a jumbo egg.

9. Divide remaining dough into 12 pieces.

10. Place in well greased muffin tins.

11. Make an indentation in the top of each brioche.

12. Roll reserved dough into 12 egg shapes.

13. Place 1 piece in each indentation.

14. Let rise until double.

15. Baste tops with melted butter.

16. Bake at 375° for 10-12 minutes.

FIRST PRIZE CORNBREAD

Preparation time: 10 minutes
Baking time: 15- 18 minutes

Serves: 9-12

1 cup flour	½ teaspoon soda
1 cup yellow cornmeal, freshly ground	½ teaspoon salt
	1 cup buttermilk
¼ cup sugar	1 egg
2 teaspoons baking powder	3 Tablespoons lard, melted

1. Mix dry ingredients.

2. Add remaining ingredients, mixing well after each addition.

3. Pour into a preheated, greased cornbread pan or cast iron skillet, or use a greased 9-inch square or pie pan.

4. Bake at 425-450° for 15-18 minutes. Serve hot with honey or sorgum.

A first prize winner from the Greene County, Ohio, Fair.

ZUCCHINI - RAISIN BREAD

Preparation time: 10-12 minutes
Baking time: 1 hour

Yield: 2 loaves

2 cups zucchini, shredded, drained	2 cups flour, measured after sifting
3 eggs, beaten until light	2 teaspoons baking soda
¾ cup oil	3 teaspoons cinnamon
1½ cups sugar	1 teaspoon salt
2 teaspoons vanilla	1 cup walnuts, chopped
¼ teaspoon baking powder	1 cup raisins

1. Place prepared zucchini in a large bowl.

2. Add eggs, oil, sugar, vanilla. Stir.

3. Stir in dry ingredients.

4. Fold in nuts, raisins.

5. Pour batter into 2 greased or sprayed 8-inch loaf pans.

6. Bake at 375° on the center oven rack for 1 hour.

The zucchini may be shredded in a blender or grated finely in a food processor. Refrigerates well for 1 week or may be frozen after baking.

ALOHA BREAD

Preparation time: 15 minutes
Baking time: 60-70 minutes

Yield: 1 loaf

2 cups flour
1 teaspoon baking soda
½ teaspoon salt
2 teaspoons baking powder
½ cup butter or margarine, softened
1 cup sugar

2 eggs
1 cup bananas, mashed
1 cup crushed pineapple in own juice, undrained
Juice of 1 orange
1 cup nuts, chopped
Almonds, shredded, for top (optional)

1. Preheat oven to 350°.

2. Sift together dry ingredients.

3. Cream butter, sugar. Add eggs; blend well.

4. Add dry ingredients to creamed mixture; mix well.

5. Add remaining ingredients; mix well.

6. Pour into a greased, floured 9x5-inch loaf pan.

7. If desired, sprinkle almonds on top.

8. Bake on the center oven rack for 60-70 minutes.

Refrigerates well for a week; may also be frozen after baking.
A nice variation of banana bread.

ORANGE BREAD

Preparation time: 1 hour　　　　　　　　　　　　　　　　*Yield: 16 thin slices*
Baking time: 1 hour

2　oranges	1　egg
Boiling water, salted	2½ cups all-purpose flour
¼ cup boiling water	Pinch salt
1　cup sugar	4　teaspoons baking powder
1　Tablespoon butter	1　cup whole milk

1. Squeeze juice from oranges.

2. Cut oranges in quarters; remove all white membrane.

3. Cut orange peel into narrow strips.

4. Boil strips in salted water to cover, about 15-20 minutes. Drain.

5. Return peel to pan; add ¼ cup boiling water and sugar. Stir well.

6. Boil over very low heat 20-25 minutes until peel is sugared, transparent.

7. Remove from heat. Add butter. Cool.

8. When cool, add egg. Beat.

9. Sift together flour, salt, baking powder. Sift again.

10. Add milk alternately with flour mixture. Mix well.

11. Pour into a greased 9¾x5¾x2¾-inch loaf pan.

12. Bake at 350° on the center oven rack for 1 hour.

Great toasted if sliced ½-inch thick.
Lovely for breakfast or brunch. Delicious alone or could be enhanced with an orange glaze.

RHUBARB BREAD

Preparation time: 15 minutes   *Yield: 2 loaves*
Baking time: 1 hour

1½ cups brown sugar
⅔ cup oil
1 egg
1 teaspoon baking soda
1 teaspoon salt

1 teaspoon vanilla
1 cup sour milk
2½ cups flour
1½ cups rhubarb, diced into
   small pieces
½ cup nuts, chopped

1. Beat sugar, oil, egg, soda until smooth.

2. Add salt, vanilla, milk, flour. Beat until smooth.

3. Add rhubarb, nuts.

4. Pour into 2 greased 9x5½x2½-inch loaf pans.

5. Bake at 350° for 1 hour.

To sour milk, use 1 Tablespoon vinegar in enough milk to yield 1 cup.

A moist, attractive loaf with a pretty pink color. Freezes well after baking.

Accompaniment: Fruit salad or luncheon plate.

CRANBERRY BREAD

Preparation time: 10 minutes
Baking time: 1 hour

Yield: 1 large or 3 small loaves

1   cup sugar
2   Tablespoons solid shortening
1   egg, beaten
2   cups flour, sifted
2   teaspoons baking powder
½   teaspoon baking soda

½   teaspoon salt
Grated rind of 1 orange
½   cup orange juice
¼   cup water
1   cup cranberries, cut in half
1   cup walnuts, chopped

1. Blend sugar, shortening.
2. Sift dry ingredients together.
3. Add sifted ingredients, beaten egg to sugar mixture.
4. Add rind, juice, water. Mix well.
5. Fold in cranberries, walnuts.
6. Pour batter into a large greased 5x8-inch loaf or 3 small greased 3½x5-inch loaf pans.
7. Bake at 350° on the center oven rack for 1 hour.

After grating rind from orange, squeeze fresh juice for bread.

Freezes well after baking.

Great to serve for Thanksgiving and Christmas meals. Also a wonderful holiday gift.

APPLE DANISH

Preparation time: 30 minutes
Baking time: 45 minutes

3   cups flour
½   teaspoon salt
1   cup solid shortening
½   cup milk
1   egg yolk, beaten
6   apples, pared, sliced
1½   cups sugar

2   Tablespoons flour
1   teaspoon cinnamon
¼   cup butter
1   egg white, slightly beaten
1¼   cups powdered sugar
¼   cup butter, melted
½   teaspoon vanilla
Milk

1. Mix together flour, salt; cut in shortening.
2. Mix milk, egg yolk; add to flour mixture.
3. Knead dough until smooth on a floured surface.
4. Roll out half of dough to fit an 11x16-inch jelly roll pan.
5. Place dough in greased pan.
6. Place apples on dough.
7. Stir together sugar, flour, cinnamon. Sprinkle over apples.
8. Dot with butter.
9. Roll out remaining pastry; place over mixture in pan.
10. Brush with egg white.
11. Slit pastry in several places.
12. Bake at 375° for 45 minutes.
13. Combine powdered sugar, butter, vanilla; thin with milk to correct consistency for glaze. Spread over pastry.

Peaches, cherries, or blueberries may be substituted for apples.
Good for breakfast or dessert.

TUTTI-FRUTTI STRUDEL

Preparation time: 20 minutes each part
Baking time: 30-40 minutes

Serves: 48

Dough

2½ cups unbleached flour
1 cup unsalted butter, chilled,
  or ½ cup each butter and
  margarine, chilled, cut into pieces

1 cup sour cream

1. Place flour in a large bowl.

2. Add butter; cut in until mixture resembles coarse meal.

3. Add sour cream; blend well.

4. Gather dough into a ball.

5. Divide into 4 pieces; form each into a flat rectangle.

6. Wrap in plastic; refrigerate at least 24 hours.

Filling

1½ cups sugar
1 Tablespoon cinnamon
4 heaping Tablespoons apricot
  preserves
4 heaping Tablespoons cherry
  preserves

¾ cup (3 ounces) pecans,
  coarsely chopped
¾ cup (3 ounces) shredded
  or flaked coconut
1½ cups dried mixed fruit,
  including raisins, diced

1. Preheat oven to 350°. Grease a jelly roll pan.

2. Mix sugar with cinnamon in a small bowl.

3. Spread ½ cup of mixture evenly over a pastry cloth, linen towel, or waxed paper.

4. Top with 1 piece of dough.

5. Roll dough out to about a 10x14-inch rectangle; sprinkle with cinnamon mixture as needed to prevent sticking.

(Continued on facing page)

6. Spread 2 Tablespoons of one flavor of preserves in a 2-inch wide strip along edge of the dough.

7. Sprinkle with 3 Tablespoons each of pecans, coconut, and 6 Tablespoons of mixed fruit.

8. Using cloth or waxed paper, roll dough up lengthwise into cylinder, folding ends in as you roll.

9. Place in a prepared jelly roll pan, seam side down.

10. Repeat with remaining dough and filling to form 4 strudels.

11. Using a sharp knife, score each strudel into ½-inch pieces, being careful not to cut through dough.

12. Sprinkle some of remaining cinnamon mixture on top.

13. Bake on the center oven rack for 30-40 minutes until firm, golden brown.

14. Cut immediately on score lines.

15. Cool on wire rack.

16. Store in an airtight container lined with waxed paper.

Filling may be prepared ahead.

Very professional in appearance.

OVERNIGHT CINNAMON ROLLS

Preparation time: 45 minutes   *Yield: 36*
Baking time: 30 minutes

2   packages yeast
⅔   cup warm water
2   teaspoons sugar
1   cup milk, warmed
¼   cup butter or margarine, softened
2   eggs, at room temperature
½   cup sugar
1   teaspoon salt

5 to 6 cups all-purpose flour, divided
¾ cup raisins
½ cup butter or margarine, melted, divided
6 Tablespoons cinnamon, divided
4 Tablespoons sugar, divided
Powdered sugar, milk for frosting (optional)

1. Place yeast, water, sugar into a small bowl. Mix; let sit until bubbly.
2. Mix milk, butter, eggs in a large bowl.
3. Stir in sugar, salt, 2 cups flour. Mix well by hand or with an electric mixer.
4. Add yeast mixture; mix well.
5. Stir in raisins and 2-3 cups flour, enough to make a stiff dough.
6. Turn onto a floured surface; knead 8-10 minutes until smooth, elastic.
7. Cover with plastic wrap, then a towel; let rest 20 minutes.
8. Divide dough in half. Roll each half into a 12-inch square.
9. Brush with ¼ cup melted butter, 3 Tablespoons cinnamon, 2 Tablespoons sugar.
10. Roll up in jelly roll fashion. Cut into 1-inch pieces.
11. Place in a greased pan. Cover with waxed paper, then plastic wrap.
12. Refrigerate overnight.
13. Preheat oven to 375° when ready to bake.
14. Uncover rolls; let stand at room temperature 10-20 minutes.
15. Bake on the center oven rack for 30 minutes.
16. Remove from pan; cool on wire racks.
17. If desired, top with powdered sugar and milk frosting.

Cooks Incorporated

CRANBERRY SOUR CREAM COFFEE CAKE

Preparation time: 15 minutes *Serves: 12-16*
Baking time: 40-45 minutes

½ cup butter
1 cup sugar
2 eggs
2 cups flour
1 teaspoon baking powder
1 teaspoon baking soda
½ teaspoon salt
8 ounces sour cream

1 teaspoon almond extract
1 16-ounce can whole
   cranberry sauce
½ cup pecans, chopped
¾ cup powdered sugar
1 Tablespoon warm water
½ teaspoon almond or vanilla extract

1. Cream butter. Add sugar gradually, beating until light, fluffy.

2. Add eggs, one at a time. Beat well after each addition.

3. Combine dry ingredients. Add to creamed mixture alternately with sour cream.
   Beat well after each addition.

4. Stir in almond or vanilla extract.

5. Spread half the batter in a greased, floured 9x13-inch pan.

6. Spoon half the cranberry sauce over batter; spread evenly.

7. Repeat layers.

8. Sprinkle with pecans.

9. Bake at 350° for 40-45 minutes.

10. Cool slightly.

11. Combine powdered sugar, water, extract to make glaze. Beat until lump free.

12. Drizzle glaze on warm coffee cake.

Dorothy Lane Market
Dayton, Ohio

Freezes well if wrapped air tight.

APRICOT-PINEAPPLE COFFEE CAKE

Preparation time: 15 minutes　　　　　　　　　　　　　*Serves: 8-10*
Baking time: 30 minutes

½ cup dried apricots, finely cut
½ cup crushed pineapple in own juices,
　　well drained (reserve liquid)
¼ cup sugar
2 Tablespoons pineapple juice
1½ Tablespoons orange juice
1½ Tablespoons orange rind,
　　grated

⅓ cup flaked coconut
1½ cups flour
2 teaspoons baking powder
¾ teaspoon salt
½ cup sugar
⅓ cup shortening
1 egg, well beaten
¾ cup milk

1. Combine apricots, pineapple, sugar, pineapple juice in a saucepan. Cook, stir over low heat 3 minutes until fruit is clear. Cool.

2. Add orange juice, rind, coconut.

3. Sift together dry ingredients. Cut in shortening.

4. Combine egg, milk. Add to flour mixture; stir only until flour is dampened.

5. Spread ⅔ batter in a greased 9-inch pie pan.

6. Top with alternating Tablespoons of fruit mixture and remaining batter.

7. Run a spatula or knife in a spiral through batter to give a marbled effect.

8. Bake at 375° for 30 minutes.

CREAM TEA SCONES

Preparation time: 10 minutes
Baking time: 12-15 minutes

Yield: 12-16

2 cups all-purpose flour
2 Tablespoons sugar
4 teaspoons baking powder
½ teaspoon salt
⅓ cup butter, at room
   temperature

1 egg
1 egg yolk
½ cup light cream or half and half
1 egg white, lightly beaten
Sugar

1. Mix together dry ingredients.

2. Cut in butter until mixture resembles coarse crumbs.

3. Combine egg, egg yolk, cream in a small bowl. Beat with a fork to blend.

4. Add egg mixture all at once to dry mixture, stirring with a fork to make a soft, slightly sticky dough.

5. Press into a ball; knead gently 10 times on a floured surface.

6. Roll out dough to ½-inch thickness. Cut into rounds.

7. Place on an ungreased cookie sheet.

8. Brush with egg white; sprinkle lightly with sugar.

9. Bake at 425° on the center oven rack for 12-15 minutes until golden brown.

A standard at tea time in Canada. Serve warm with butter and raspberry or strawberry jam.

PEPPERONI APPETIZER BREAD

Preparation time: 20 minutes + rising
Baking time: 25-30 minutes

Serves: 30

2¼ cups warm water (105-115°)
2 packages active dry yeast
1 Tablespoon sugar
1 Tablespoon salt

1 Tablespoon margarine, softened
6½ cups all-purpose flour, divided
18 thin slices provolone cheese
1½ cups pepperoni, chopped
1 egg, beaten

1. Measure warm water into a large warm bowl. Sprinkle in yeast; stir until dissolved.

2. Add sugar, salt, margarine, 3 cups flour; beat until smooth.

3. Stir in enough additional flour to make a soft dough.

4. Knead on a lightly floured surface about 8-10 minutes until smooth, elastic.

5. Place in a greased bowl; turn to grease top.

6. Cover; let rise in warm, draft-free place until double in size, about 1 hour.

7. Punch dough down; divide into 3 pieces. Roll each into a 12x8-inch rectangle.

8. Place 6 slices provolone, ½ cup pepperoni on each rectangle.

9. Roll from long side as for jelly roll; seal.

10. Place on 3 greased baking sheets.

11. Cover; let rise until double, about 1 hour.

12. Slash tops; brush loaves with egg.

13. Bake at 400° for 25-30 minutes.

14. Cool slightly. Slice. Serve warm.

Refrigerate leftovers; reheat to serve.
May be prepared 1 day ahead.

Accompaniment: Soup or salad. Also a good appetizer.

SPICED OATMEAL MINI-MUFFINS

Preparation time: 10 minutes + standing　　　　　　　　*Yield: 36*
Baking time: 15 minutes

1 cup uncooked oatmeal	1 teaspoon salt
1 cup buttermilk	1¾ cups all-purpose flour
1 egg, beaten	¾ teaspoon ground cinnamon
1 cup brown sugar	¼ teaspoon ground cloves
1 teaspoon baking powder	½ cup vegetable oil
1 teaspoon baking soda	¾ cup raisins
	¾ cup walnuts, chopped

1. Combine oatmeal, buttermilk in a large bowl; let stand 1 hour.

2. Add egg, brown sugar; mix well.

3. Combine dry ingredients; stir into oatmeal mixture.

4. Stir in remaining ingredients.

5. Fill greased mini-muffin tins ½ full.

6. Bake at 400° for 15 minutes.

A perfect mini-muffin which is moist, holds its shape, and freezes well.
Serve in a bread basket at meals with French bread and rye bread sticks.

FRUITED BRAN MUFFINS

Preparation time: 30 minutes   *Yield: 48*
Baking time: 25 minutes

8 ounces bran
¾ cup dark brown sugar
¾ cup light brown sugar
1½ cups sugar
5 cups flour, sifted
5 teaspoons baking soda

2 teaspoons salt
1 cup butter, melted
4 eggs, beaten
1 quart buttermilk
3 cups walnuts, chopped
1 cup dried apricots, chopped
1 cup dates, chopped

1. Preheat oven to 400°.

2. Mix together dry ingredients in a large bowl.

3. Add butter, eggs, buttermilk.

4. Pour batter into greased or sprayed muffin tins, filling ¾ full.

5. Bake on the center oven rack for 25 minutes.

Batter stores covered in the refrigerator for several days and may also be frozen.
Delicious, chewy muffins with excellent taste and texture.

NUTRIENT ANALYSIS (Per Serving)

Carbohydrate .... 30 grams
Protein .... 4 grams
Fat .... 7 grams
Calories .... 192 (33% from fat)
Cholesterol .... 19 milligrams
Sodium .... 194 milligrams

FRUITED BRAN MUFFINS - LIGHT OPTION

Preparation time: 30 minutes   *Yield: 48*
Baking time: 25 minutes

8   ounces bran
¾ cup dark brown sugar
¾ cup light brown sugar
1½ cups sugar
5   cups flour, sifted
5   teaspoons baking soda

2   teaspoons salt
⅔ cup margarine, melted
4   eggs, beaten
1   quart buttermilk
1   cup dried apricots, chopped
1   cup dates, chopped

1. Preheat oven to 400°.

2. Mix together dry ingredients in a large bowl.

3. Add margarine, eggs, buttermilk.

4. Pour batter into greased or sprayed muffin tins, filling ¾ full.

5. Bake on the center oven rack for 25 minutes.

NUTRIENT ANALYSIS (Per Serving)

Carbohydrate .... 29 grams
Protein .... 4 grams
Fat .... 3 grams
Calories .... 155 (17% from fat)
Cholesterol .... 19 milligrams
Sodium .... 182 milligrams

MOIST BRAN MUFFINS

Preparation time: 10 minutes
Baking time: 20 minutes

Yield: 18

½ cup butter or margarine, softened
1¼ cups sugar
2 eggs
1½ cups flour

1½ cups bran or raisin bran cereal
1 teaspoon baking soda
1 cup regular or low-fat sour cream
1 cup nuts or raisins (optional)

1. Cream butter, sugar.

2. Add eggs one at a time, mixing after each addition.

3. Add flour, bran, soda, sour cream. Mix well.

4. If desired, fold in nuts, raisins. Pour batter into greased muffin tins.

5. Bake at 350° on the center oven rack for 20 minutes until light brown.

A moist, light, easy muffin.

DRIED APPLE MUFFINS

Preparation time: 10-12 minutes
Baking time: 20 minutes

Yield: 18 regular or
36 mini-muffins

1½ cups flour
1 teaspoon cinnamon
1 teaspoon soda
Pinch salt
1 large egg

1 cup regular or light sour cream
1 cup dark brown sugar
1 teaspoon vanilla
6 ounces dried apples, chopped
½ cup raisins

1. Mix together dry ingredients.

2. Mix egg, sour cream, sugar. Gradually add mixture to dry ingredients.

3. Add remaining ingredients.

4. Place in muffin tins lined with paper baking cups.

5. Bake at 350° on the center oven rack for 20 minutes

Dried apples give a crisp taste to these moist muffins.

A nice mini-muffin for a dinner bread basket.

MINI APPLESAUCE MUFFINS

Preparation time: 20 minutes *Yield: 36-40*
Baking time: 12 minutes

½ cup vegetable oil
1 cup sugar
1 cup unsweetened applesauce
1 teaspoon baking soda
2 cups flour
1 teaspoon cinnamon

½ teaspoon cloves
¼ teaspoon nutmeg
¼ teaspoon salt
¼ cup raisins
½ cup chopped nuts
   (optional)

1. Cream oil, sugar until fluffy.

2. Combine applesauce, soda; blend into sugar mixture.

3. Sift together, add dry ingredients; add to applesauce mixture.

4. Stir in raisins; blend until smooth.

5. Add nuts.

6. Spoon into mini-muffin pans which have been sprayed with no-stick cooking spray and floured, or use paper baking cups.

7. Bake at 350° on the center oven rack for 12-15 minutes.

Freeze well after baking.

A low fat, low cholesterol recipe with no eggs.

Place in a basket for a nice gift.

BLUEBERRY PECAN MUFFINS

Preparation time: 10-15 minutes   *Yield: 12*
Baking time: 20-25 minutes

1¼ cups all-purpose flour
¼ cup whole wheat flour
⅓ cup sugar
1 teaspoon baking powder
½ teaspoon salt

1 cup fresh or frozen blueberries
⅓ cup pecans, broken
½ cup milk
¼ cup oil
1 egg, broken by stirring

1. Sift together dry ingredients.

2. Mix in blueberries, pecans.

3. Mix together milk, oil, egg.

4. Make a well in center of dry ingredients; pour liquid ingredients into well. Mix only until barely combined. Batter will be lumpy.

5. Pour batter into muffin tins which have been well greased or lined with lightly sprayed paper baking cups.

6. Bake at 400-425° for 20-25 minutes.

7. Remove immediately; serve hot.

Easy to make and great for breakfast guests.

Variation: Increase sugar to ½ cup: ¼ cup white and ¼ cup brown.

CELEBRATION MUFFINS

Preparation time: 10-15 minutes
Baking time: 20-25 minutes

Yield: 12 regular or
24 mini-muffins

1½ cups all-purpose flour
⅓ cup sugar
½ cup light brown sugar
1 teaspoon baking powder
½ teaspoon salt
½ cup milk

¼ cup butter, melted,
   slightly cooled
1 egg
1 cup fresh blueberries
1 cup sour cherries, halved, pitted
1 cup pecans, broken

1. Combine dry ingredients.

2. Add liquid ingredients; blend until combined.

3. Add fruits, pecans.

4. Spoon into 12 well greased or sprayed muffin tins or 24 mini-muffin tins.

5. Bake at 400° on the center oven rack for 20-25 minutes.

6. Serve warm.

For mini-muffins, use ¾ cup blueberries.

Freeze sour cherries in ½ cup portions when available fresh to be able to make muffins for a longer time when blueberries are in season.

Freeze well, but best right out of the oven.

Great for Fourth of July!

ENGLISH MUFFINS

Preparation time: 20 minutes + rising   *Yield: 8-10*
Cooking time: 6-8 minutes

¼ cup water (105-115 degrees)
1 package dry yeast
½ teaspoon sugar
¼ cup raw potato, grated
1 cup water

½ cup cold milk
2½ cups unbleached all-purpose flour
1 teaspoon salt
3 Tablespoons tepid water
2 Tablespoons butter, melted

1. Remove both ends from 8-10 tuna cans.

2. Proof yeast in water with sugar.

3. Simmer potato in water.

4. Stir in milk. Add flour, then proofed yeast. Batter will be very thick.

5. Cover with plastic wrap; let rise until bubbly.

6. Stir down batter.

7. Combine salt, water. Beat into batter. Beat well.

8. Cover with plastic wrap; let rise until bubbly.

9. Brush tuna can rings with butter.

10. Butter griddle.

11. Scoop batter into rings, filling ½ full.

12. Cook 6-8 minutes until bubbles form on top. Turn to brown.

13. Cool on a rack.

14. Split with a fork before serving.

Good toasted and served with jam or eggs Benedict.

RIVIERA TOAST

Preparation time: 10 minutes　　　　　　　　　　　　　　　*Serves: 12*
Baking time: 15-20 minutes

2　loaves French bread	1　teaspoon sugar
8　eggs	1　teaspoon orange rind, grated
2　cups milk	½　teaspoon cinnamon
¾　teaspoon vanilla	¼　teaspoon nutmeg
	Powdered sugar

1. Slice rounds of bread a bit diagonally to 1½-inch thick slices.

2. Mix remaining ingredients.

3. Dip each slice into mixture.

4. Place slices on buttered large flat pan. Do not place slices too close together.

5. Bake at 325° on the center oven rack for 15-20 minutes until centers are golden. (Turning usually not necessary.)

6. Sprinkle lightly with powdered sugar.

An easy, tasty breakfast for a group of any size. If multiplying the recipe, reduce the amount of milk.

SOUR CREAM - COTTAGE CHEESE PANCAKES

Preparation time: 30 minutes   *Yield: 8-10*

2 large or extra large eggs   ½ cup flour, sifted
⅓ cup cottage cheese   ½ teaspoon baking soda
¾ cup sour cream   ½ teaspoon salt

1. Beat eggs in a blender at low speed until thick, lemon-colored.

2. Add cheese; blend well on high speed.

3. Add sour cream; mix thoroughly at low speed.

4. Combine dry ingredients. Add to blender; blend at low speed, scraping sides of blender with a spatula.

5. Let stand 10-15 minutes.

6. Fry on a buttered griddle or skillet using medium to medium-high heat.

Very light pancakes.

MOTHER'S PANCAKES

Preparation time: 10-15 minutes   *Yield: 24 small pancakes*

2 cups buttermilk   2 teaspoons baking powder
1 teaspoon baking soda   4 Tablespoons sugar
2 eggs, beaten well   ⅔ cup flour
1⅓ teaspoons salt   1⅓ cups cornmeal

1. Stir soda into buttermilk; let foam.

2. Add to beaten eggs.

3. Add additional ingredients; beat well.

4. Cook on griddle.

A Kentucky family recipe with a unique taste.
Good served with maple syrup.

OVERNIGHT YEAST WAFFLES

Preparation time: 10 minutes   *Yield: 6*

2   cups milk
1   package active dry yeast
½   cup warm water
⅓   cup butter, melted

1   teaspoon salt
1   teaspoon sugar
3   cups flour, sifted
2   eggs, slightly beaten
½   teaspoon baking soda

1. Scald milk; cool to lukewarm.

2. Put water in a large bowl; sprinkle in yeast. Stir until dissolved.

3. Add milk, butter, salt, sugar, flour. Mix thoroughly until smooth with a rotary beater.

4. Cover; let stand at room temperature overnight.

5. Add eggs, soda. Beat well.

6. Cook on high on a waffle iron until brown.

UNCLE MEL'S HEARTY WAFFLES

Preparation time: 10-15 minutes   *Yield: 6-8*

2   cups unbleached flour
½   teaspoon salt
1   Tablespoon baking powder
1   Tablespoon wheat germ (optional)

2   egg yolks, slightly beaten
2   Tablespoons vegetable oil
2   egg whites, beaten until stiff
1   cup plain nonfat yogurt
1 to 1¼ cups skim milk

1. Sift together flour, salt, baking powder.

2. If desired, add wheat germ.

3. Mix beaten egg yolks with yogurt, milk. Stir into flour mixture, blending until smooth with a spoon or mixer.

4. Stir in oil.

5. Fold beaten egg whites into mixture.

6. Pour onto a preheated very hot waffle iron; cook until golden.

For variety add blueberries, slivered almonds, or apples with a tablespoon of cinnamon to the batter.

TIPS ON BREADS

(From Our Good Cooks!)

Bread is suitable to every time of day, every age of life, and every temperament.

Proofing yeast: Place yeast in warm water or milk heated to 105-115°. Add ½ teaspoon sugar; mix. If mixture bubbles up quickly, yeast is good. If mixture does not bubble, yeast is dead. Fluid that is above 115° will kill yeast.

Using milk rather than water makes a richer bread. Potato water may also be used.

Use unbleached, hard wheat flour to make the best yeast dough.

Add skim milk powder to regular milk to provide more nutrition.

Choose and stick with one flour for predictable results. Because there is no standardization of flours, no two flours react alike.

Salt is necessary in yeast breads to add flavor and stabilize fermentation.

Use large or extra large eggs for baking.

Banana bread – Place darkened, over-ripe unpeeled bananas in the freezer. When ready to make banana bread, remove bananas from freezer, thaw, mash.

Pancakes – Keep pancakes warm until ready to use by placing them on a platter or baking dish in a 200° oven. Layer paper towels between pancakes to absorb steam and prevent sogginess.

Crystallized jam, jelly, or honey – Microwave on high in a jar 1-2 minutes per cup, stirring often until crystals dissolve.

Muffins – Remove muffins easily from tins by first placing the hot tin on a wet towel.

Soften butter for spreading by inverting a small heated pan over the butter dish for a while.

Piqua, Ohio

This interesting city may contain some of the finest examples of 19th and 20th Century architecture in this part of the country.

Twenty-three blocks in the downtown area – known as the Piqua-Caldwell Historic District – were entered in the National Register of Historic Places in 1985. Matthew Caldwell, an early landowner built his residence at 626 Caldwell Street in 1888. Featuring a pedimented front gable end, the home is recognized as one the finest examples of the Queen Anne style.

Piqua lends itself to leisurely strolling with the opportunity to study the striking examples of residential architecture. Represented in the historic district are buildings of Federal, Colonial, Romanesque, and art deco styles. The ambiance of the city is complemented by a corps of fine restaurants, taverns, and coffee shops as well as bed and breakfast, hotel, and motel accommodations.

The Labor Day *Heritage Festival* attracts thousands of visitors for a weekend of amusements, history, and craft demonstrations as well as military French-Indian War drills provided by a company of French Marines from Detroit. Watching the preparation of apple butter, cider, and fresh baked bread and feasting on a full menu of other homemade specialties including chicken, pork, sausage, funnel cakes, shish kabobs, and dumplings provide visitors with a glimpse of life in earlier times. Various competitions - a bicycle tour, five kilometer marathon, plus a children's zoo - round out a weekend hard to equal.

Piqua's commitment to preserving its heritage will delight histroy buffs of all ages.

Eggs & Cheese

Cooks Incorporated

ASPARAGUS QUICHE

Preparation time: 30 minutes
Baking time: 40 minutes

Serves: 8

1 pie shell for 10" quiche dish
   (Pillsbury All-Ready Pie Crust
   suggested)
1½ pounds asparagus, cut up, or 2
   packages frozen asparagus
8 slices bacon, cut up
½ pound grated Gruyère cheese, grated

4 ounces mushrooms, sliced
3 to 4 Tablespoons shallots,
   chopped
4 eggs
1½ cups half and half or 2% milk
¼ teaspoon salt
Pepper
Asparagus tops

1. Bake pie shell at 400° for 10 minutes.

2. Steam asparagus until tender.

3. Sauté bacon until crisp. Drain

4. Sauté mushrooms, shallots in a small amount of bacon fat.

5. Beat eggs, milk. Add salt, pepper.

6. Layer bacon, asparagus, mushrooms, shallots, cheese in baked pie shell.

7. Pour egg/milk mixture over layered ingredients.

8. Decorate top of quiche with extra asparagus tops.

9. Bake at 375° for 40 minutes until a knife inserted in center comes out clean.

10. Cool slightly before cutting and serving.

CHRISTMAS BREAKFAST QUICHE

Preparation time: 20 minutes
Baking time: 45 minutes

Serves: 4

1 9" quiche pastry crust
1 cup shredded Swiss cheese
1 Tablespoon flour
¼ cup onion, sliced
1 teaspoon parsley, chopped

Salt, pepper to taste
1½ cups half and half
4 eggs
5 sausage links, cooked
5 slices bacon, cooked, crumbled

1. Toss cheese with flour.

2. Add onion, parsley, salt, pepper; sprinkle on base of pastry shell.

3. Whisk eggs with half and half; pour over cheese mixture.

4. Bake at 375° for 35 minutes.

5. Arrange sausage links, crumbled bacon on top; bake an additional 10 minutes.

Pie crust should be partially cooked before filling to prevent sogginess.

CONTINENTAL ONION QUICHE

Preparation time: 20 minutes
Baking time: 30-35 minutes

Serves: 4-6

1 unbaked 9" deep dish pastry shell
2 cups onions, thinly sliced
5 slices bacon, fried crisp, drained, crumbled
1 Tablespoon butter or margarine, melted

1 cup shredded Swiss cheese, divided
3 eggs
1½ cups half and half
¼ teaspoon salt
⅛ teaspoon white pepper
½ teaspoon basil

1. Bake pastry shell at 400° for 10 minutes.

2. Sauté onion in melted butter until golden.

3. Sprinkle half of cheese over bottom of pastry shell.

4. Spoon in onions. Top with remaining cheese.

5. Beat eggs with cream, salt, pepper, basil.

6. Pour over onions, cheese; sprinkle with bacon.

7. Bake at 400° on the center oven rack for 10 minutes; reduce to 350°; bake for 20-25 minutes.

Cooks Incorporated

CRUSTLESS LEEK QUICHE

Preparation time: 20-25 minutes　　　　　　　　　　　　　*Serves: 8*
Baking time: 45 minutes

1　⅞-ounce package leek soup mix
　　(Knorr suggested)
1½ cups milk (Farm Rich may be used)
½ cup light cream
3　eggs, beaten, or egg substitute
1　cup cottage cheese
¾ cup Swiss or Monterey Jack cheese

¾ cup sharp Cheddar cheese
1　teaspoon dry mustard
1　teaspoon Dijon mustard
½ teaspoon pepper, freshly ground
1　cup fresh broccoli florets
2　Tablespoons rye bread crumbs
Fresh parsley

1. Combine soup mix, milk. Cook over medium heat, stirring until thickened. Cool.

2. Stir in cream.

3. Mix eggs, cheeses, mustards, pepper in mixer or food processor.

4. Add to quiche mixture.

5. Steam broccoli or microwave 4 minutes with 2-3 Tablespoons water. Cool.

6. Add 2 Tablespoons bread crumbs to broccoli.

7. Place broccoli mixture in an 8-inch cake or pie pan.

8. Pour egg mixture over broccoli mixture.

9. Bake at 350° for 45 minutes until knife inserted in center comes out clean.

10. Let stand for 10 minutes before cutting.

CRUSTLESS MEXICAN QUICHE

Preparation time: 55 minutes   *Serves: 10-12*
Baking time: 55 minutes

10 eggs
½ cup flour
1 teaspoon baking powder
½ teaspoon salt
¼ cup butter, melted

1 cup green chilies, chopped
1 pound Monterey Jack cheese, grated
2 cups low fat cottage cheese
Salsa or chili sauce

1. In a large bowl, beat eggs until frothy.

2. Add flour, baking powder, salt; blend well. Mix in melted butter, chilies, cheeses.

3. Pour into a buttered 9x13-inch dish; bake at 400° on the center oven rack for 15 minutes; lower heat to 350°; bake 40 minutes longer.

4. Cut into small squares. Serve warm with salsa or chili sauce.

An excellent brunch dish with a different flavor.
Accompaniments: Green salad, corn muffins.

QUICK CHILI RELLENO CASSEROLE

Preparation time: 20 minutes   *Serves: 4-6*
Baking time: 45 minutes

1 7-ounce can whole chilies, cut in half
½ pound Monterey Jack cheese, grated
½ pound Cheddar or longhorn cheese, grated

1 3-ounce can evaporated milk
2 eggs
1 Tablespoon flour
1 7-ounce can tomato sauce or mild salsa

1. Place half of chilies in greased 9x9-inch baking dish.

2. Add Monterey Jack cheese, other half of chilies, Cheddar cheese.

3. Mix together milk, eggs, flour.

4. Pour over casserole; bake at 350° for 30 minutes.

5. Remove from oven; pour tomato sauce or salsa on top.

6. Bake for another 15 minutes.

Accompaniment: Tacos

CHEESE BAKE

Preparation time: 25-30 minutes
Baking time: 30-35 minutes

Serves: 6

2 medium onions, sliced
1 Tablespoon butter, melted
8 hard boiled eggs, sliced
2 cups Swiss cheese, shredded
1 10¾-ounce can mushroom soup
¾ cup milk

1 teaspoon prepared mustard
½ teaspoon seasoned salt
¼ teaspoon dill weed
¼ teaspoon pepper
24 pieces small caraway rye bread
Paprika

1. Sauté onions in butter.

2. Place in 9x12-inch casserole.

3. Top with egg slices; sprinkle with cheese.

4. Blend soup, milk, mustard, salt, dill weed, pepper in an electric mixer.

5. Pour soup mixture over eggs and cheese. Overlap bread in rows on top.

6. Bake at 350° on the center oven rack for 30-35 minutes. Broil 1 minute to toast bread.

Variation: Add bacon or Canadian bacon. An excellent brunch or holiday breakfast.

Accompaniment: Fruit.

BLUSHING BUNNY

Preparation time: 15 minutes

Serves: 4

½ pound Cheddar cheese, grated
1 10¾ can condensed tomato soup

½ teaspoon dry mustard
4 slices enriched toast, buttered
8 slices bacon, cooked

1. Mix together cheese, soup, mustard in a glass microwave bowl.

2. Heat in microwave oven 2 minutes at medium. Stir. Continue to cook about 4 ½ minutes until cheese melts. Stir once more.

3. To serve, place one slice of toast on a luncheon plate. Spoon cheese sauce over top to cover. Criss-cross two bacon strips on each serving.

Variations: Use shrimp or other cooked seafood, sliced hard cooked eggs, cubed ham, cooked vegetables. Just use your imagination and your leftovers.

Accompaniment: Fresh fruit or salad

BROCCOLI AND CHEESE PIE

Preparation time: 20 minutes   *Serves: 8*
Baking time: 40-45 minutes

Phyllo dough
¼ cup butter, melted
½ cup onion, finely chopped
3 10-ounce packages frozen chopped
   broccoli, thawed, well drained
3 eggs, beaten

½ pound feta cheese, crumbled
¼ cup parsley, chopped
2 Tablespoons fresh dill, chopped
1 teaspoon salt
⅛ teaspoon pepper
½ to 1 cup butter, melted

1. Preheat oven to 350°. Sauté onions 5 minutes in hot butter until golden.

2. Add broccoli; stir to combine with onion. Remove from heat.

3. Combine eggs, cheese, parsley, dill, salt, pepper with broccoli and onion mixture. Mix well.

4. Line a 9-inch round pan with removable bottom, or a 9-inch springform pan with rim in place with 6-8 phyllo pastry leaves, overlapping and brushing top of each with melted butter.

5. Pour filling mixture into pastry-lined pan. Fold overlapping edges of pastry leaves over the top of filling.

6. Cut 6-8 phyllo leaves in 9-inch circles. Brush each with butter; layer one over the other on top of mixture. With a knife, cut through leaves to make servings.

7. Pour remaining butter on top.

8. Place on jelly roll pan.

9. Bake 40-45 minutes or until top is golden brown, crust puffy.

Good as a side dish, entrée, or appetizer.

Truffles Café and Catering
Centerville, Ohio

EGG BLOSSOMS

Preparation time: 45 minutes
Baking time: 10-15 minutes

1 **Tablespoon margarine**	4 **sheets phyllo pastry**
1 **clove garlic, minced**	2 **Tablespoons butter, melted**
½ **cup onion, chopped**	4 **teaspoons grated Parmesan cheese**
¼ **teaspoon oregano**	4 **eggs**
½ **teaspoon salt**	4 **teaspoons green onion, minced**
1 **16-ounce can whole tomatoes,**	**Salt, pepper to taste**
drained, chopped	

1. Combine first 6 ingredients for tomato sauce. Set aside.

2. Preheat oven to 350°.

3. Grease four 2½-inch muffin cups.

4. Brush 1 sheet of phyllo with butter. Top with another sheet; brush with butter. Cut stack into 6 4-inch squares. Repeat with remaining 2 sheets. Stack 3 layers of 4-inch squares together, rotating layers so that corners do not overlap.

5. Press into muffin cups. Repeat with remaining squares.

6. Sprinkle 1 teaspoon cheese into each phyllo cup.

7. Break 1 egg into each cup; sprinkle onion over eggs.

8. Season with salt, pepper.

9. Bake at 350° for 15-20 minutes until pastry is golden, eggs set.

10. Serve with tomato sauce.

BREAKFAST CASSEROLE

Preparation time: 30 minutes   *Serves: 12*
Baking time: 1 hour

2½ cups salad croutons
2 cups Cheddar cheese, grated
1½ cups canned mushrooms, diced, drained
2 pounds sausage, cooked, crumbled, well drained
8 whole fresh eggs, beaten

2½ cups skim milk, powdered cream substitute, half and half, or milk
2 10¾-ounce cans cream of mushroom soup, undiluted
¾ teaspoon prepared yellow mustard
1 cup shredded Cheddar cheese
¼ cup fresh parsley, chopped

1. Place croutons in bottom of a greased 9x12-inch pan.

2. Mix cheese, mushrooms, sausage. Spread over croutons.

3. Combine eggs, milk, soup, mustard. Mix well.

4. Pour egg mixture over ingredients in pan. Do not stir.

5. Cover; refrigerate at least one hour.

6. Bake at 350° for 1 hour until set. If necessary, cover with foil to prevent excess browning.

7. Sprinkle with cheese, parsley before serving.

May be prepared a day ahead and refrigerated before baking.
Variation: Omit sausage.

Accompaniments: Fruit, muffins.

NUTRIENT ANALYSIS (Per Serving)

Carbohydrate .... 5 grams
Protein .... 26 grams
Fat .... 41 grams
Calories .... 534 (69% from fat)
Cholesterol .... 238 milligrams
Sodium .... 1509 milligrams

BREAKFAST CASSEROLE - LIGHT OPTION

Preparation time: 25 minutes + refrigeration   *Serves: 12*
Baking time: 1 hour

5   slices bread, toasted, cubed
1½ cups reduced fat Cheddar cheese, grated
1½ cups canned mushrooms, drained, diced
2   pounds turkey sausage, cooked, crumbled, well drained
1½ cups egg substitute
2   eggs, beaten

2½ cups ½% milk
2   10¾-ounce cans low fat cream of mushroom soup (Healthy Request suggested)
¾   teaspoon yellow mustard
¾   cup reduced fat Cheddar cheese, grated
¼   cup fresh parsley, chopped

1. Place toasted bread cubes in bottom of a 9x12-inch pan sprayed with non-stick cooking spray.

2. Combine cheese, mushrooms, turkey sausage. Spread over croutons.

3. Combine egg substitute, eggs, milk, soup, mustard. Mix well.

4. Pour egg mixture over ingredients in pan. Do not stir.

5. Cover; refrigerate at least 1 hour or overnight.

6. Bake at 350° for 1 hour until set. (If necessary, cover with foil to prevent excess browning.)

7. Sprinkle with cheese, parsley before serving.

NUTRIENT ANALYSIS (Per Serving)

Carbohydrate .... 15 grams
Protein .... 26 grams
Fat .... 17 grams
Calories .... 318 (48% from fat)
Cholesterol .... 100 milligrams
Sodium .... 802 milligrams

ARTICHOKE & EGG CASSEROLE

Preparation time: 20 minutes
Baking time: 30 minutes

Serves: 4

6 hard-boiled eggs, peeled, quartered
1 package frozen artichoke hearts, defrosted
1 2½-ounce jar sliced mushrooms, drained

4 Tablespoons butter, melted
4 Tablespoons flour
2 cups milk
2 teaspoons lemon juice
½ cup herb seasoned stuffing (Pepperidge Farm suggested)

1. Mix first 3 ingredients together. Arrange in a buttered baking dish.

2. Add flour to melted butter. Mix until well blended.

3. Stir milk into flour mixture, whisking until thick.

4. Add lemon juice.

5. Cover mixture in baking dish with sauce; top with stuffing.

6. Bake at 350° on the center oven rack for 30 minutes.

SHRIMP SOUFFLÉ

Preparation time: 15 minutes + refrigeration
Baking time: 1 hour

Serves: 4

6 slices white bread, crusts removed
1 pound medium shrimp, cooked, deveined
1½ pounds sharp Cheddar cheese
¼ cup butter, melted

1 pint milk
3 eggs, well beaten
½ teaspoon dry mustard
Salt to taste
Paprika, fresh parsley

1. Break bread, cheese into bite-sized pieces.

2. Layer bread, shrimp, cheese in a buttered soufflé or casserole dish. Repeat layers.

3. Pour melted butter over layers.

4. Combine milk, eggs, dry mustard, salt. Pour mixture over layered ingredients.

5. Cover. Refrigerate 8-14 hours. Bake, covered, at 350° for 1 hour.

6. Sprinkle with paprika before serving. Garnish with parsley.

Accompaniment: Broiled tomato, hot bread, and fruit.

GRITS CASSEROLE

Preparation time: 15 minutes
Baking time: 40 minutes

Serves: 10-12

4 cups skim milk
1 cup quick grits
½ cup butter, melted, divided

6 ounces Gruyère cheese, cubed or grated
¼ teaspoon salt
½ cup grated Parmesan cheese

1. Boil milk.

2. Gradually add grits. Cook 3-4 minutes, stirring constantly until thickened.

3. Add ¼ cup melted butter, cheeses.

4. Add salt. Let thicken.

5. Pour into buttered casserole.

6. Pour remaining ¼ cup butter over casserole. Cut in with knife.

7. Sprinkle with Parmesan cheese.

8. Bake at 400° on the center oven rack for 40 minutes. Serve hot.

A nice picnic dish.

Accompaniment: Ham or sandwiches.

PINEAPPLE NOODLE KUGEL

Preparation time: 20 minutes   *Serves: 8*
Baking time: 1 hour, 15 minutes

1 pound noodles, cooked
½ cup butter, melted
3 eggs, slightly beaten
¾ cup sugar
1 cup sour cream
16 ounces creamed cottage cheese

1 cup milk
1 teaspoon vanilla
1 20-ounce can crushed pineapple,
   drained
Cinnamon, sugar

1. Add all ingredients to noodles.

2. Pour into greased a 9x13-inch baking dish.

3. Sprinkle cinnamon and sugar on top.

4. Bake at 325° on the center oven rack for 1 hour, 15 minutes.

May be frozen after baking. A good buffet dish.

Accompaniment: Ham.

STUFFED FRENCH TOAST

Preparation time: 45 minutes   *Yields: 10-12 slices*

8 ounces cream cheese, softened
1 teaspoon vanilla
½ cup walnuts, chopped
1 16-ounce loaf French bread, cut
   into 1½-inch thick slices

4 eggs, beaten
1 cup heavy cream or half and half
½ teaspoon vanilla
½ teaspoon ground nutmeg
1 12-ounce jar apricot preserves
½ cup orange juice

1. Combine cream cheese, vanilla in a small bowl. Beat until fluffy with mixer at medium speed or by hand.

2. Stir in walnuts.

3. Cut a pocket in each slice of bread.

4. Fill each pocket with 1½ Tablespoons cheese mixture.

5. Combine eggs, cream, vanilla, nutmeg in a small bowl. Stir.

6. Dip bread slices into egg mixture.

7. Cook in a lightly greased skillet until golden, turning once. Keep warm in a 200° oven.

8. Warm preserves, juice. Spoon over warm bread slices.

An elegant brunch item.

Accompaniments: Crisp bacon, champagne.

TIPS ON EGGS AND CHEESE

(From Our Good Cooks!)

Keep cottage cheese fresh longer by storing container upside down in the refrigerator.

Substitute for 2 whole eggs by using 1 whole egg plus 1 egg white or 1/4 cup egg substitute. In some recipes, 2 egg whites can substitute for 1 whole egg.

Immerse an egg in a pan of cool, salted water to determine its freshness. If egg sinks, it is fresh. If it rises to the surface, discard it.

Fresh eggs are rough, chalky; old eggs are smooth, shiny.

A fresh egg will wobble, not spin; a hard-boiled egg will spin.

Prevent cheese from hardening by buttering the exposed edges before storing.

Prevent the cheese from drying out by wrapping a cloth dampened with vinegar around it.

Dip bacon into cold water before frying; no more "curly" bacon.

Rolling a bacon package into tube shape secured with rubber bands will prevent the slices from sticking together.

Separate frozen bacon by heating a spatula over a burner and sliding it under each slice.

Use sharp instead of mild Cheddar cheese in recipes. Because of the stronger flavor, only half as much is needed.

Oxford, Ohio

The establishment of Oxford and the founding of Miami University were not isolated events, nor was the partnership an accidental relationship. Oxford was one of Ohio's first planned communities.

President George Washington signed a bill in 1792 which directed that one complete township be set aside for the "sole and exclusive intent and purposing of erecting and establishing therein an academy and other public schools...." Joel Collins, one of the original settlers in the area, led three commissioners through a forest to the present site of Oxford. Following their inspection, they directed that Oxford be platted. Work began in 1803, and on February 17, 1809, Miami University was founded.

Over the years Miami University has attracted a distinguished faculty holding advanced degrees in 101 areas of study. William Holmes McGuffey, a professor of education at Miami University, published a reader that quickly achieved "best seller" status. Still in print, McGuffey Readers have sold more than 130,000,000 copies - second only to the Bible.

The City of Oxford, with its wide, red brick paved streets and its striking red brick Georgian colonial buildings, is one of the few university communities to maintain an architectural symmetry and an aura of stately dignity not unlike its namesake in England. One almost expects to see a gown-clad undergraduate emerge from a pizzeria with a "slice" in hand.

Oxford has a modest blend of industry, retail, and professional businesses, providing a pleasing environment for its 18,000 residents. Parks and recreation facilities, combined with the university's many cultural and artistic activities, make for a fruitful and satisfying lifestyle.

Pasta & Rice

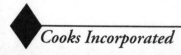
Cooks Incorporated

CHICKEN AND PASTA PRIMAVERA

Preparation time: 45-60 minutess
Baking time: 30 minutes

Serves: 16

1 chicken
16 ounces spiral macaroni, cooked drained, cooled
1 medium zucchini, sliced
1 bunch broccoli, chopped
3 stalks celery, chopped
1 green pepper, chopped
1 yellow pepper, chopped (optional)
1 red pepper, chopped (optional)
1 medium onion, chopped

1 tomato, chopped
2 cloves garlic, chopped
4 Tablespoons flour
½ cup butter
3 cups milk
2 5-ounce jars Old English cheese
Salt, pepper to taste
1½ cups shredded Cheddar cheese
1½ cups shredded mozzarella cheese

1. Stew chicken ½ hour until tender. Cool. Remove skin and bones; cut into pieces.

2. Steam zucchini, broccoli until tender.

3. Sauté celery, peppers, onion, tomato, garlic. Combine with zucchini, broccoli.

4. For cheese sauce, make a roux of butter, flour; add milk. Cook until thickened. Add Old English cheese. Stir until cheese is melted. Add salt, pepper to taste.

5. Layer macaroni, chicken, Cheddar, mozzarella cheeses, vegetables in two 13x9x4-inch casseroles. Cover with cheese sauce.

6. Bake at 350° on the center oven rack for 30 minutes.

May be prepared a day before serving. Refrigerates well.

A lump of butter or several teaspoons of cooking oil added to water when boiling rice, noodles, or spaghetti will prevent boiling over. Or, rub the inside of the cooking vessel with cooking oil.

CHICKEN TETRAZZINI

Preparation time: 30 minutes   *Serves: 6*

3   cups (8 ounces) rotini, cooked in
    salted water, drained
¼   cup margarine, melted
¼   cup flour
1   cup chicken broth
1   cup whipping cream

½   cup shredded Swiss cheese
⅓   cup grated Parmesan cheese
3   cups cooked chicken, cubed
4   ounces canned mushrooms
Salt, pepper to taste
Pimentos (for color)

1. In a large saucepan, blend flour into melted margarine.

2. Gradually stir in broth, cream.

3. Cook over low heat, stirring constantly until sauce thickens.

4. Blend in cheeses.

5. Continue heating, stirring constantly until cheeses melt.

6. Stir in rotini and remaining ingredients; heat thoroughly.

A good Saturday night supper to serve to friends at the kitchen table. May be prepared 2 days ahead. Refrigerates well for 2 days after cooking.

Accompaniments: Tossed salad, garlic bread, wine.

NUTRIENT ANALYSIS (Per serving)
Carbohydrate .... 46 grams
Protein .... 29 grams
Fat .... 31 grams
Calories .... 579 (48% from fat)
Cholesterol .... 116 milligrams
Sodium .... 760 milligrams

CHICKEN TETRAZZINI–LIGHT OPTION

Preparation time: 30 minutes   *Serves: 6*

3 cups (8 ounces) rotini, cooked in unsalted water, drained
2 Tablespoons margarine, melted
1 green pepper, seeded, diced
⅓ cup scallions, sliced
¾ cup fresh mushrooms, sliced, or 4 ounces no-salt added canned mushrooms
¼ cup flour
1 cup evaporated skim milk
1 cup defatted, low sodium chicken broth

1 teaspoon reduced sodium Worcestershire sauce
½ cup reduced fat shredded Swiss, Monterey Jack, or sharp Cheddar cheese
¼ cup grated Parmesan cheese
3 cups cooked chicken, cubed
¼ teaspoon salt
Pepper to taste
2 ounces pimentos (optional)

1. Spray skillet with cooking spray.

2. Sauté pepper, scallions, mushrooms in margarine. Blend in flour.

3. Gradually stir in milk, broth, Worcestershire sauce.

4. Cook over low heat, stirring constantly, until sauce thickens.

5. Blend in cheeses.

6. Continue heating, stirring constantly, until cheeses melt.

7. Stir in rotini and remaining ingredients; heat thoroughly.

If desired, substitute 2 cups regular skim milk for broth and evaporated skim milk. Green pepper and scallions have been added to this version to enhance flavor.

NUTRIENT ANALYSIS (Per serving)
Carbohydrates .... 49 grams
Protein .... 31 grams
Fat .... 11 grams
Calories .... 423 calories (24% from fat)
Cholesterol .... 57 milligrams
Sodium .... 307 milligrams

PASTA ROMA

Preparation time: 45 minutes   *Serves: 1-2*

Olive oil
4   ounces fettuccine, cooked, drained
4   ounces chicken breast, cut into
    small chunks
1   ounce sun-dried tomatoes,
    roughly chopped

¼   small Spanish onion, thinly sliced
¼   leek, sliced (both green and white)
3 to 4 ounces heavy cream
Dash garlic powder
Salt, pepper to taste
2   ounces Parmesan or Romano cheese

1. In a sauté pan, cook chicken in heated oil.

2. Add tomatoes, onion, leeks.

3. When all ingredients are cooked, drain off excess oil.

4. Add cream; allow mixture to come to a boil.

5. Add fettuccine, seasonings.

6. When cream begins to thicken, add cheese.

7. Toss; serve immediately.

A good main course dish.

Peasant Stock Restaurant
Kettering, Ohio

Accompaniments: Green salad, sourdough bread.

AVOCADO AND SHRIMP FETTUCCINE

Preparation time: 20 minutes   *Serves: 3*

1 Tablespoon butter, melted
1 teaspoon garlic, minced
2 Tablespoons fresh parsley, chopped
1½ pounds shrimp, peeled, deveined
2 Tablespoons dry vermouth
3 Tablespoons butter
½ cup heavy cream
¼ cup Parmesan cheese, freshly grated

Pinch crushed red pepper flakes
¼ teaspoon salt
⅛ teaspoon black pepper, freshly ground
9 ounces fettuccine, cooked, drained
1 avocado, peeled, pitted, cubed

1. In a 10-inch or larger skillet, cook garlic 1 minute in melted butter.

2. Add parsley, shrimp, vermouth; cook 2 minutes, stirring constantly until shrimps turn pink. Do not overcook.

3. Add remaining butter; reduce heat to low.

4. Add cream, Parmesan, pepper flakes.

5. Cook 3 minutes, stirring constantly until cheese melts.

6. Stir in salt, pepper.

7. Toss shrimp mixture, avocado with fettuccine.

It is important not to overcook shrimp. If necessary, transfer to a small bowl while finishing the sauce.

Accompaniments: A green salad and crusty bread.

BEST LASAGNA

Preparation time: 2 hours
Baking time: 45 minutes

Serves: 8-10

1 pound hot Italian sausage
½ pound ground beef
½ cup onion, finely chopped
2 cloves garlic, crushed
2 Tablespoons sugar
1½ teaspoons salt
1½ teaspoons dried basil
½ teaspoon fennel seed
¼ teaspoon pepper
¼ cup parsley, chopped

2 6-ounce cans tomato paste
4 cups canned tomatoes, undrained
½ cup water
1 Tablespoon salt
12 lasagna noodles
1 15-ounce container ricotta or
    cottage cheese, drained
1 egg
½ teaspoon salt
¾ pound mozzarella cheese
¾ cup grated Parmesan cheese

1. Sauté sausage, ground beef (breaking up with a wooden spoon), onion, garlic until well browned, about 20 minutes.

2. Add sugar, salt, basil, fennel, pepper, ½ of parsley, tomato paste, tomatoes, water.

3. Mix well. Bring to a boil. Simmer, covered, 1½ hours.

4. Cook noodles in 3 quarts water with 1 Tablespoon salt 10 minutes. Drain.

5. Combine ricotta, egg, remaining parsley, salt. Mix well.

6. In a 9x13-inch pan, layer sauce, 6 noodles (overlapping to cover), ½ ricotta mixture, ⅓ mozzarella, 1½ cups sauce, ¼ cup Parmesan.

7. Repeat layers, beginning with 6 noodles and ending with 1½ cups sauce. Sprinkle top with remaining Parmesan.

8. Bake uncovered at 375° on the center oven rack for 45 minutes.

May be prepared days ahead. Refrigerates (2 days) and freezes well. Freeze before putting Parmesan on top.

Accompaniments: Lettuce, onion, and orange salad and garlic bread.

MICHELLE'S STUFFED SHELLS

Preparation time: 45 minutes *Yield: 24 shells*
Baking time: 20-30 minutes

24 jumbo macaroni shells, cooked, drained
1 pound ground beef
½ cup minced onion
½ teaspoon pepper
¼ teaspoon garlic powder
¼ teaspoon red pepper, crushed
1¼ cups beef broth
1 7-ounce jar sun-dried tomatoes in oil, drained
¼ cup pine nuts, toasted

¼ cup fresh basil leaves
2 Tablespoons fresh parsley, chopped
2 cloves garlic, sliced
¼ cup olive oil
⅓ cup grated Parmesan cheese
1 32-ounce jar spaghetti sauce
1½ cups (6 ounces) shredded mozzarella cheese
1 to 2 Tablespoons fresh parsley, chopped

1. In a large skillet, brown ground beef, onion; drain.

2. Add pepper, garlic powder, red pepper; cover; set aside.

3. In an electric blender, combine beef broth and next 5 ingredients. Cover; process until well blended.

4. Add olive oil in a slow, steady stream, processing until combined.

5. Stir tomato mixture into ground beef mixture.

6. Stir in Parmesan cheese.

7. Place 1 heaping Tablespoonful of ground beef mixture into each shell.

8. Arrange shells in a lightly greased or sprayed 13x9x2-inch baking dish. Pour spaghetti sauce over top.

9. Cover. Bake at 375° on the center oven rack for 20-30 minutes until thoroughly heated.

10. Uncover; sprinkle with mozzarella; bake an additional 5 minutes until cheese melts.

11. Sprinkle with parsley.

Best when eaten immediately but may be refrigerated or frozen.

Accompaniment: Red Italian wine.

PEASANT PASTA

Preparation time: 20 minutes   *Serves: 1-2*

6 ounces angel hair pasta, cooked, drained
2 ounces olive oil, heated
2 ounces Shitake mushrooms

1 large or 2 small tomatoes, coarsely chopped
1 Tablespoon pesto sauce
Salt, pepper to taste
Parmesan cheese to taste

1. In a sauté pan, add mushrooms, tomatoes, pesto to heated oil.

2. Add seasonings; cook 30-40 seconds.

3. Add pasta; toss.

4. When hot, transfer to serving plate; top with Parmesan.

A simple pesto sauce is made from fresh basil leaves with garlic finely ground with olive oil. Salt, pepper, pine nuts are optional. Traditionally a mortar and pestle were used, but a food processor works fine.

Peasant Stock Restaurant
Kettering, Ohio

BASIL PESTO WITH PASTA

Preparation time: 15-20 minutes

2 cups fresh basil, firmly packed
3 cloves garlic
½ cup pine nuts
¾ cup fresh Parmesan
    cheese, grated

¼ cup fresh Romano cheese, grated
½ cup + 3 Tablespoons olive oil
1 pound pasta or noodles, cooked
    until al dente, drained

1. Combine basil, garlic, ⅓ cup pine nuts in a blender or food processor; puree to desired smoothness.

2. Add ½ cup Parmesan and all of Romano cheese; blend briefly.

3. Add ½ cup olive oil. Mix well; set aside.

4. In a large bowl, toss cooked pasta with 3 Tablespoons olive oil. Cool to room temperature.

5. Mix pesto, pasta, remaining Parmesan cheese.

6. Garnish with remaining pine nuts, basil.

Variation: Walnuts may be substituted for pine nuts.

This excellent, slightly different pesto has a delicate, slightly sweet flavor.

Accompaniments: As a main dish: salad, and sourdough bread.
As a side dish: grilled salmon or chicken.

HERBED PASTA

Preparation time: 20 minutes   *Serves: 10*

8 ounces 3-color rotini, cooked, drained
8 ounces oil-free Italian dressing
½ package dry Italian salad dressing mix
1 tomato, peeled, chopped

1 medium onion, chopped
½ medium green pepper, chopped
½ cup fresh carrot, julienned
⅓ cup fresh zucchini, julienned
¼ cup red wine vinegar
2 Tablespoons whole basil

1. Mix oil-free dressing with dry dressing mix.

2. Add chopped tomato, onion, pepper to dressing.

3. Mix carrots, zucchini into pasta.

4. Combine all ingredients.

5. Cover; refrigerate overnight.

6. Toss well before serving.

Even better the second or third day.

VEGETARIAN LINGUINE ALFREDO

Preparation time: 30 minutes   *Serves: 6*

1 pound linguine, cooked, drained
½ cup olive oil
½ teaspoon fresh garlic, minced
½ cup cauliflower florets
½ cup broccoli florets
½ cup carrots, julienned

½ cup snow peas, diagonally sliced into ½-inch strips
½ cup zucchini, thinly sliced
½ cup yellow squash, thinly sliced
2 Tablespoons herbs (thyme, oregano, sage, or dill)

1. Sauté garlic in oil.

2. Add vegetables; sauté until hot.

3. Add mixture to cooked linguine.

4. Add seasonings; toss.

*Benham's Restaurant and Catering
Dayton, Ohio*

LINGUINE WITH ZUCCHINI

Preparation time: 30 minutes   *Serves: 6-8*

10 to 12 ounces fresh linguine or 8
   ounces dry linguine
3 Tablespoons olive oil, heated
3 cloves garlic, pressed
3 cups zucchini, shredded
¼ cup parsley

2 Tablespoons butter
½ cup half and half
½ cup grated Parmesan cheese
1½ cups shredded Monterey
   Jack cheese
Salt, pepper to taste

1. Cook pasta until barely tender.

2. In a 12 or 14-inch skillet, add garlic, zucchini to heated olive oil. Stir fry 3-4 minutes until tender-crisp.

3. Reduce heat to low. Add parsley, butter, half and half.

4. When butter melts, add linguine, cheeses.

5. Toss lightly. Add seasonings to taste.

Accompaniment: Grilled chicken

CREAMY PASTA PRIMAVERA

Preparation time: 1 hour   *Serves: 6*

1½ cups carrots, sliced
2 cups broccoli, cut into
   bite-sized pieces
6 ounces fresh or frozen (thawed in
   warm water, drained) snow peas

10 ounces fettuccine or medium
    noodles, cooked, drained
2 cups prepared buttermilk or milk
   ranch dressing (Hidden Valley
   suggested)
¼ cup grated Parmesan cheese

1. Cook vegetables until tender, crisp; drain well.

2. In a large skillet over moderate heat, warm salad dressing until almost simmering. Do not boil.

3. Add pasta, vegetables. Toss to coat. Remove from heat.

4. Sprinkle with Parmesan cheese. Serve immediately.

Accompaniment: Meat, poultry, or fish.

PENNE WITH BROCCOLI SAUCE

Preparation time: 45 minutes

Serves: 4 as main dish
6 as first course

4 cups broccoli florets, cut
  to 1½ inches
4 cups water
2 Tablespoons olive oil, heated
2 teaspoons fresh garlic, minced
¼ cup tomato paste

1 teaspoon dried red pepper flakes
½ teaspoon salt
1 pound penne or tubular pasta
  (imported Italian Di Cecco suggested)
2 Tablespoons salt
4 to 6 Tablespoons grated Romano or
  Parmesan cheese

1. Drop broccoli florets into boiling water. Boil a few minutes until barely tender.

2. Drain; set aside; reserve cooking water.

3. In a 12-inch non-stick skillet, sauté the garlic in heated olive oil over low heat until tender but not brown.

4. Add tomato paste and the broccoli cooking water. Smooth mixture with the back of a spoon while stirring.

5. Add seasonings; lower heat to a slight simmer.

6. Add penne, salt to 6 quarts of rapidly boiling water.

7. Lower heat to medium high; cook penne 8-11 minutes until just al dente. Do not overcook.

8. While cooking pasta, add broccoli florets to tomato mixture in skillet. Simmer while pasta cooks.

9. If necessary, add ¼ to ½ cup of pasta cooking water to skillet to maintain 3 cups liquid.

10. When just less than done, drain pasta.

11. Add pasta to skillet mixture; continue cooking about 45 seconds, stirring gently but thoroughly.

(Continued on facing page)

12. Portion into heated pasta bowls.

13. Sprinkle with cheese.

A light, nearly fat-free sauce. Cauliflower may be substituted for broccoli.

Accompaniments: Serve as a main course with spinach salad, bread, and wine. As a first course, follow the penne with broiled fish and a salad of sliced oranges and pitted calamata olives drizzled with olive oil.

BROCCOLI - VERMICELLI CASSEROLE

Preparation time: 20 minutes　　　　　　　　　　　　　　　　*Serves: 6*
Baking time: 45 minutes

½ **pound vermicelli, cooked, drained**
¼ **pound butter, melted**
1 **pint fresh mushrooms, sliced**
1 **large onion, chopped**
2 **stalks celery, chopped**
1 **16-ounce box frozen chopped broccoli, defrosted, drained**

1 **10¾-ounce can cream of mushroom soup**
½ **cup milk**
3 **cups sharp New York Cheddar cheese, shredded**

1. In a large skillet sauté mushrooms, onion, celery in melted butter until slightly tender.

2. Add broccoli, soup, milk.

3. In a 13x9x2-inch baking dish layer half the vermicelli, half the broccoli mixture, half the cheese.

4. Repeat the layers.

5. Bake uncovered at 350° for 45 minutes until hot.

PASTITSIO

Preparation time: 45 minutes
Baking time: 50 minutes

Serves: 8-10

1 pound elbow macaroni, cooked, drained
4 Tablespoons butter, melted to golden brown

¾ cup grated Parmesan cheese
¼ teaspoon nutmeg
3 eggs, lightly beaten

Cream Sauce

⅓ cup butter, melted
½ cup flour
3 cups milk

¼ teaspoon nutmeg
Salt, pepper to taste
1 egg, slightly beaten

Meat Sauce

2 Tablespoons butter, melted
1 large onion, chopped
1½ pounds ground chuck
¼ cup tomato paste
½ cup dry red wine

1½ cups stock or water
2 Tablespoons parsley, chopped
½ teaspoon sugar
Salt, pepper to taste

1. Pour melted butter over macaroni.

2. Add ½ cup cheese, spices. Let cool.

3. Add eggs. Toss well; set aside.

4. Prepare cream sauce:

    • Stir flour into melted butter; cook 2 minutes.

    • Add milk all at once; bring to a boil, stirring constantly; boil 1 minute. Add spices.

    • Cool slightly; add egg.

5. Prepare meat sauce:

    • In melted butter, fry onion until soft.

    • Add meat; cook until brown; drain.

    • Add remaining ingredients; cover; simmer 20 minutes.

    • Add ½ cup cream sauce to meat mixture.

(Continued on facing page)

6. Butter a 13x9x3-inch baking dish.

7. Spoon half the macaroni mixture evenly into bottom.

8. Spread meat mixture evenly over macaroni.

9. Spoon remaining macaroni over meat.

10. Spread cream sauce over top, covering macaroni completely.

11. Sprinkle with remaining cheese.

12. Bake at 350° on the center oven rack for 50 minutes until golden brown.

13. Let stand 15 minutes before cutting into squares.

A delicious, hearty dish. Freezes well before baking.

Accompaniments: Salad, crusty bread

LEMON TORTELLINI WITH ARTICHOKES

Preparation time: 15 minutes   *Serves: 4-6*

9 **ounces cheese-filled tortellini, cooked, drained, cooled**
3 **Tablespoons olive oil**
1 **Tablespoon lemon juice**
½ **teaspoon pepper, freshly ground**
1 **clove garlic, minced**

4 **green onions, sliced**
1 **4-ounce jar artichoke hearts, drained, quartered**
10 **cherry tomatoes, halved**
Parmesan cheese

1. Mix olive oil, lemon juice, pepper, garlic in a large bowl.

2. Add tortellini, onions, artichokes; toss to coat.

3. Just before serving, add tomatoes; sprinkle with Parmesan cheese.

This salad may be prepared ahead and refrigerated. Remove from refrigerator an hour before serving to bring to room temperature.

GRANDMA'S NOODLES

Preparation time: 10 minutes   *Serves: 4*
Drying time: 4-5 hours   *Cooking time: 15-20 minutes*

Making Noodles

1 cup flour
½ teaspoon salt
2 eggs

1. Measure flour and salt into a medium-sized bowl.

2. Make a well in the center of the flour mixture; put eggs into the well.

3. Stir with a fork until mixture forms a ball, adding a little flour if necessary.

4. Turn out dough onto a well-floured surface.

5. Knead flour from surface into dough until no longer sticky.

6. Add additional flour to surface as needed to be sure dough does not stick when rolled out.

7. With a floured rolling pin, roll dough, flipping occasionally to keep lightly floured on both sides. Roll thinly to about 1/16-inch.

8. Cut into 3-inch strips.

9. Allow noodles to dry for ½ hour.

10. Turn strips over (loosen with metal spatula if sticking to surface); dry for about 3 hours.

11. Stack dough strips; cut ¼-inch strips off short side. (Dough should be dry enough to stick together but not brittle.)

12. Pick up noodles by the handful; drop to separate.

13. Dry about 1 hour.

14. Use immediately or freeze.

(Continued on facing page)

Cooking Noodles

Method 1

1. In a medium saucepan, bring 2 ½ cups water and 2 teaspoons chicken or beef bouillon to a rapid boil.

2. Add noodles; return to a boil.

3. Reduce heat until noodles bubble gently.

4. Cook approximately 15-20 minutes until tender, stirring often. Add a little water if necessary to prevent drying and sticking.

5. Drain; serve.

Method 2

1. In a medium saucepan, bring 4 cups water to a rapid boil.

2. Add noodles; continue cooking as above.

POLISH NOODLES AND CABBAGE

Preparation time: 1 hour   *Serves: 6-8*

8 ounces egg noodles, cooked, drained   **1 teaspoon caraway seed**
¼ cup butter or margarine, melted   **½ teaspoon salt**
½ cup onion, chopped   **⅛ teaspoon pepper**
4 cups cabbage, coarsely chopped   **½ cup sour cream**

1. In a large skillet in melted butter, sauté onion until soft.

2. Add cabbage; sauté 5 minutes until crisp-tender.

3. Stir in seasonings.

4. Stir cooked noodles into cabbage mixture.

5. Add sour cream.

6. Cook 5 minutes, stirring frequently.

If preparing ahead, omit the sour cream and add when re-heating.

Accompaniment: Pork

SOUBISE

Preparation time: 20-30 minutes
Baking time: 1 hour, 15 minutes

Serves: 8

⅔ cup long-grain rice
1⅔ cups water
¼ cup butter or margarine, melted
2 pounds yellow onions,
   thinly sliced

1½ teaspoons salt
⅛ teaspoon pepper
½ cup grated Swiss cheese
¼ cup light cream or half and half
1 Tablespoon fresh parsley, minced

1. Place rice, water into a 3-quart casserole.
2. Combine butter, onions; stir until well coated.
3. Stir in salt, pepper.
4. Place onion mixture over rice in casserole. Cover.
5. Bake at 375° on the center oven rack for 1 hour until rice is tender.
6. Stir in cheese, cream.
7. Add additional seasonings, if necessary.
8. Return to oven; bake uncovered for 15-20 minutes until crusty brown.
9. Sprinkle with parsley; serve hot.

May be partially prepared 1 day ahead. Combine ingredients except cheese, cream, and parsley; cover and refrigerate.

A good buffet dish.

NUTRIENT ANALYSIS (Per serving)
Carbohydrate .... 22 grams
Protein .... 3 grams
Fat .... 9 grams
Calories .... 189 (44% from fat)
Cholesterol .... 11 milligrams
Sodium .... 503 milligrams

SOUBISE–LIGHT OPTION

Preparation time: 20-30 minutes   *Serves 8*
Baking time: 1 hour, 15 minutes

⅔ cup long-grain rice   ⅛ teaspoon pepper
1⅔ cups water   ¼ cup grated reduced fat Swiss cheese
2 Tablespoons margarine, melted   ¼ cup evaporated milk
2 pounds yellow onions, thinly sliced   1 Tablespoon fresh parsley, minced
¼ teaspoons salt

1. Place rice, water into a 3-quart casserole.

2. Combine margarine, onions; stir until well coated.

3. Stir in salt, pepper.

4. Place onion mixture over rice in casserole. Cover.

5. Bake at 375° on the center oven rack for 1 hour until rice is tender.

6. Stir in cheese, milk.

7. Add additional seasonings, if necessary.

8. Return to oven; bake uncovered for 15-20 minutes until crusty brown.

9. Sprinkle with parsley; serve hot.

NUTRIENT ANALYSIS (Per serving)
Carbohydrate .... 24 grams
Protein .... 6 grams
Fat .... 4 grams
Calories .... 157 (25% from fat)
Cholesterol .... 5 milligrams
Sodium .... 12 milligrams

TASTY RICE

Preparation time: 10 minutes
Cooking time: 1 hour
Serves: 6-8

½ cup plus 2 Tablespoons butter, melted

1 cup rice

1 medium onion, chopped

1 medium green pepper, chopped

1⅓ cups chicken broth

1 4-ounce can mushroom pieces, undrained

1 4-ounce jar diced pimentos

¼ Tablespoon ground saffron (optional - for color only)

1 Tablespoon grated Parmesan cheese

1. Sauté rice, onion, pepper in melted butter.

2. Add broth, mushrooms, pimentos, saffron.

3. Cover; cook 1 hour. Add water or additional broth if mixture becomes too dry.

4. Place mixture in an 8x8x2-inch casserole.

5. Sprinkle with cheese.

6. Bake at 350° for 5 minutes.

A good variation to basic rice. May be frozen before baking.

CONFETTI RICE

Preparation time: 35-40 minutes
Serves: 4

1 cup rice, cooked

¼ cup butter or margarine, melted

3 eggs, slightly beaten

⅓ cup pimentos, chopped

2½ cups bean sprouts, drained

1 cup green onions, finely chopped

Salt, pepper to taste

1. In a large skillet, scramble eggs loosely in melted butter until moist but firm.

2. Add cooked rice and remaining ingredients.

3. Mix well; heat.

A colorful dish best when made a few hours before serving. Doubles nicely for a larger group.

Accompaniment: *Ham or barbecued chicken.*

WILD RICE CASSEROLE

Preparation time: 20 minutes   *Serves: 4*
Baking time: 30-35 minutes

1½ cups wild rice	¼ cup butter
3 quarts boiling water	1½ cups brown stock or canned
1½ Tablespoons salt	beef bouillon
3 Tablespoons carrots, minced	1 bay leaf
3 Tablespoons onions, minced	¼ to ½ teaspoon thyme
3 Tablespoons celery, minced	Salt, pepper to taste

1. Drop rice into boiling, salted water; boil uncovered 5 minutes. Drain thoroughly.

2. While rice is cooking, cook vegetables in butter in casserole 5-6 minutes until tender.

3. Add drained rice; stir over moderate heat 2 minutes.

4. Add remaining ingredients.

5. Bring to a boil; cover.

6. Set in the lower third of a 350° oven for 30-35 minutes until rice is tender, all liquid absorbed. (Add more liquid if all has been absorbed before rice is tender.)

7. Discard bay leaf. Fluff rice with a fork.

Vegetables add color and taste.

Accompaniment: Beef or poultry.

RICE WITH PINE NUTS, GREEN ONIONS, AND PARSLEY

Preparation time: 45 minutes   *Serves: 10*

¼ cup butter, melted
2 cups rice
4 cups chicken broth
¼ cup butter, melted

¾ cup pine nuts
2 bunches green onions, chopped
1 cup fresh parsley, minced
Salt, pepper to taste

1. In a skillet over medium heat, add rice to melted butter. Stir 3 minutes until milky.

2. Add stock; cover; bring to a boil.

3. Reduce heat; simmer 20-25 minutes until all liquid is absorbed.

4. In another skillet over medium heat, add pine nuts to melted butter. Stir 4 minutes until golden brown.

5. Add onions, parsley. Stir until heated through.

6. Mix into rice; season.

Accompaniments: Barbecued turkey breast or marinated chicken and seafood.

GARLIC GRITS

Preparation time: 15 minutes   *Serves 12*
Baking time: 45 minutes

4½ cups boiling water
1 cup grits
1 Tablespoon salt
1 cup butter

1 roll garlic cheese
   (Kraft link suggested)
2 eggs
½ cup milk

1. Pour grits into salted boiling water; cook over low heat until done.

2. Cool.

3. Melt butter and ¾ roll of cheese; add to grits.

4. Beat eggs with milk; stir slowly into grits.

5. Pour into casserole.

6. Grate remaining cheese; sprinkle over top.

7. Bake at 350° for 45 minutes.

Eaton, Ohio

On April 1, 1987, a roaring fire completely destroyed the gallery, prize-winning paintings, classrooms, and studios of one of Eaton's most treasured cultural assets, the Preble County Art Association.

The asset which defied destruction was the indomitable spirit of the community. Within six months of the fire, the decision was made to raise $300,000 and to build a fine arts center. It seemed improbable but not impossible. In a community where residents are no strangers to barn raisings, eager volunteers began fund raising.

To the surprise of some and the joy of all, the goal was reached, and at the end of three years "The Miracle Building," as some called it, was dedicated as the Preble County Fine Arts Center. The fund-raising effort produced a total of $306,000 without a cent of public tax funds! This stands not only as a cultural landmark but as a monument to the spirit of the possible.

Eaton's reputation for staging successful community affairs is widespread. Ranking fifth in Ohio for hog production, Eaton appropriately stages the two-day *Pork Festival* in September which attracts 100,000 people with hearty appetites! Visitors start the day with a sausage and pancake breakfast and move on to a barbecued pork chop smorgasbord, where short orders are continuously available.

The antiques show in Fairhaven Village and the County Fair are favorite summer activities while house tours, a garden and trade show, and a *White Christmas* celebration serve to puncuate the calendar with special events.

The 15,000 families in the county, including the 3,000 residing in Eaton, all agree there are plenty of things to keep the spirit alive!

Entrees

FLANK STEAK

Preparation time: 10 minutes + marinating   *Serves: 3 per pound of steak*
Grilling time: 14 minutes

1 cup soy sauce
½ cup brown sugar
½ cup vinegar
½ cup pineapple juice

2 teaspoons salt
1 teaspoon garlic powder
1 flank steak

1. Combine all ingredients except steak. Bring to a boil.

2. Cover steak with the sauce; marinate in refrigerator for at least 4 hours.

3. For a medium finish, grill steak on high 7 minutes on each side.

4. Slice diagonally across the grain.

Leftovers refrigerate well for a week.

STEAK WITH GREEN CHILE CHUTNEY

Preparation time: 20-25 minutes   *Serves: 4*

½ pound fresh mushrooms, sliced
1 medium onion, finely chopped
2 Tablespoons olive oil
2 4-ounce cans chopped green chilies
¼ teaspoon oregano

¼ to 1 teaspoon fresh cilantro
¼ teaspoon salt
1 teaspoon Tabasco
4 filet mignon or New York-cut steaks

1. Sauté mushrooms in a 10-12 inch skillet. Set aside.

2. Combine onion, olive oil in a skillet. Cook until onion is transparent.

3. Add mushrooms, remaining sauce ingredients. Keep sauce warm.

4. Grill steak to desired doneness.

5. Place sauce on plates. Top with steak.

NO-FAIL FILLET OF BEEF

Preparation time: 10 minutes *Serves: 8*
Baking time: 20 minutes

1 3½-pound fillet of beef,   **Seasonings as desired**
at room temperature

1. Preheat oven to 450°.

2. Rub beef with desired seasonings.

3. Place in a baking pan with ends of fillet tucked under.

4. Bake uncovered for 20 minutes.

5. To slice very thinly, allow to cool before slicing.

Suggested seasonings: Brandy, garlic, soy sauce, Kitchen Bouquet, salt, freshly ground pepper.
Results in a pink-centered medium rare fillet.

ROAST BEEF BRAVO!

Preparation time: 15 minutes + marinating *Serves: 6*
Roasting time: 1½ hours

1½ Tablespoons salt   **½ Tablespoon dried bouquet garni,**
1 teaspoon pepper   **rubbed to accent flavor**
1 Tablespoon seasoned salt   **½ Tablespoon onion powder**
1 Tablespoon garlic powder   **1 5-pound standing rib roast**
½ Tablespoon dried thyme, rubbed
to accent flavor

1. Combine first 7 ingredients to make a dry marinade.

2. Place beef in a roasting pan.

3. Rub roast on top and ends with as much of mixture as meat will absorb.

4. Let stand 2 hours at room temperature.

5. Preheat oven to 325°.

6. Roast uncovered for 1½ hours or 18 minutes per pound.

Juicy, tender, delicious, and so easy to prepare.

FOOLPROOF RIB ROAST

Preparation time: 10 minutes
Roasting time: 1½ hours

Yield: 3-4 servings per pound

1   standing rib roast (any size)
Salt, pepper to taste

1. Allow meat to stand at room temperature at least 1 hour. If frozen, thaw completely, bring to room temperature.

2. Preheat oven to 375°.

3. In the morning, rub roast with seasonings.

4. Place on a rack in a roasting pan, rib side down.

5. Roast for 1 hour.

6. Turn off oven. Leave roast in the oven; do not open oven door.

7. 30-40 minutes before serving, set oven temperature at 375°.

8. Roast 30-40 minutes.

Results in a lusciously browned on the outside, rare on the inside roast, regardless of size. For a more well done roast, increase final roasting time by 15-30 minutes.

Very important not to remove roast or open oven door from the time roast is put in in the morning until ready to serve. This really works!

BRISKET WITH VEGETABLES

Preparation time: 40 minutes
Baking time: 3 hours

Serves: 12-14

8 pounds beef brisket (1 large or 2 smaller briskets)
2 cloves garlic, crushed
2 onions, coarsely chopped
Freshly ground pepper to taste
1 Tablespoon Worcestershire sauce

2 envelopes onion soup mix
1 12-ounce bottle chili sauce
1 12-ounce can beer
8 or more carrots, scraped
3 slices rye bread
Chopped parsley

1. Preheat oven to 350°.

2. Rub brisket with garlic; place on a bed of chopped onions in a large roasting pan.

3. Over the brisket place in this order: pepper, Worcestershire sauce, onion soup mix, chili sauce, beer.

4. Arrange carrots around the brisket in the pan.

5. Tear bread into small pieces; tuck under the brisket so that the liquid is covering the bread. Cover tightly. Bake on the lower oven rack for 45 minutes.

6. Reduce oven temperature to 275°; braise another 2¼ hours, or until done.

7. Remove brisket from oven; let stand until cool.

8. Slice meat; arrange on an oven-proof platter; surround with carrots; cover with foil.

9. To make gravy, take bread, half of the onions, 2 cups liquid from the pan.

10. Place in blender container; process until smooth.

11. Return to pan; blend with remaining liquid.

12. About ½ hour before serving, reheat meat, carrots.

13. Arrange on a warm serving platter.

14. Pour part of gravy over sliced meat; serve remaining gravy in a sauce bowl.

15. Sprinkle chopped parsley over meat.

May be prepared ahead and refrigerates well. Put the brisket into the oven in the evening, set the cooking time. It will be cool by morning and ready to slice.

Accompaniments: Delmonte potato casserole, layered salad (both prepared a day ahead), zinfandel wine.

BELGIAN BEEF STEW

Preparation time: 15 minutes
Cooking time: 2-2½ hours

Serves: 6

¼ cup flour
3½ teaspoons salt
½ teaspoon pepper
2 pounds beef stew meat, cubed
¼ cup salad oil
1 clove garlic, crushed

2 medium onions, sliced or diced
12 ounces lite beer
1 Tablespoon soy sauce
1 Tablespoon Worcestershire sauce
1 Tablespoon steak sauce
2 bay leaves
1 teaspoon thyme

1. Combine flour, seasonings; coat meat with flour mixture.

3. Sauté garlic, onions in oil in a pot. Brown meat in oil.

4. Add remaining ingredients; mix well. Simmer, covered, 2-2½ hours.

5. Serve with noodles or mashed potatoes.

May be prepared and refrigerated 2-3 days ahead. Also freezes well after cooking.

BEEF STEW WITH WALNUTS AND FETA CHEESE

Preparation time: 20 minutes
Cooking time: 2 hours, 5 minutes

Serves: 6-8

2 Tablespoons butter, melted
1 medium onion, chopped
3 pounds lean beef, cubed
Salt, pepper to taste
3 ounces tomato paste
½ cup red wine
2 Tablespoons vinegar

½ cup water
1 clove garlic, minced
1 bay leaf
2 pounds small onions, peeled, or
   small canned pearl onions
¾ cup walnut halves
½ pound feta cheese

1. In a large heavy pan in melted butter, sauté onion until transparent, not brown.

2. Add meat, seasonings. Stir to coat with butter. Do not brown.

3. Mix tomato paste, wine, vinegar, water, garlic. Pour over meat. Add bay leaf.

4. Cover. Simmer 1 hour.

5. Add onions. Cover. Simmer 1 hour until meat, onions are fork tender.

6. Add walnuts, cheese. Simmer an additional 5 minutes.

Accompaniment: Orzo.

BAVARIAN POT ROAST

Preparation time: 15 minutes
Cooking time: 4-5 hours

Serves: 6-10

5 pounds boneless chuck roast
2 Tablespoons fat
1 can beer
1 cup tomato sauce
⅔ cup onion, chopped

1 Tablespoon vinegar
2 Tablespoons sugar
2 teaspoons salt
1 teaspoon cinnamon
½ teaspoon ginger
1 large bay leaf

1. Brown meat in hot fat in a heavy kettle.

2. Combine remaining ingredients; pour over meat.

3. Simmer, covered, 4-5 hours until tender, or bake, covered, at 350° for 4-5 hours.

Very tender, sweet.

Accompaniments: Carrots, onions, and potatoes cooked in broth from the roast, green salad, rolls.

BEEF CURRY

Preparation time: 30 minutes

Serves: 4-6

1½ Tablespoons salad oil
1 medium onion, sliced into rings
1 to 2 teaspoons curry to taste
1½ pounds lean flank steak, cut into 1-inch cubes
½ pound fresh mushrooms, sliced

1 tomato, diced
1 large clove garlic
2 teaspoons salt
2 teaspoons sugar
2 Tablespoons cornstarch
2 Tablespoons water

1. Sauté onion until tender in heated oil in a 10 to 12-inch heavy skillet.

2. Stir in curry powder. (Taste before adding full amount.) Cook 1 minute.

3. Add beef, next 5 ingredients. Cook until beef cubes are lightly browned.

4. Add enough water (about 2 cups) just to cover beef.

5. Cover. Simmer gently until tender.

6. Combine cornstarch, water. Thicken beef mixture.

May be prepared and refrigerated 2 days ahead. Also freezes well after cooking.

Accompaniment: Steamed rice.

BEEF BURGERS BAKED IN WINE

Preparation time: 30 minutes   *Serves: 4*
Baking time: 1½ hours

1 pound ground chuck
1 large tomato, diced
2 carrots, thickly sliced
2 medium onions, thinly sliced
¼ pound fresh mushrooms, sliced
2 ribs celery, diagonally sliced

1 clove garlic, crushed, or
   ⅛ teaspoon garlic powder
1 cup canned beef broth
½ cup dry red wine or sherry
2 teaspoons salt
⅛ teaspoon pepper
3 Tablespoons cornstarch

1. Form beef into 4 patties; brown in a skillet.

2. Place patties in bottom of a 2-quart casserole; sprinkle with vegetables.

3. Mix garlic, broth, wine, seasonings.

4. Combine cornstarch with a small amount of cold broth mixture. Mix until smooth.

5. Slowly add cornstarch mixture to remaining liquid. Pour over patties.

6. Bake at 350° on the center oven rack for 1½ hours.

CRANBERRY MEAT BALLS

Preparation time: 25 minutes   *Yield: 24*
Baking time: 45 minutes

2 pounds ground chuck
1 cup cornflake crumbs
⅓ cup dried parsley
2 eggs
2 Tablespoons soy sauce
¼ teaspoon pepper
½ teaspoon garlic salt

⅓ cup catsup
2 Tablespoons dried minced onion
2 Tablespoons brown sugar
1 16-ounce can whole cranberry
   sauce
1 12-ounce bottle chili sauce
2 Tablespoons lemon juice

1. Blend first 9 ingredients. Form into small balls.

2. Place in a 15½ x 10½-inch baking dish.

3. Combine remaining ingredients in a saucepan to make sauce.

4. Cook sauce over medium heat until smooth; pour over meat balls.

5. Bake at 350° on the center oven rack for 45 minutes.

Make smaller meat balls for use as an appetizer. Moist and delicious.

CABBAGE ROLLS

Preparation time: 45 minutes
Baking time: 2-3 hours

Serves: 20

2 medium heads cabbage
1 32-ounce can sauerkraut
6 cups fresh tomatoes, diced, or canned whole tomatoes, drained, divided
4 pounds ground beef
¾ cup catsup
¼ cup water
½ teaspoon garlic salt

1 Tablespoon seasoned salt
1 cup uncooked long grain white rice (Uncle Ben's suggested)
2 to 3 drops Tabasco sauce
1 onion, chopped
2 Tablespoons margarine, melted
2 Tablespoons flour
1 Tablespoon paprika
2 cups hot water

1. Core cabbage; separate leaves. Steam.

2. Place sauerkraut in bottom of a large roasting pan.

3. Add half of tomatoes.

4. Mix beef, catsup, water, seasonings, rice. Form into small rolls; roll into cabbage leaves.

5. Brown onion in margarine in a skillet. Add flour, paprika. Stir in hot water to make a thin sauce.

6. Pour over rolls. (If sauce does not cover rolls, add more water.)

7. Add remaining tomatoes.

8. Cover. Bake at 350° on the center oven rack for 2-3 hours.

Refrigerates for 2 days or may be frozen after baking. If more liquid is needed after freezing, pour tomato soup over top before reheating.

A never-fail Hungarian recipe.

Accompaniments: Mashed potatoes, green beans.

Cooks Incorporated

FAJITAS

Preparation time: 30 minutes + marinating   *Serves: 6*

¾ cup light oil
¼ cup soy sauce
3 Tablespoons honey
2 Tablespoons white or rice vinegar
1½ teaspoons garlic powder
1½ teaspoons powdered ginger

1 pound boneless sirloin or top round steak, trimmed of all fat, sliced into thin strips
1 large onion, sliced into rings
1 large red or green bell pepper, seeded, sliced
8 9-inch flour tortillas, warmed

Condiments

1 large fresh tomato, chopped
¼ pound mozzarella cheese, shredded
¼ pound Cheddar cheese, shredded

1 4-ounce can black olives, chopped
½ head iceberg lettuce, shredded
½ cup sour cream
1 cup chunky salsa

1. In a large bowl, combine first 6 ingredients to make marinade.
2. Add beef to marinade.
3. Add onion, bell pepper.
4. Cover. Marinate 4-6 hours, stirring occasionally.
5. Heat a large skillet over medium-high heat.
6. Spoon beef into skillet. (Do not add additional oil.) Sauté until desired doneness.
7. Add vegetables; sauté just until tender crisp.
8. Serve immediately wrapped in warm tortillas.
9. Pass condiments in separate dishes to be added as desired.

Accompaniment: A large assortment of summer fruits.

BAKED LIVER IN WINE

Preparation time: 30 minutes + marinating   *Serves: 6*
Baking time: 30 minutes

½ cup vegetable oil
2 Tablespoons lemon juice
2 Tablespoons white vinegar
1 teaspoon salt
½ teaspoon oregano
2 pounds calf or beef liver, ¼-inch thick
6 slices bacon, crisp cooked, crumbled

Bacon drippings
2 cups onion, sliced
4 ounces fresh mushrooms, sliced
½ cup flour
2 Tablespoons margarine
½ cup dry white wine
1 teaspoon salt
⅛ teaspoon pepper
2 Tablespoons parsley

1. Combine first 5 ingredients for marinade.

2. Place liver in a shallow dish.

3. Pour marinade over liver.

4. Refrigerate. Marinate 2 hours.

5. In a skillet, cook and stir onions, mushrooms in bacon drippings 5 minutes until golden. Remove to a bowl.

6. Drain liver. Coat with flour.

7. Add margarine to bacon drippings in skillet.

8. Fry liver, a few pieces at a time, 3 minutes per side until brown.

9. Remove to a baking dish.

10. Stir wine, seasonings into drippings in skillet. Heat to boiling, scraping browned pieces from skillet.

11. Place onions, mushrooms over liver. Pour wine sauce over all.

12. Sprinkle with bacon, parsley.

13. Bake at 350° for 30 minutes until tender.

CELESTIAL ROAST LOIN OF PORK

Preparation time: 10 minutes *Serves: 8-10*
Roasting time: 2¾ hours

2 **Tablespoons flour**
1½ **teaspoons salt**
1 **teaspoon dry mustard or**
   caraway seed
½ **teaspoon sugar**
¼ **teaspoon black pepper**
¼ **teaspoon ground sage**

1 **4 to 5-pound pork loin roast**
1½ **cups applesauce**
½ **cup brown sugar**
¼ **teaspoon cinnamon or allspice**
¼ **teaspoon mace**
¼ **teaspoon salt**

1. Mix first 6 ingredients. Rub over surface of meat.

2. Place meat fat side up in a roasting pan.

3. Roast at 325° for 2 hours.

4. Meanwhile, mix remaining ingredients to make sauce.

5. Spread over meat.

6. Roast an additional 45 minutes.

C'est magnifique!

Accompaniments: Mushroom casserole, rice pilaf, orange-glazed carrots, mini croissants.

GRILLED PORK TENDERLOIN WITH MUSTARD CREAM SAUCE

Preparation time: 30 minutes + marinating　　　　　　*Serves: 6*
Cooking time: 25 minutes

¾ cup vegetable oil　　　　　　3　garlic cloves, lightly crushed
¼ cup dry white wine　　　　　2　pounds pork tenderloin, trimmed

1. In a small deep dish just large enough to hold the pork, combine oil, wine, garlic.
2. Add pork, turning to coat thoroughly. Cover. Marinate overnight.
3. Drain pork; discard marinade.
4. Grill pork on an oiled rack about 6 inches above glowing coals, turning, for 25 minutes or until meat thermometer registers 155°. Remove to cutting board.
5. Let stand 10 minutes before slicing into ½-inch slices.

Mustard Sauce

¾ cup dry white wine　　　　　　3　Tablespoons Dijon mustard
1　Tablespoon shallot, minced　　　White pepper to taste
1　cup heavy cream　　　　　　　　Salt to taste

1. In a small, heavy saucepan, boil wine, shallot until reduced to about 2 Tablespoons.
2. Add cream; bring to a boil; simmer 2 minutes until slightly thickened.
3. Strain through a sieve into a bowl.
4. Whisk in mustard, seasonings.
5. Serve over pork.

Sauce may be made a day ahead and kept in a double boiler.

Accompaniments: Steamed miniature carrots or other vegetables.

NUTRIENT ANALYSIS (Per Serving)
Carbohydrate .... 3 grams
Protein .... 26 grams
Fat .... 28 grams
Calories .... 393 (64% from fat)
Cholesterol .... 136 milligrams
Sodium .... 172 milligrams

GRILLED PORK TENDERLOIN WITH MUSTARD CREAM SAUCE - LIGHT OPTION

Preparation time: 30 minutes + marinating
Cooking time: 25 minutes

Serves: 6

¾ cup red wine vinegar
¼ cup dry white wine

3 garlic cloves, lightly crushed
1½ pounds pork tenderloin, trimmed

1. In a small deep dish just large enough to hold the pork, combine vinegar, wine, garlic.
2. Add pork, turning to coat thoroughly. Cover. Marinate overnight.
3. Drain pork; discard marinade.
4. Grill pork on an oiled rack about 6 inches above glowing coals, turning, for 25 minutes or until meat thermometer registers 155°. Remove to cutting board.
5. Let stand 10 minutes before slicing into ½-inch slices.

Mustard Sauce

2 Tablespoons dry white wine
1 Tablespoon shallot, minced

1 cup evaporated skim milk
3 Tablespoons Dijon mustard
1 teaspoon white pepper

1. In a small, heavy saucepan, boil wine, shallot.
2. Add milk; bring to a boil; simmer 2 minutes until slightly thickened.
3. Strain through a sieve into a bowl.
4. Whisk in mustard, seasonings.
5. Serve over pork.

NUTRIENT ANALYSIS (Per Serving)
Carbohydrate .... 8 grams
Protein .... 32 grams
Fat .... 5 grams
Calories .... 209 (22% from fat)
Cholesterol .... 81 milligrams
Sodium .... 206 milligrams

ORANGE PORK CHOPS

Preparation time: 20 minutes
Cooking time: 45-60 minutes

Serves: 3-4

1 to 2 pork chops per person
2 to 4 Tablespoons water
Salt, pepper, paprika to taste
5 Tablespoons sugar
1½ teaspoons cornstarch
¼ teaspoon salt

¼ teaspoon cinnamon
10 whole cloves
2 Tablespoons orange rind
½ cup orange juice
4 to 6 orange slices, halved, or 10 to 12 mandarin orange slices

1. Sprinkle chops with seasonings. Brown in a sauté pan.

2. Add water. Cover tightly; cook over low heat 45-60 minutes, turning several times.

3. About 20 minutes before chops are done, combine remaining ingredients, except orange slices, in a saucepoan to make glaze.

4. Cook over medium heat, stirring constantly, until thick, clear.

5. Add orange slices to glaze. Cover tightly; remove from heat.

6. Serve over chops.

SWEET-SOUR PORK

Preparation time: 15 minutes
Cooking time: 1 hour

Serves: 6

1½ pounds boneless pork, trimmed of fat, cut into 1-inch cubes
Flour, salt, pepper
2 Tablespoons oil
½ cup barbeque sauce

¼ cup vinegar
¼ cup water
1 green pepper, cut into strips
½ to 1 cup pineapple preserves
Cooked rice

1. Coat meat with seasoned flour. Brown in oil in an electric wok or skillet.

2. Add barbeque sauce, vinegar, water.

3. Cover. Simmer 45 minutes, stirring occasionally to prevent sticking. Add more water if necessary.

4. Add green pepper, preserves. Simmer an additional 15 minutes.

5. Serve with rice.

May be prepared 1-2 hours before serving. Add green pepper, preserves 15 minutes before serving.

PORK BARBEQUE

Preparation time: 15 minutes *Serves: 14-16*
Baking time: 5 hours

3 medium onions, peeled, halved
3 cloves garlic
2 1-pound cans tomatoes with liquid
1 3 to 4-pound boneless
   pork loin roast
½ cup white vinegar

½ cup brown sugar
4 Tablespoons soy sauce
6 Tablespoons Worcestershire sauce
Salt to taste
2 to 3 drops hot sauce or more
   to taste

1. Chop onions, garlic cloves in a food processor.

2. Place in a large 5-quart Dutch oven.

3. Chop tomatoes in food processor.

4. Add tomatoes and all other ingredients.

5. Cover. Bake at 325° for 5 hours.

6. Remove from oven; cool.

7. Shred pork loin. (Will fall apart easily.)

8. If necessary, simmer on top of range to reduce extra juice.

9. Serve on buns.

Prepare a day ahead to enhance flavor.
Makes a great after-tennis supper! Kids love it, too.
Also good as a hot hors d'oeuvre served on miniature buns.

Accompaniments: Soup, potato or fruit salad.

KENTUCKY CASSOULET

Preparation time: 4-5 hours   *Serves: 6*

1 cup navy beans
Cold water
½ bay leaf
1½ teaspoons salt
1¾ cups water
1 Tablespoon red wine vinegar
½ teaspoon Tabasco
1 teaspoon fennel seeds (optional)
4 teaspoons salad oil, divided
1 pound lean pork or pork tenderloin, cubed

6 chicken thighs, skinned, boned
1 cup onion, finely chopped
4 cloves garlic, finely chopped
6 tomatoes, peeled, sliced, or 1 32-ounce can whole tomatoes, drained
½ teaspoon salt
⅓ cup parsley, chopped
1 cup raw spinach, shredded (optional)

1. Soak beans 2 hours in enough cold water to cover. Drain.

2. Place beans, bay leaf, salt, water, vinegar, Tabasco, fennel seeds in a 3-quart saucepan.

3. Cover; simmer gently 1 hour.

4. Heat 2 teaspoons oil in a large skillet. Add pork; brown 5 minutes, turning constantly to brown all sides.

5. Add pork to bean mixture. Cook 30 minutes.

6. Heat remaining oil in the same skillet. Add chicken: brown 3-4 minutes on each side.

7. Add chicken to bean mixture.

8. Sauté onion, garlic in the same skillet until onions are soft.

9. Add to bean mixture.

10. Add tomatoes, salt to bean mixture. Cover. Simmer gently 40 minutes.

11. Just before serving, stir in parsley, spinach. Cook 2 minutes.

HAM BALLS

Preparation time: 30 minutes
Baking time: 1 hour

Yield: 60-65 balls or
8-10 individual loaves

1   pound ground ham
1½ pounds ground pork
2   cups fresh bread crumbs
2   eggs, beaten
1   cup milk
½ cup celery, finely chopped

2   Tablespoons green pepper, finely chopped
1   teaspoon parsley, chopped
1   cup brown sugar
1   teaspoon dry mustard
½ cup water
¼ cup vinegar

1.   Mix together first 8 ingredients.

2.   Form into balls, using 1 heaping Tablespoon per ball, or place in 8-10 individual loaf pans.

3.   Mix remaining ingredients to make glaze. Pour over ham.

4.   Bake at 325° on the center oven rack for 1 hour, basting frequently with glaze.

ITALIAN SAUSAGES AND PEPPERS

Preparation time: 10 minutes
Cooking time: 15-20 minutes

Serves: 4

1   pound Italian sausage, cut into serving sizes
2   green peppers, cut into large pieces
1   tomato, diced into large pieces
6   ounces beer
1   teaspoon garlic powder

1   teaspoon paprika
½ teaspoon black pepper
½ teaspoon salt
1   teaspoon chili powder
½ teaspoon thyme
Dash red pepper (optional)
Cooked rice

1.   Cook sausage until done in an electric skillet. Drain.

2.   Add all remaining ingredients, except rice. Cover skillet.

3.   Cook at 375° for 15-20 minutes.

4.   Serve over rice.

Variation: Substitute hot dogs for sausage.
Very spicy.

STROMBOLI

Preparation time: 20 minutes
Baking time: 25 minutes

Serves: 4

1 Tablespoon olive oil
1 can refrigerated pizza dough
8 thin slices hard salami
8 thin slices provolone
8 thin slices capocollo or Virginia ham
1½ teaspoons Dijon mustard

¼ cup Parmesan cheese, freshly grated
½ teaspoon garlic salt
½ teaspoon dried oregano, crumbled
½ teaspoon seasoned salt
¾ cup shredded mozzarella cheese
Water
Pizza sauce or sun-dried tomatoes
   (optional)

1. Preheat oven to 375°.

2. Brush an 11x17-inch baking sheet with oil.

3. Unroll dough on sheet to edges.

4. Arrange salami pieces in a lengthwise row down center of dough, leaving ½-inch space at ends.

5. Top with provolone, then capocollo.

6. Spread with mustard.

7. Sprinkle with Parmesan, garlic salt, oregano, seasoned salt.

8. Cover with mozzarella.

9. Bring long sides of dough together atop filling; brush with water. Pinch to close.

10. Brush short ends with water; pinch to close.

11. Bake on the center oven rack for 25 minutes until golden brown.

12. Cut into slices; serve warm.

13. Top with sauce or tomatoes, if desired.

Variations: Add other ingredients, such as mushrooms, onions, tomatoes.
Make ahead and freeze to give as a gift.

Accompaniment: Salad of romaine lettuce, radishes, red bell pepper, and mushrooms tossed with olive oil, lemon juice, and grated Romano cheese.

PIZZA PARTY

Preparation time: 50 minutes
Baking time: 7-9 minutes

20 10-inch flour tortillas
1 30-ounce jar pizza sauce
1 pound sliced pepperoni
3 large onions, thinly sliced
3 large green peppers, finely diced

1 pound mushrooms, sliced
1 16-ounce can black olives, sliced
2 pounds mozzarella cheese, shreddedd
8 ounces Parmesan cheese, grated
¼ ounce oregano

1. Place tortillas on sheet pans.

2. Distribute remaining ingredients in individual bowls. Place a tablespoon to use for building pizzas in each bowl.

3. Build pizzas, placing sauce, meat, vegetables, cheeses, oregano on each tortilla.

4. Bake at 400° on the center oven rack for 7-9 minutes until cheese bubbles. Pizzas should be crisp.

5. Cut each pizza into 4-6 pieces.

Prepare all items ahead.
Children love to create their own pizzas.

ROAST RACK OF LAMB

Preparation time: 10 minutes
Roasting time: 30 minutes

Serves: 4-5

2 racks of lamb, 7 ribs each, trimmed, Frenched
¼ teaspoon garlic powder
½ teaspoon salt
2 Tablespoons Dijon mustard

1½ teaspoons ground rosemary
1½ teaspoons ground thyme
2 Tablespoons lemon juice
¼ cup olive or peanut oil
Mint jelly or wine sauce

1. Preheat oven to 500°. Lightly score fat side of each rack.
2. Combine remaining ingredients, except mint jelly or wine sauce.
3. Rub mustard mixture over racks, covering all sides completely.
4. Place lamb in a pan. Fold a strip of foil over rib ends to prevent burning.
5. Roast lamb for 10 minutes to sear. Reduce heat to 400°. Roast for 20 minutes to rosy rare. (Meat will be springy to touch.)
6. Let stand 5 minutes before cutting into serving portions.
7. Serve with mint jelly or a wine sauce made by combining white wine, orange marmalade, orange juice.

Accompaniments: Wild rice, Belgian endive salad with vinaigrette dressing, Merlot wine.

EASY LAMB SHANKS

Preparation time: 5 minutes
Baking time: 3 hours

Yield: 1 per person

1 lamb shank per person

1 Tablespoon onion soup mix per shank

1. Place each shank on heavy aluminum foil.
2. Sprinkle soup mix on each shank.
3. Seal foil.
4. Place in a baking pan to fit number of prepared shanks.
5. Bake at 275° on the center oven rack for 3 hours.

Accompaniment: Mint jelly or sauce.

LAMB SHANKS KAPAMA

Preparation time: 10 minutes *Serves: 8*
Baking time: 2 hours

6 lamb shanks
Salt, pepper, garlic powder to taste
1 medium onion, chopped
1 Tablespoon olive oil or vegetable oil
2 cups tomato sauce

1 teaspoon salt
½ teaspoon pepper
¼ teaspoon ground cinnamon
¼ teaspoon ground cloves

1. Rinse shanks. Place side by side in a baking dish.

2. Lightly sprinkle both sides with seasonings.

3. Bake at 400° on the center oven rack for at least 15 minutes on each side to sear, developing a good color, cooking off excess fat.

4. While lamb browns, combine remaining ingredients for sauce.

5. Remove lamb from oven. Drain off all fat, leaving a dry pan.

6. Reduce oven temperature to 350°. Pour sauce over lamb. Bake for 1½ hours.

7. After the first hour, check consistency of sauce. If too thick, add a small amount of water. Skim fat from surface if necessary.

Greek Festival, Dayton, Ohio

BROILED BUTTERFLY LAMB

Preparation time: 15-20 minutes + marinating *Serves: 6*
Grilling time: 30 minutes

1 leg of lamb, boned, butterflied,
   trimmed of excess fat
½ cup Dijon mustard
⅓ cup soy sauce

⅓ cup olive oil
1 teaspoon dried rosemary
½ teaspoon powdered ginger
1 large clove garlic, minced
   Wine (optional)

1. Place lamb in a shallow pan.

2. Combine all other ingredients; pour over lamb. Marinate at least 12 hours.

3. Grill over charcoal 15 minutes per side. (Lamb should be pink in center.)

Marinade excellent and also good for beef, poultry, or pork.

Accompaniments: Rice pilaf, tossed salad, muffins.

MOUSAKA

Preparation time: 1-1½ hours   *Serves: 8*
Baking time: 30 minutes

2 pounds ground lamb or beef
2 Tablespoons olive oil
1 large onion, chopped
2 Tablespoons parsley, chopped
2 cloves garlic, crushed
2 Tablespoons tomato paste
1 cup tomatoes, peeled, chopped

½ cup white wine
1 teaspoon sugar
¼ teaspoon cinnamon
Salt, pepper to taste
2 pounds (3 medium) eggplant, sliced
Salted water
Vegetable oil

Cream sauce

¼ cup butter, melted
⅓ cup flour
2 cups milk
⅛ teaspoon nutmeg

¼ cup grated Parmesan cheese,
    divided
Salt, pepper to taste
1 egg, slightly beaten

1. Brown meat in oil in a skillet. Drain.

2. Add next 9 ingredients. Simmer 15 minutes.

3. Soak eggplant slices in a deep pan of salted water 15 minutes. Drain. Squeeze slices gently to remove excess water.

4. Brush slices with vegetable oil. Place on a broiling pan; broil on both sides until browned.

5. In a 9x13-inch baking dish, arrange layers of eggplant slices alternately with meat, ending with eggplant.

6. Make cream sauce:
   - Stir flour into melted butter in a saucepan. Cook 2 minutes.
   - Add milk all at once; bring to a boil, stirring constantly.
   - Let sauce bubble gently 1 minute. Remove from heat.
   - Add nutmeg, half of cheese, seasonings.
   - Add egg. Cook over low heat until thickened.

(Continued on facing page)

7. Pour sauce over meat, eggplant layers.

8. Sprinkle with remaining cheese.

9. Bake at 350° on the center oven rack for 30 minutes.

10. Let cool. Cut into squares before serving.

A very good combination of flavors.

Accompaniments: Salad, crusty bread, feta cheese, calamata olives.

VIDALIA VEAL

Preparation time: 30 minutes   *Serves: 4*
Cooking time: 15-20 minutes

2 Tablespoons flour	**2 to 3 teaspoons capers**
2 Tablespoons grated Parmesan cheese	**½ teaspoon thyme**
2 Tablespoons olive oil	**1 teaspoon salt (optional)**
4 to 6 veal medallions, thinly sliced	**1 teaspoon black pepper**
2 Tablespoons raspberry or balsamic vinegar	**4 cups Vidalia onions, sliced**
	2 cups fresh mushrooms, sliced
2 Tablespoons lemon juice	**1 green or red pepper, diced**
½ cup white wine	**Fresh parsley**
1 Tablespoon fresh or dried parsley	**Cherry tomatoes**

1. Combine flour, cheese.

2. Dredge meat in flour mixture.

3. Heat a skillet to 400-450°. Brown meat in hot olive oil.

4. Reduce heat to medium; add seasonings.

5. Top meat slices with onions, mushrooms, peppers.

6. Cover; cook 15-20 minutes.

7. Garnish serving platter or plates with parsley, cherry tomatoes.

Deliciously tender veal and spicy vegetables.

Accompaniments: Rice, green vegetable.

VEAL SCALOPPINE WITH ASPARAGUS

Preparation time: 30 minutes   *Serves: 6*

1½ pounds veal cutlet, cut for scaloppine
2 Tablespoons butter, melted
⅓ cup sherry (optional)
1½ cups beef consommé (1 cup if using sherry)
4 large mushrooms, thinly sliced

1 Tablespoon flour
1 Tablespoon concentrated liquid beef bouillon (Bovril suggested)
1 Tablespoon tomato paste
½ teaspoon salt
Dash cayenne pepper
12 fresh asparagus spears

1. Cook meat in butter over high heat 2 minutes per side.

2. Remove veal. Deglaze pan with sherry or ½ cup consommé.

3. Add mushrooms to pan. Cook 2 minutes. Remove from pan.

4. Stir flour into a little consommé.

5. Add flour mixture, remaining consommé, Bovril, tomato paste to pan, stirring continuously. Heat to a boil.

6. Return veal, mushrooms to pan. Add seasonings.

7. Place asparagus over top. Cover tightly.

8. Cook slowly 10 minutes.

Variation: Use thinly sliced beef tenderloin or pork tenderloin instead of veal.

CHICKEN WITH CASHEWS AND SNOW PEAS

Preparation time: 30 minutes   *Serves: 2*

1 whole chicken breast, skinned, boned, cut into 1-inch cubes
2 cloves garlic, peeled, minced
1 Tablespoon soy sauce
1 Tablespoon dry sherry
2 Tablespoons cornstarch
1 teaspoon hoisin sauce
1 Tablespoon peanut oil

20 snow peas
½ red bell pepper, seeded, cut into strips
½ cup sliced water chestnuts, drained
½ cup hot chicken stock
½ teaspoon salt
½ cup unsalted raw cashews

1. Combine garlic, soy sauce, sherry, cornstarch, hoisin sauce.

2. Marinate chicken in mixture 15 minutes.

3. Heat oil in a wok, uncovered, at 375°.

4. Add chicken mixture; stir fry 3 minutes.

5. Add snow peas, red pepper, water chestnuts; stir-fry 30 seconds.

6. Add stock, salt; stir-fry until slightly thickened.

7. Stir in cashews.

9. Serve immediately.

If unsalted cashews are unavailable, use salted ones and omit salt from recipe. Hoisin sauce is available in large groceries.

Refrigerates well for 2 days after cooking.

Accompaniment: White rice.

CHICKEN ALMONDINE

Preparation time: 35 minutes + marinating   *Serves: 6*

6½ Tablespoons olive oil, divided
5 Tablespoons lemon juice
3 Tablespoons Dijon mustard
2 cloves garlic, finely chopped
¼ teaspoon white pepper
3 whole chicken breasts, halved, boned
1 cup natural almonds, sliced

2 cups chicken broth
1 teaspoon cornstarch dissolved in 1 Tablespoon water
2 Tablespoons orange marmalade
2 Tablespoons butter, cut into bits
2 Tablespoons fresh parsley, chopped
¼ teaspoon red pepper flakes
Lemon slices for garnish

1. Heat 5 Tablespoons olive oil in a skillet.
2. Combine lemon juice, mustard, garlic, white pepper. Heat in olive oil.
3. Add chicken; marinate 1 hour at room temperature.
4. In a large skillet sauté almonds until golden in ½ Tablespoon oil. Remove; set aside. Wipe out pan.
5. Drain chicken. Reserve marinade.
6. Cook chicken over high heat in remaining 1 Tablespoon oil 6-10 minutes until tender, brown on each side. Remove from pan; set aside.
7. Strain marinade into pan.
8. Add chicken broth, cornstarch mixture.
9. Cook 5 minutes over high heat, stirring occasionally until sauce reduces one half.
10. Add marmalade; stir over medium heat until melted.
11. Over high heat stir in butter, parsley, pepper flakes.
12. Return chicken to pan; heat through.
13. Add almonds.
14. Garnish with lemon slices.

Accompaniments: Wild rice, green beans or sugar snaps, green salad, Chablis.

CHICKEN SUPERB

Preparation time: 1½ hours
Baking time: 35-40 minutes

Serves: 6 - 8

4 large chicken breast halves, skinned, boned
6 Tablespoons butter or margarine, melted
6 Tablespoons flour
2 cups chicken broth (canned acceptable)
1½ teaspoons salt
½ teaspoon celery salt
Dash beau monde seasoning
½ teaspoon marjoram
3 Tablespoons fresh parsley, chopped
½ cup slivered almonds, toasted
6 ounces medium noodles, cooked, drained
2 cups heavy cream
2 Tablespoons dry sherry
2 Tablespoons butter, melted
10 ounces fresh mushrooms, sliced
½ cup grated Cheddar cheese

1. Preheat oven to 350°.
2. Wrap chicken in foil; bake 1 hour. Cool. Cut into large strips. Set aside.
3. Combine flour with melted butter in a large skillet over low heat. Do not brown.
4. Stir in broth, seasonings, herbs. Cook, stirring constantly until thickened.
5. Add cream, sherry; set aside.
6. Sauté mushrooms in melted butter in a small skillet.
7. Add mushrooms, almonds to sauce.
8. Combine sauce with chicken, noodles.
9. Pour into a flat 11x7½-inch casserole.
10. Top with cheese.
11. Bake on the center oven rack for 35-40 minutes.

ALPINE CHICKEN CASSEROLE

Preparation time: 25 minutes
Baking time: 30 - 40 minutes

Serves: 6

4   cups cooked chicken, cubed
2   cups celery, sliced
2   cups seasoned croutons
1   cup mayonnaise
½   cup milk

1   teaspoon salt
⅛   teaspoon pepper
½   small onion, grated
8   ounces Swiss cheese, cut into strips
¼   cup almonds, toasted

1. Combine chicken, celery, croutons.

2. Combine mayonnaise, milk, seasonings; mix well. Fold in onion, cheese.

3. Pour over chicken mixture; toss until well blended.

4. Spoon into a buttered 2-quart casserole. Sprinkle with almonds.

5. Bake at 350° on the center oven rack for 30-40 minutes.

NUTTY CHICKEN

Preparation time: 30 minutes

Serves: 4

3   Tablespoons soy sauce
2   teaspoons cornstarch
2   Tablespoons dry sherry
1   teaspoon fresh ginger root, grated
1   teaspoon sugar
½   teaspoon crushed red pepper
2   Tablespoons cooking oil

2   medium green peppers, cut into
    ¾-inch pieces
4   scallions, cut into 1-inch lengths
1   cup walnuts, coarsely chopped
1½ pounds chicken breasts, skinned,
    boned, cubed
Cooked rice

1. Combine first 6 ingredients. Blend; set aside.

2. Preheat a wok with cooking oil.

3. Stir-fry peppers, onions 2 minutes. Remove from wok.

4. Cook walnuts 2 minutes. Remove.

5. Stir-fry half of the chicken 2 minutes. Remove.

6. Stir-fry remaining chicken. If necessary, add more oil to prevent chicken from sticking.

7. Return all chicken to wok. Stir sauce into chicken. Cook until thick, bubbly.

8. Add peppers, onions, walnuts. Cover; cook 1 minute. Serve with rice.

CHICKEN IN WHITE WINE

Preparation time: 1 hour | *Serves: 8*

4 Tablespoons oil
2 medium onions, chopped
1 large clove garlic, chopped
4 large chicken breasts, halved, boned
1 Tablespoon cornstarch dissolved
   in 1 Tablespoon water
1 cup dry white wine

1 Tablespoon brandy (optional)
1 teaspoon salt
⅛ teaspoon pepper
1 teaspoon dried thyme leaves
2 Tablespoons parsley, finely
   chopped
½ pound mushrooms, sliced, sautéed
Chopped parsley

1. Slowly heat oil in a large heavy skillet or Dutch oven.

2. Add onions, garlic. Sauté until golden. Remove onions; set aside.

3. Add chicken; sauté until browned on both sides. Remove; set aside.

4. Drain all but 2 Tablespoons fat from skillet.

5. Stir in cornstarch mixture, wine, brandy, seasonings, thyme, parsley.

6. Return chicken, onions to pan. Cover; simmer 30 minutes.

7. Add mushrooms. Simmer 10 minutes.

8. Serve with sauce. Sprinkle with parsley.

If sauce is too thin, add additional cornstarch.

Accompaniments: Wild rice, fresh green beans, spiced peaches, green salad, dry white wine.

CHICKEN DE - LITE

Preparation time: 30 minutes   *Serves: 4*

4 **large chicken breast portions, skinned, boned**
½ **teaspoon paprika**
1 **teaspoon seasoning (Mrs. Dash original suggested)**

½ **teaspoon basil**
¾ **to 1 cup dry white wine or cranberry juice**
2 **Tablespoons grated Parmesan cheese**
Fresh parsley

1. Spray a skillet with a non-stick surface with no-stick cooking spray.

2. Brown chicken on both sides.

3. Sprinkle with spices.

4. Add liquid ¼ cup at a time.

5. Cover; simmer on low heat 15-20 minutes until tender.

6. Sprinkle with Parmesan the last 5 minutes.

7. Garnish with parsley.

To save time, use skinned, boned chicken portions straight from your freezer. Sliced leftovers make wonderful hot or cold sandwiches.

LAZY DAY CHICKEN

Preparation time: 15 minutes + marinating   *Serves: 4*
Baking time: 1 hour, 15 minutes

4 **chicken breasts, boned**
½ **cup honey**

½ **cup Dijon mustard**
½ **teaspoon curry powder**
1 **teaspoon Worcestershire sauce**

1. Place chicken breasts skin side down in a baking dish.

2. Mix remaining ingredients. Pour mixture over chicken. Cover.

3. Refrigerate 6 hours or overnight.

4. Turn chicken skin side up.

5. Uncover. Bake at 350° for 1 hour.

6. Baste. Bake an additional 15 minutes.

CHICKEN WITH 40 CLOVES OF GARLIC

Preparation time: 20 minutes   *Serves: 6 - 8*
Baking time: 1½ hours

8 **chicken thighs, rinsed, patted dry**
¼ **cup olive oil, divided**
2 **teaspoons salt**
¼ **teaspoon nutmeg**
3 **bulbs garlic, peeled into 40 whole
   cloves**

4 **stalks celery, thinly sliced**
2 **teaspoons pepper**
6 **sprigs parsley**
½ **cup white wine**
   Juice of 1 lemon
   Rind of 1 lemon, minced

1. Preheat oven to 375°.

2. Coat chicken with oil; sprinkle with salt, nutmeg.

3. Place in a 3-quart casserole with remaining oil.

4. Add remaining ingredients except lemon juice, rind.

5. Squeeze lemon juice over chicken. Scatter rind on top.

6. Seal casserole with foil. Bake for 1½ hours.

The softened garlic is delicious on French bread.

TWO - STEP CHICKEN BREASTS

Preparation time: 10 minutes + marinating   *Serves: 6*
Grilling time: 10 - 15 minutes

½ **cup orange juice**
½ **cup soy sauce**
½ **cup red wine**

2 **Tablespoons oil**
2 **to 3 whole chicken breasts,
   halved, boned**

1. Combine first 4 ingredients. Mix well.

2. Pour over chicken.

3. Marinate 3 hours.

4. Grill over medium low flame for 10-15 minutes, or broil for 10 minutes
    on each side.

Accompaniments: Corn on the cob, mixed green salad, fruit.

OVEN-FRIED CHICKEN PICCATA

Preparation time: 15 minutes   *Serves: 4*
Baking time: 40 minutes

1   Tablespoon soy sauce
½ teaspoon salt (optional)
½ teaspoon pepper
¼ cup canola oil
¼ cup lemon juice
2   teaspoons grated lemon peel
1   clove garlic, minced

½ cup flour
1   teaspoon salt (optional)
¼ teaspoon pepper
2   teaspoons paprika
4   chicken breast halves, skinned, boned
2   Tablespoons margarine, melted

1. Combine first 7 ingredients to make sauce. Refrigerate sauce at least 1 hour.

2. Preheat oven to 400°.

3. Combine flour, seasonings. Coat chicken.

4. Spray bottom of a shallow baking pan with non-stick cooking oil; arrange chicken in a single layer.

5. Spoon margarine over chicken. Bake uncovered for 20 minutes.

6. Turn; pour sauce over chicken. Bake an additional 20 minutes.

7. Pour pan juices over each piece before serving.

YOUNG MOTHER'S CHICKEN

Preparation time: 15 minutes   *Serves: 6 - 8*
Baking time: 1 hour

2½ to 3 pounds frying chicken pieces, washed, dried, or 8 chicken breasts, skinned, boned

¼ cup butter, melted
1   clove garlic, pressed
2   cups potato chips, crushed

1. Combine butter, garlic.

2. Dip chicken into butter mixture.

3. Roll in crushed chips.

4. Place chicken pieces so that they do not touch in a 9x13-inch baking dish. (If chicken has skin, place skin side up.)

5. Bake at 375° on the center oven rack for 1 hour. Do not turn.

CHICKEN SCALLOPS PROVENCALE

Preparation time: 35 minutes
Baking time: 10 - 15 minutes

Serves: 4

4 Tablespoons olive oil
½ cup onion, chopped
1 Tablespoon garlic, minced
1 red or green bell pepper, chopped
½ cup celery, chopped
8 medium tomatoes, peeled, seeded, chopped, or 1 32-ounce can tomatoes, drained

1 teaspoon dried basil
1 teaspoon dried oregano
Salt, pepper to taste
2 large whole chicken breasts, halved, skinned, boned
½ cup flour
¼ cup butter, melted
6 ounces Gruyère, Jarlsburg, or Swiss cheese, grated

1. Sauté onion, garlic, pepper, celery in olive oil 5 minutes.
2. Add tomatoes, spices, seasonings. Cook uncovered 20 minutes.
3. Preheat oven to 350°.
4. Slice chicken pieces in half lengthwise.
5. Place chicken scallops between waxed paper; pound gently to flatten.
5. Lightly flour scallops. Sauté quickly in butter.
6. Place scallops in a single layer in an oblong baking dish.
7. Coat with vegetable mixture; top with grated cheese.
8. Bake for 10-15 minutes until cheese melts.

Accompaniments: Tossed salad, garlic bread, lemon sherbert.

HERBED CHICKEN AU JUS

Preparation time: 20 minutes   *Serves: 4*
Baking time: 65 minutes

1   cup carrots, thinly sliced   ½ teaspoon rosemary
1   cup onion, thinly sliced   ½ teaspoon thyme
1   3 ½-pound broiler chicken, cut   ½ teaspoon marjoram
    into pieces, or 4 chicken breasts   1 teaspoon salt
1   cup chicken stock, divided   ¼ teaspoon freshly ground pepper
2   Tablespoons lemon juice   ⅓ cup fresh parsley, chopped

1. Preheat oven to 325°.

2. Arrange carrots, onions in a shallow baking dish.

3. Place chicken, skin side up, over vegetables.

4. Pour ½ cup stock over chicken.

5. Cover tightly. Bake for 45 minutes.

6. While chicken bakes, combine ½ cup stock with remaining ingredients, except parsley, in a saucepan.

7. Bring herb mixture to a boil. Remove from heat.

8. Remove chicken from oven. Increase oven temperature to 400°.

9. Uncover chicken. Bake, basting liberally with herb mixture, for 20 minutes until chicken is tender, skin lightly browned.

10. Spoon vegetables, pan juices over chicken.

11. Garnish with parsley. Serve immediately.

NUTRIENT ANALYSIS (Per Serving)
Carbohydrate .... 8 grams
Protein .... 28 grams
Fat .... 11 grams
Calories .... 246 (40% from fat)
Cholesterol .... 74 milligrams
Sodium .... 869 millgrams

HERBED CHICKEN AU JUS - LIGHT OPTION

Preparation time: 20 minutes
Baking time: 65 minutes

Serves: 4

1 **cup carrots, thinly sliced**	½ **teaspoon rosemary**
1 **cup onion, thinly sliced**	½ **teaspoon thyme**
4 **chicken breasts, skinned, boned**	½ **teaspoon marjoram**
1 **cup chicken stock, divided**	¼ **teaspoon freshly ground pepper**
2 **Tablespoons lemon juice**	⅓ **cup fresh parsley, chopped**

1. Preheat oven to 325°.
2. Arrange carrots, onions in a shallow baking dish.
3. Place chicken over vegetables.
4. Pour ½ cup stock over vegetables.
5. Cover tightly. Bake for 45 minutes.
6. While chicken bakes, combine ½ cup stock with remaining ingredients, except parsley, in a saucepan.
7. Bring herb mixture to a boil. Remove from heat.
8. Remove chicken from oven. Increase oven temperature to 400°.
9. Uncover chicken. Bake, basting liberally with herb mixture, for 20 minutes until chicken is tender.
10. Spoon vegetables, pan juices over chicken.
11. Garnish with parsley. Serve immediately.

NUTRIENT ANALYSIS (Per Serving)
Carbohydrate .... 8 grams
Protein .... 31 grams
Fat .... 5 grams
Calories .... 204 (22% from fat)
Cholesterol .... 77 milligrams
Sodium .... 296 milligrams

CHICKEN OLÉ

Preparation time: 30 minutes
Baking time: 55 minutes

Serves: 6

⅔ cup yellow cornmeal
1 teaspoon chili powder
1 teaspoon garlic powder
1 teaspoon pepper
½ teaspoon salt (optional)
½ cup milk
1 small can diced green chilies
1 2 ½-ounce jar sliced mushrooms

4 ounces shredded sharp Cheddar cheese
4 ounces shredded Monterey Jack cheese
6 whole chicken breasts, skinned, boned, pounded to ¼ to ½-inch thickness
¼ cup butter or margarine, melted

1. Combine first 5 ingredients. Set aside.

2. Mix chilies, mushrooms.

3. Mix cheeses. Add to mushroom mixture.

4. Dip chicken in milk, then in cornmeal mixture.

5. Stuff each breast with cheese-mushroom mixture. Secure with toothpicks.

6. Place in a glass baking dish.

7. Drizzle butter over chicken.

8. Cover. Bake at 350° for 45 minutes.

9. Uncover. Bake an additional 10 minutes.

An interesting, spicy blend.

Accompaniments: Corn, green salad, light dessert.

ORANGE BAKED CHICKEN

Preparation time: 15 minutes + marinating　　　　　　　　*Serves: 4*
Baking time: 45 minutes

2　pounds chicken breasts, skinned,
　boned
1　6-ounce can frozen orange juice
1　Tablespoon orange rind, grated

2　Tablespoons low-sodium soy sauce
1　Tablespoon minced onion
1　teaspoon dried parsley
1　clove garlic, minced
¼　teaspoon black pepper

1.　Place chicken in a 9x12-inch baking dish.

2.　Combine remaining ingredients to make marinade.

3.　Pour marinade over chicken. Cover. Refrigerate several hours or overnight.

4.　Bake, covered, at 400° on the lower oven rack for 45 minutes.

5.　Uncover. Continue baking until tender, basting several times with the sauce.

Accompaniments: Rice, broccoli and carrots, white zinfandel wine.

APRICOT CHICKEN

Preparation time: 10 minutes　　　　　　　　*Serves: 6*
Baking time: 1 1/2 hours

1　12-ounce jar apricot preserves
1　package dry onion soup mix
　(Lipton suggested)
1　8-ounce bottle Russian salad
　dressing

10 dried apricot halves
6 to 8 chicken breast halves, skinned,
　boned
Red raspberries
Wild or long grain rice

1.　Combine first 4 ingredients.

2.　Place chicken in a flat baking dish.

3.　Pour sauce over chicken. Cover.

4.　Bake at 350° for 1 hour.

5.　Uncover. Baste. Bake an additional 30 minutes.

6.　Garnish with red raspberries. Spoon some sauce over raspberries.

7.　Serve with rice.

CALIFORNIA CHICKEN

Preparation time: 1 hour   *Serves: 4*

4 Tablespoons margarine, melted
3½ pounds broiler-fryer chicken, cut
    into pieces
¾ teaspoon salt
⅛ teaspoon cayenne
1 cup orange juice
1 Tablespoon cornstarch

2 Tablespoons cold water
2 Tablespoons orange liqueur
¼ teaspoon ground cloves
1 clove garlic, pressed
1½ cups orange sections, cut into
    bite-size pieces
1 cup avocado, cubed
1½ teaspoons grated orange rind

1. In a large skillet, sauté chicken in melted margarine until brown on both sides.

2. Turn chicken skin side up. Season.

3. Add orange juice. Cover.

4. Simmer 30 minutes until tender.

5. Remove chicken to a heated platter.

6. Blend cornstarch, water, liqueur.

7. Add mixture to skillet; bring to a boil.

8. Reduce heat. Add cloves, rind, garlic.

9. Cook, stirring until sauce thickens.

10. Remove from heat. Stir in orange sections, avocado cubes.

11. Return chicken to skillet.

12. Baste with sauce over low heat until chicken is heated through.

13. Serve immediately.

RASPBERRY GLAZED CHICKEN

Preparation time: 15 minutes
Baking time: 15 minutes

Serves: 2 - 4

4   chicken breast halves, skinned,
    boned
Flour
2   Tablespoons butter, melted

¼   cup red raspberry preserves
1   Tablespoon raspberry vinegar
1   Tablespoon fresh lemon juice
Grated rind of 1 lemon

1. Dredge chicken with flour, shaking off excess.

2. Brown chicken quickly on both sides in a skillet in melted butter.

3. Place breasts in a single layer in a shallow baking dish.

4. Combine remaining ingredients in a small saucepan. Heat to boiling, stirring to combine.

5. Brush chicken with glaze.

6. Bake at 400° on the center oven rack for 15 minutes, basting every 5 minutes.

To prevent leftovers from turning dark, do not store in aluminum foil.

Elegant, easy, and delicious.

Accompaniments: New potatoes, asparagus, tossed salad, rolls.

CHICKEN WITH APRICOT GLAZE

Preparation time: 20 minutes
Cooking time: 45 minutes

Serves: 4

1   3-pound chicken, cut into 8 pieces
¼   cup flour
2   Tablespoons margarine, melted
2   Tablespoons salad oil
1   16-ounce can peeled apricot halves
    with juice
Water

½   cup apricot jam
2   teaspoons sherry
1   teaspoon marjoram
1   teaspoon grated lemon peel
1   teaspoon soy sauce
Dash hot sesame oil
Pinch ground ginger
1   green pepper, diced

1.   Coat chicken pieces with flour.

2.   Brown chicken in margarine and oil in a large skillet over medium high heat.

3.   Drain juice from apricot halves. Set fruit aside. Combine juice with enough water to measure 1½ cups liquid.

4.   Combine liquid with all remaining ingredients except apricots, green pepper.

5.   Pour mixture over chicken.

6.   Reduce heat to low. Cover. Simmer 40 minutes until chicken is tender.

7.   Add green pepper. Cook 5 minutes.

8.   Add apricots just before serving. Heat thoroughly.

A tasty, colorful combination.

CHUTNEY CHICKEN

Preparation time: 10 minutes Serves: 6
Baking time: 40 minutes

6 chicken breasts, boned
12 ounces chutney (Major Grey sug-
    gested)
6 ounces frozen orange juice
    concentrate
½ cup water

1 large onion, peeled, sliced
½ cup white raisins
1 cup dry white wine
Salt, pepper to taste
1 large mango, peeled, sliced
Fresh parsley, chopped

1. Preheat oven to 400°.

2. Spread both sides of chicken with 1 Tablespoon chutney.

3. Place in a baking dish, skin side up.

4. Mix orange juice with water. Pour over chicken.

5. Sprinkle onion, raisins over all.

6. Cover dish with foil.

7. Bake on the center oven rack for 20 minutes. Uncover. Bake an additional 20 minutes. Remove from oven.

8. Place sauce in a saucepan.

9. Add wine, seasonings. Heat. Add mango.

10. Place chicken on a serving dish. Pour sauce over chicken.

11. Garnish with parsley.

May be prepared and refrigerated 2-3 days in advance. Also freezes well after baking.

PARADISE EN PAPILLOTE

Preparation time: 15 minutes + marinating   *Serves: 6*
Baking time: 45 minutes

6   uncooked chicken breast halves, skinned, boned
Italian dressing
6   12x20-inch pieces heavy aluminum foil
12 large mushrooms
1½ cups fast cooking rice (Minute Rice suggested)
1½ cups frozen peas

12 cherry tomatoes
1½ small onions
6   2-inch piece Polish sausage in casing, cut lengthwise into 2 pieces
18 large uncooked shrimp, peeled
4½ teaspoons soy sauce
¾ cup tomato juice or vegetable juice (V-8 suggested)
18   green pepper strips

1. Marinate each chicken breast half in 2 teaspoons of your favorite Italian dressing 1 hour at room temperature or several hours in the refrigerator.

2. Rub mushrooms with Italian dressing.

3. Divide ingredients onto 6 foil rectangles in this order: rice, mushrooms, peas, tomatoes, onion, sausage, shrimp, chicken breast, soy sauce, pepper strips.

4. Fold each tightly into a pouch.

5. Place pouches on a cookie sheet.

6. Bake at 300° on the center oven rack for 45 minutes, or place pouches directly on an outdoor grill for 30 minutes.

7. Serve pouches on individual plates or a serving platter.

May be prepared 2 hours in advance.
Great for cookouts or camping trips.

Accompaniments: Salad, garlic bread, dessert.

CREAMED CHICKEN ON PHYLLO

Preparation time: 35 minutes   *Serves: 6 - 8*

1 1-pound package phyllo dough	2 cups milk
½ cup butter, melted, divided	2 chicken bouillon cubes
¼ cup onion, chopped	3 cups cooked chicken breast, cubed
1 cup fresh mushrooms, sliced	¼ cup pimento, diced
⅓ cup flour	1 to 2 Tablespoons sherry (optional)

1. For each serving fold 1 sheet phyllo dough in half, then in half again. Brush with butter.

2. Butter small individual baking dishes. Place a folded sheet of phyllo in each.

3. Bake at 350° until golden brown. The shell will curve to form a cup.

4. Cool. Remove from baking dishes, or leave in dishes to serve.

5. Sauté onion, mushrooms in a skillet in ¼ cup melted butter.

6. Blend flour with ¼ cup melted butter in a saucepan.

7. Slowly add milk, bouillon cubes. Cook until smooth, boiling.

8. Add chicken, mushroom mixture, pimentos.

9. Add sherry if desired.

10. Fill phyllo shells with chicken mixture. Serve immediately.

Truffles Café and Catering
Centerville, Ohio

SAVORY CRESCENT CHICKEN SQUARES

Preparation time: 35 minutes   *Serves: 8*
Baking time: 20 - 25 minutes

1 **3-ounce package cream cheese, softened**
2 **Tablespoons margarine, melted**
2 **cups cooked skinless chicken breast, cubed**
¼ **teaspoon salt**
⅛ **teaspoon pepper**
2 **Tablespoons milk**
1 **Tablespoon chives, chopped**

1 **Tablespoon pimento, chopped**
2 **cans crescent rolls (Pillsbury suggested)**
1 **Tablespoon margarine, melted**
¾ **cup seasoned croutons or crackers, crushed**
1 **10 ¾-ounce can cream of mushroom or chicken mushroom soup**
½ **cup white wine**

1. Mix first 8 ingredients well.

2. Separate crescents into 8 squares, 4 from each can, sealing the perforations.

3. Place on an ungreased cookie sheet.

4. Spoon ⅓ cup chicken mixture into the center of each square.

5. Pull 4 corners of each square of dough to the center. Seal.

6. Brush tops with margarine.

7. Coat with crushed croutons or crackers.

8. Bake at 350° for 20-25 minutes.

9. Combine soup, wine. Heat.

10. Spoon a little of soup mixture over each serving. Pass remaining soup mixture.

Excellent flavor, texture. Make smaller crescents for a ladies' luncheon.

Accompaniments: Cranberry sauce, fruit salad, baked custard or mousse.

NUTRIENT ANALYSIS (Per Serving)
Carbohydrate .... 40 grams
Protein .... 29 grams
Fat .... 33 grams
Calories .... 590 (50% from fat)
Cholesterol .... 83 milligrams
Sodium .... 1657 milligrams

SAVORY CRESCENT CHICKEN SQUARES - LIGHT OPTION

Preparation time: 35 minutes
Baking time: 20 - 25 minutes

Serves: 4

1 **3-ounce package light cream cheese, softened**
2 **cups cooked skinless chicken breast, cubed**
⅛ **teaspoon pepper**
2 **Tablespoons ½% milk**
1 **Tablespoon chives, chopped**
1 **Tablespoon pimento, chopped**

1 **can crescent rolls (Pillsbury suggested)**
1 **Tablespoon margarine, melted**
¾ **cup (16) saltines, crushed**
1 **10¾-ounce can low fat cream of mushroom soup (Healthy Request suggested)**
½ **cup white wine**

1. Mix first 6 ingredients well.

2. Separate crescents into 4 squares, sealing the perforations.

3. Place on an ungreased cookie sheet.

4. Spoon ⅓ cup chicken mixture into the center of each square.

5. Pull 4 corners of each square of dough to the center. Seal.

6. Brush tops with margarine.

7. Coat with crushed crackers.

8. Bake at 350° for 20-25 minutes.

9. Combine soup, wine in a saucepan. Heat.

10. Spoon a little of soup mixture over each serving. Pass remaining soup mixture.

NUTRIENT ANALYSIS (Per Serving)
Carbohydrate .... 42 grams
Protein .... 29 grams
Fat .... 20 grams
Calories .... 497 (36% from fat)
Cholesterol .... 73 milligrams
Sodium .... 1269 milligrams

MICROWAVE CHICKEN IN A POUCH WITH VEGETABLES

Preparation time: 15 minutes
Microwave time: 6-8 minutes

Serves: 4

2 Tablespoons butter, melted
4 chicken breasts, skinned, boned
4 teaspoons Dijon mustard
2 small carrots, thinly julienned

1 stalk celery, thinly julienned
1 green onion, thinly julienned
1 teaspoon dried thyme
Salt, pepper to taste

1. Fold 4 15x10-inch pieces of microwave wrap in half crosswise. Trim corners to form ovals. Brush with butter, leaving a 1-inch border.

2. Place 1 chicken breast in center of 1 end of each oval.

3. Spread with mustard.

4. Sprinkle evenly with remaining ingredients.

5. Fold paper over chicken; crimp edges to seal. Slash each top to vent slightly.

6. Arrange on a shallow microwave baking dish with thickest portions to the outside.

7. Microwave 6-8 minutes until chicken is no longer pink inside. Rotate dish halfway through cooking time.

8. Let stand 3 minutes before serving.

Dorothy Lane Market
Dayton, Ohio

LEMON CHICKEN KABOBS

Preparation time: 15 minutes + marinating　　　　　　　*Serves: 4*
Grilling time: 25 - 30 minutes

1　package chicken breasts or thighs,
　　skinned, boned, cubed
2　small zucchini, diced
16　medium mushrooms
1　red pepper, seeded, cut into chunks
1　Tablespoon grated lemon peel

⅓　cup lemon juice
¼　cup vegetable oil
1　Tablespoon sugar
1　Tablespoon cider vinegar
Salt, pepper to taste
½　teaspoon paprika
1　clove garlic, minced

1. Place chicken, zucchini, mushrooms, pepper in a glass bowl.

2. Combine remaining ingredients for marinade. Reserve ¼ cup marinade.

3. Pour remaining over chicken, vegetables. Stir to coat. Cover; refrigerate 2 hours.

4. Drain marinade from chicken, vegetables. Discard marinade.

5. Alternately thread chicken, zucchini, mushrooms, red peppers onto 4 metal skewers. Brush with reserved marinade.

6. Grill over coals for 25-30 minutes, turning and brushing with marinade often.

GRILLED CHICKEN MUSHROOM KABOBS

Preparation time: 35 minutes　　　　　　　　　　*Serves: 4*
Grilling time: 15 minutes

1　cup orange marmalade (Spreadable
　　Fruit suggested)
¼　cup orange juice
¼　cup reduced sodium soy sauce
1　teaspoon ground ginger

2　large whole chicken breasts,
　　skinned, boned
24　whole fresh mushrooms
2　green peppers, cut into 16 wedges
24　cherry tomatoes

1. Combine first 4 ingredients in a medium bowl. Set aside.

2. Cut each chicken breast into 8 pieces.

3. Add chicken, remaining ingredients to marmalade sauce, mixing to coat. Marinate 20 minutes.

4. Alternately thread chicken, mushrooms, green peppers, tomatoes onto 4 10-inch all metal skewers. Arrange skewers on grill or broiler pan.

5. Grill or broil 15 minutes until chicken is tender, turning and brushing occasionally with marmalade sauce.

CURRY ROAST TURKEY BREAST

Preparation time: 15 minutes　　　　　　　　　　　　*Serves: 8*
Roasting time: 2 hours

1 Tablespoon curry powder	***Gravy***
¼ cup soy sauce	
¼ cup vegetable oil	**2 cups juice from cooking bag**
2 Tablespoons lemon juice	**Flour, water for thickening**
2 Tablespoons orange juice	**8 ounces cream or half and half**
1 fresh or frozen (thawed) turkey breast	**Salt, pepper to taste**

1. Mix first 5 ingredients for marinade.

2. Place turkey breast in a cooking bag.

3. Pour half of marinade over turkey. Secure bag.

4. Roast at 325° on the center oven rack for 1 hour, 40 minutes.

5. Open bag; slit to lay back. Pour remaining marinade over turkey. Roast uncovered an additional 20 minutes until tender.

6. Remove turkey to a cutting board. Let sit 20 minutes.

7. Make gravy:
   • Skim excess fat from pan juices.
   • Whisk in thickening in a saucepan; simmer until smooth, thick.
   • Add cream to desired consistency; season. Keep warm.

8. Serve sliced turkey with gravy.

An interesting change from the traditional holiday roast turkey.

Accompaniment: Stuffing made from a mixture of herb stuffing mix and cooked wild rice mix. Add sautéed onion and celery to the mixture.

NUTRIENT ANALYSIS (Per Serving)
Carbohydrate ....6 grams
Protein ....63 grams
Fat ....28 grams
Calories ....548 (46% from fat)
Cholesterol ....175 milligrams
Sodium ....561 milligrams

CURRY ROAST TURKEY BREAST - LIGHT OPTION

Preparation time: 15 minutes　　　　　　　　　　　　　　　　*Serves: 8*
Roasting time: 2 hours

1 Tablespoon curry powder
¼ cup reduced sodium soy sauce
¼ cup red wine vinegar
2 Tablespoons lemon juice
2 Tablespoons orange juice
1 5-pound fresh or frozen (thawed)
　　turkey breast, skinned before
　　cooking

Gravy

2 cups juice from cooking bag
¼ cup flour
Water
1 cup skim milk

1. Mix first 5 ingredients for marinade.

2. Place turkey breast in a cooking bag.

3. Pour half of marinade over turkey. Secure bag.

4. Roast at 325° on the center oven rack for 1 hour, 40 minutes.

5. Open bag; slit to lay back. Pour remaining marinade over turkey.

6. Roast uncovered an additional 20 minutes until tender.

7. Remove turkey to a cutting board. Let sit 20 minutes.

8. Make gravy:

   • Skim excess fat from pan juices. Place juices in a saucepan.

   • Combine flour, water for thickening.

   • Whisk thickening into juices; simmer until smooth, thick.

   • Add skim milk to desired consistency; keep warm.

9. Serve sliced turkey with gravy.

NUTRIENT ANALYSIS (Per Serving)
Carbohydrate .... 7 grams
Protein .... 66 grams
Fat .... 7 grams
Calories .... 371 (17% from fat)
Cholesterol .... 148 milligrams
Sodium .... 484 milligrams

AFTER CHRISTMAS CASSEROLE

Preparation time: 30 minutes   *Serves: 6 - 7*
Baking time: 40 minutes

½ cup wild rice, cooked
½ cup brown rice, cooked
1½ cups mayonnaise
½ teaspoon salt
Dash thyme
2 Tablespoons lemon juice
1 teaspoon seasoned salt
1 red bell pepper, coarsely chopped

2 Tablespoons onion, chopped
1 14-ounce can chicken broth
4 cups cooked turkey or chicken, cubed
2 cups celery, chopped
¾ cup slivered almonds
3½ ounces cornbread stuffing mix (Brownberry or Pepperidge Farm suggested)

1. Add seasonings to mayonnaise.

2. Combine all ingredients except stuffing mix.

3. Spoon into a greased 3½ or 4-quart casserole. Sprinkle with stuffing mix.

4. Bake at 350° on the center oven rack for 40 minutes until well heated.

CORNISH HEN AU VIN

Preparation time: 25 minutes   *Serves: 4*
Baking time: 1 hour

4 Cornish hens
Salt, pepper
4 Tablespoons Dijon mustard

10 crackers, crushed (Ritz suggested), or ½ cup dry bread crumbs
2 Tablespoons green onion, chopped
12 Tablespoons white wine

1. Rub each hen with salt, pepper and 1 Tablespoon mustard.

2. Place each on a square of foil; fold foil to center. Place on a cookie sheet.

3. Sprinkle ¼ crumbs, ¼ onion, 3 Tablespoons wine over each package.

4. Fold foil tightly. Bake at 400° for 45 minutes.

5. Open foil. Baste hens. Bake an additional 15 minutes until browned.

6. Remove from foil. Serve juices separately in a small serving dish.

Accompaniments: Wild rice, green vegetable.

CORNISH HEN CASSEROLE ITALIENNE

Preparation time: 45 mnutes
Baking time: 2 hours

Serves: 4

4 **Cornish hens**
Salt
Chopped parsley
3 **to 4 Tablespoons butter, melted**
1 **large onion, finely chopped**
1½ **Tablespoons tomato paste**
1½ **cups chicken stock**
Salt, pepper to taste

Bouquet garni to taste
1 **cup (¼ pound) fresh mushrooms, sliced**
1 **teaspoon arrowroot or cornstarch**
1 **Tablespoon stock or water**
½ **cup cooked ham, cut into julienne strips**
Parsley

1. Rub insides of hens with salt, parsley.

2. Brown hens on all sides in melted butter. Remove hens from pan.

3. Brown onion, cooking slowly over low heat, scraping drippings from hens, until onions are golden brown.

4. Mix tomato paste, stock, seasonings, bouquet garni.

5. Add to onion. Bring to a boil.

6. Place hens in a 5-quart baking dish. Pour onion mixture over hens.

7. Bake at 350° for 2 hours, basting every 20-30 minutes.

8. Transfer liquid mixture to a saucepan.

9. Add mushrooms; cook 15 minutes.

10. Mix arrowroot or cornstarch with stock or water. Simmer 2 minutes. (If using arrowroot, remove from heat.)

11. Add ham to gravy. Taste for seasoning.

12. Sprinkle hens with fresh parsley.

13. Serve gravy on the side.

A gourmet dinner.

Accompaniments: Wild rice, asparagus, cucumber and onion salad with a light sweet and sour dressing, clover leaf dinner rolls.

BEER DUCK

Preparation time: 30 minutes
Cooking time: 1½-2 hours

Serves: 4

1   **5 to 6-pound duckling**
1   **12-ounce can beer**
¾   **cup soy sauce**
¼   **cup sugar**

1   **head romaine lettuce or equivalent**
    amount fresh spinach
1   **Tablespoon cornstarch**
1   **Tablespoon water**

1. If frozen, defrost duckling completely.

2. Clean duck well. Remove excess skin at neck, fat at tail.

3. Immerse duck in a large pot of cold water using just enough water to cover duck.

4. Heat until boiling.

5. Remove; rinse duck with cold water. Clean pot.

6. Place duck into clean pot, breast side down.

7. Combine beer, soy sauce, sugar; pour into pot.

8. Heat until boiling.

9. Cover; reduce heat; simmer 45 minutes.

10. Turn duck; cook an additional 45 minutes, breast side up.

11. Test for tenderness. (Cooking may take up to 2 hours.) Discontinue cooking when tender.

12. Remove duck from pan.

13. Refigerate duck and sauce separately.

14. When sauce is cold, remove fat.

15. At serving time, reheat duck in sauce.

16. Remove duck; place on a serving platter.

17. Add lettuce or spinach to pot; remove when limp. Place around duck on platter.

18. Combine cornstarch, water to make a thin paste. Add to 1 cup of remaining sauce.

19. Stir until sauce thickens. Pour over duck.

Cook a day ahead to remove solidified grease. Excellent, moist, not greasy.

SAUTÉED FISH

Preparation time: 30 minutes   *Serves: 3-4*

2 Tablespoons peanut oil, heated
1 pound orange roughy or sole fillets
Salt, pepper to taste
¼ cup flour
2 to 3 cloves garlic, minced

¼ cup white wine
4 small whole green onions, cut into ¼-inch pieces
12 medium mushrooms, sliced

1. Season fillets with salt, pepper; flour lightly.

2. In a large skillet or wok over moderately high heat, sauté fillets in heated oil until lightly browned, not crisp.

3. Remove from heat; place on an oven-proof plate.

4. Keep fillets warm in a 250° oven.

5. Barely glaze garlic in a pan. Do not let it turn black.

6. Deglaze pan with wine.

7. Add onions, mushrooms; stir 1-2 minutes.

8. Simmer 2 minutes until slightly thickened.

9. Pour over fish.

Accompaniments: Rice pilaf, tossed salad, buttermilk biscuits.

VEGETABLE FISH MEDLEY

Preparation time: 15 minutes   *Serves: 4*
Baking time: 20-25 minutes for fresh fish, 35 minutes for frozen

4 **12-inch lengths heavy**
   aluminum foil
4 **4-ounce fresh or frozen fish fillets,**
   ½-inch thick
¼ **cup reduced calorie ranch-type**

   salad dressing
2 **cups fresh or frozen broccoli florets**
1 **red or green sweet pepper, sliced**
   into thin strips
1 **small onion, thinly sliced**

1. Preheat oven to 450°.
2. Place 1 fillet on each length of foil.
3. Spoon 1 Tablespoon dressing onto each fillet.
4. Divide vegetables evenly over fillets.
5. Fold foil; seal tightly to form a packet.
6. Place packets on a baking sheet.
7. Bake 20-25 minutes for fresh fillets, 35 minutes for frozen fillets.
8. Let stand 1-2 minutes before serving.

This easy, tasty recipe may be prepared a day ahead. Bake just before serving.

FLUKE DAUFAUSKIE

Preparation time: 45 minutes   *Serves: 4*

1 **2-pound fish fillet or 4**
   8-ounce fish fillets
2 **Tablespoons margarine, melted**
½ **pound mushrooms,**
   sliced
1 **large onion, sliced**

⅔ **cup mayonnaise**
⅓ **cup prepared mustard**
¼ **teaspoon garlic salt**
3 **dashes Tabasco sauce**
2 **ounces dry vermouth**
Salt, pepper to taste
Paprika

1. Preheat oven to 350°.

2. Precook fish 15 minutes in a pan on the center oven rack.

3. Sauté mushrooms, onion in melted margarine.

4. Place mushrooms, onion on fillet(s).

5. Combine remaining ingredients, except paprika, to form sauce.

6. Place sauce over fillet(s).

7. Add paprika.

8. Bake on the center oven rack for 25 minutes until browned.

POACHED FISH WITH GREEN ONION SAUCE

Preparation time: 20 minutes   *Serves: 2-4*

Boiling water
1 **1-pound whole red snapper, pickerel, or trout, cleaned**
2 **Tablespoons peanut oil**
3 to 4 **green onions, chopped**

5 to 6 **cloves garlic, chopped**
3 **Tablespoons soy sauce**
1 **teaspoon vinegar**
1 **Tablespoon dry sherry**
1 **Tablespoon sugar**

1. Fill a pot, large enough to immerse whole fish completely, half full with water. Bring to a boil.
2. Score fish almost to the bone at 1½-inch intervals.
3. Add fish to boiling water. Cover.
4. Remove pot from heat immediately.
5. Let fish remain in the pot for 10 minutes.
6. Drain; place on a serving platter.
7. Heat oil; add onions, garlic; stir fry until fragrant.
8. Add remaining ingredients; stir until well combined.
9. Pour sauce over fish.
10. After presenting fish at the table, remove bones.

Use the recommended amount of garlic. It is not overwhelming, and the sauce is excellent.

Accompaniment: Rice.

Cooks Incorporated

PAN FRIED TROUT WITH BOURBON PECAN BUTTER

Preparation time: 35 minutes   *Serves: 2-4*

2 1-pound trout, cleaned, headless
Flour
Salt, pepper
Vegetable oil
6 Tablespoons unsalted butter
¼ cup pecans, chopped, roasted
1 shallot, finely diced
1 jalapeño chili, seeded, finely chopped

2 Tablespoons red pepper, finely diced
Pinch thyme
2 Tablespoons Kentucky bourbon, or to taste
3 Tablespoons fresh lemon juice
Salt to taste

1. Dredge trout in flour seasoned with salt, pepper.

2. Heat oil in a sauté pan. Add trout; cook thoroughly 2-3 minutes on each side.

3. Remove to napkin to drain.

4. Heat butter in a sauté pan.

5. Add roasted pecans.

6. Over medium heat, brown butter 3-4 minutes. Do not shake pan until butter starts to brown.

7. Add remaining ingredients; toss 30-60 seconds.

8. Arrange trout on a serving platter; pour sauce over top.

Peasant Stock Restaurant
Kettering, Ohio

For a lighter dish, prepare with 3 Tablespoons of butter.

Accompaniments: Wild and white rice, julienne carrots, zucchini.

BAKED STUFFED FLOUNDER

Preparation time: 45 minutes
Baking time: 35- 40 minutes

Serves: 8

¾ cup margarine, divided
¼ pound raw shrimp, peeled, deveined
½ pound small mushroom caps, thinly sliced
½ cup onion, finely chopped
¼ cup fresh parsley, chopped
¼ cup green onion tops, chopped
½ teaspoon lemon juice
¼ teaspoon lemon rind, grated

6 ounces frozen fresh crabmeat, thawed, or imitation crab, finely chopped
1 cup seasoned bread crumbs
1 egg, beaten
Salt to taste
Red and black pepper to taste
8 6-ounce flounder fillets, each about 4 inches wide
½ cup margarine, melted
½ teaspoon lemon juice
¼ cup dry white wine

1. Melt half of the margarine.

2. Add shrimp. Cook over low heat until shrimp are pink.

3. Add remaining margarine.

4. Add mushrooms; cook 5 minutes.

5. Add vegetables; cook until onions are transparent, wilted.

6. Add lemon juice, rind.

7. Add crabmeat, bread crumbs, egg, seasonings.

8. Mix gently but thoroughly.

9. Starting at the larger end, place ⅛ of mixture on each fillet.

10. Roll to small end; secure with a toothpick.

11. Mix margarine, lemon juice, wine for basting.

12. Place fillets in a 9x13-inch baking pan. Baste.

13. Bake uncovered at 375° on the center oven rack for 20 minutes. Do not turn fillets.

14. Lower temperature to 300°; bake 15-20 minutes longer.

(Continued on facing page)

Sauce for Stuffed Flounder (optional)

⅓ cup light mayonnaise
⅓ cup lemon juice

2 teaspoons Dijon mustard or
   more to taste
2 teaspoons dill weed

1. Mix all ingredients well.

2. Serve in a sauce dish.

Sole may be substituted for flounder.

MARINATED SALMON

Preparation time: 20 minutes
Broiling time: 8-10 minutes

Serves: 4

1 24-ounce salmon fillet
¾ Tablespoon Kosher salt
3 Tablespoons sugar

2 to 3 Tablespoons orange zest,
   grated
1 teaspoon freshly grated black
   pepper
Olive Oil

1. Remove skin from bottom of the salmon.

2. Mix together all ingredients except oil.

3. Rub fillet on both sides with entire mixture.

4. Place on a platter; cover.

5. Marinate in refrigerator at least 4 hours or, preferably,
   overnight, turning occasionally as marinade liquefies.

6. Place fillet on a lightly oiled broiler pan or grill.

7. Broil or grill 8-10 minutes. Do not overcook.

Swordfish or any firm fish may be substituted for the salmon.

PASTA WITH SMOKED SALMON

Preparation time: 20 minutes   *Serves: 4*

12 to 16 ounces linguine or fettucine
⅓ to ½ cup extra virgin olive oil, heated
1 medium red onion, sliced into thin ½ round slices

3 Tablespoons capers, drained
¾ to 1 pound smoked salmon, broken into small chunks
Freshly ground pepper to taste
Salt to taste

1. Cook pasta according to package directions in boiling water with a little olive oil.

2. Meanwhile, sauté onion until transparent in heated olive oil.

3. When onion is almost done, add capers, salmon; heat until warm.

4. Drain pasta; mix all ingredients.

Use only the best ingredients. Because this is a simple recipe, each item needs to stand on its own.

For an interesting presentation, place shavings from a block of fresh Parmesan (with a hand grater) on the serving platter.

Accompaniments: Tossed salad with fresh tomatoes, cucumber, and celery seed dressing, sourdough bread.

GRILLED SALMON FILLET WITH DILL BUTTER

Preparation time: 10-15 minutes *Serves: 6*
Cooking time: 16-18 minutes

Salmon

1   **1 to 2 pound salmon fillet,**   **Olive oil**
    1¼ inches thick

1. Brush salmon lightly with olive oil.

2. Place skin side up in a lightly oiled wire grill basket.

3. Grill 4-6 inches above hot coals for 16-18 minutes until fish is barely opaque in the thickest part when tested with a fork.

Dill Butter

¼ cup butter or margarine, melted   **1   teaspoon minced garlic**
¼ cup dry vermouth (optional)   **1   Tablespoon fresh dill, snipped, or**
¼ cup lemon juice   **1 teaspoon dried dill weed**

1. Stir all ingredients except dill into melted butter.

2. Simmer just until hot.

3. Stir in dill just before serving the sauce with the salmon.

A garnish of fresh dill or watercress enhances the presentation.

Accompaniments: Fresh asparagus steamed tender crisp, tossed salad, sourdough baguettes, Chardonnay wine.

HERB ROASTED SALMON

Preparation time: 20 minutes
Baking time: 6 -8 minutes

Serves: 4

2   teaspoons peanut oil, heated
1   shallot, chopped
⅓ cup mushrooms, coarsely chopped
½ cup dry white wine (Hafle
    Vineyards Seyval suggested)
5   sprigs fresh tarragon
5   sprigs fresh thyme
5   sprigs fresh fennel tops
½ cup fish stock or bottled clam juice

¼ cup heavy cream
½ cup unsalted butter
1   teaspoon fresh lemon juice
½ teaspoon salt, divided
¼ teaspoon freshly ground pepper,
    divided
2   Tablespoons peanut oil, heated
4   6-ounce salmon fillets, skin on

1. Sauté shallot, mushrooms in heated oil 2-3 minutes until soft.

2. Add wine and 1 sprig each tarragon, thyme, fennel.

3. Cook 2 minutes until liquid is reduced by half.

4. Add stock, cream; cook 10 minutes until reduced to
    3 Tablespoons.

5. Remove from heat; whisk in half the butter.

6. Strain sauce.

7. Stir in lemon juice, half the salt, half the pepper.

8. Cover; set aside.

9. Preheat oven to 400°.

10. Season fish with remaining salt, pepper.

11. Sauté fillets, skin side up, in heated oil in a large, heavy skillet
    1 minute until lightly browned. Turn once to brown
    other side.

12. Using a wide spatula, remove fillets; invert into a baking dish.

13. With a knife, carefully peel back skin from each fillet, leaving it
    attached at one end.

14. On top of each fillet place 1 sprig each tarragon, thyme, fennel,
    and 1 Tablespoon butter. Cover with the skin.

(Continued on facing page)

15. Bake 6-8 minutes until fish is opaque throughout.

16. Remove skin, herbs from each fillet.

17. Scoop 2 Tablespoons of the warm sauce onto each dinner plate.

18. Place a fillet on top.

19. If desired, garnish with additional herbs. Serve immediately.

Hafle Vineyards Winery
Springfield, Ohio

Accompaniment: Dry white wine.

SHRIMP IN FOIL

Preparation time: 45 minutes   *Serves: 2 as entree or*
Baking time: 20 minutes   *4 as appetizer*

2 **12x12-inch squares heavy aluminum foil**
1 **pound raw large shrimp, peeled, deveined, washed, dried**
⅓ **cup butter, melted**
1 **cup mushrooms, thinly sliced**

¼ **cup onion, finely minced**
⅓ **cup fresh parsley, finely chopped**
½ **teaspoon salt**
½ **teaspoon Worcestershire sauce**
Dash Tabasco sauce

1. Divide shrimp into equal portions on each piece of foil.

2. Stir remaining ingredients into melted butter.

3. Pour mixture over shrimp.

4. Fold foil to make a secure pouch.

5. Cook over medium coals 10-15 minutes or bake at 350° on the center oven rack for 20 minutes.

Prepare this several hours in advance. Serve in foil packets to be opened by each diner.

Easy preparation, easy clean-up, different presentation!

SALMON WITH MUSTARD SAUCE

Preparation time: 10 minutes *Serves: 4*
Broiling time: 5-7 minutes

2 teaspoons lemon juice, freshly squeezed

4 6-ounce salmon fillets with skin, boned

2 Tablespoons fresh onion, grated

1½ Tablespoons shallots, minced

Salt to taste

Freshly ground pepper to taste

2 teaspoons honey mustard

½ teaspoon Dijon mustard

⅛ to ¼ teaspoon Tabasco, to taste

½ cup whipping cream

1 Tablespoon unsalted butter, softened

1. Preheat broiler to high.

2. Sprinkle lemon juice over salmon.

3. Rub with onions, shallots.

4. Season with salt, pepper.

5. Broil 5-7 minutes until cooked through but still moist.

6. While salmon cooks, make sauce with remaining ingredients.

7. Combine both mustards, Tabasco, cream in a small saucepan. Cook until hot over moderate heat.

8. Remove from heat; whisk in butter.

9. Place each fillet on a warm plate; spoon some sauce over each.

Heat the sauce slowly so that it will not become thin.

Accompaniments: Steamed, parsleyed new potatoes, broccoli, fresh asparagus, or zucchini.

SHRIMP AND WILD RICE CASSEROLE

Preparation time: 40 minutes
Baking time: 35-45 minutes

Serves: 6-8

2 Tablespoons butter or margarine, melted
2 Tablespoons flour
1 cup light cream or half and half
1 cup 2% milk
¼ cup butter or margarine, melted
¼ cup green pepper, thinly sliced
½ cup onion, thinly sliced

1 4-ounce can sliced mushrooms (½ cup), drained
1 Tablespoon Worcestershire sauce
Few drops Tabasco
½ teaspoon pepper
2 cups packaged wild rice and white rice, cooked without seasoning packet
1 pound cooked shrimp, deveined

1. Prepare a thin cream sauce with first 4 ingredients.

2. Sauté green pepper, onion, mushrooms in melted butter until tender.

3. Add seasonings, rice, shrimp.

4. Fold into cream sauce.

5. Place in a buttered 2-quart casserole. Cover.

6. Bake at 350° for 35-45 minutes.

This casserole may be prepared up to 1 month ahead and frozen. Do not heat before freezing. To freeze, line casserole with freezer wrap, add cooled shrimp mixture, top with freezer wrap. When frozen, remove wrapped shrimp mixture from casserole; overwrap with freezer wrap; seal. To serve, remove wrap. Return to casserole; bake at 375° for 1¼ hours.

To microwave, freeze in a microwave-proof casserole. Thaw in microwave, covered, on low for 15 minutes. Microwave, covered, on medium for 15 minutes until hot. A great buffet dish.

Accompaniments: Green beans, salad, rolls.

SHRIMP CREOLE

Preparation time: 2 hours   *Serves: 8-10*

¼ cup flour
¼ cup olive oil
2 cups onions, chopped
½ cup green onions, chopped
2 cloves garlic, minced
1 cup green pepper, chopped
1 cup celery with leaves, chopped
1 teaspoon thyme
2 bay leaves
3 teaspoons salt
½ teaspoon pepper

6 ounces tomato paste
1 16-ounce can tomatoes, coarsely chopped, with liquid
8 ounces tomato sauce
1 cup stock made from boiling shrimp shells
4 pounds raw shrimp, peeled, deveined
1 teaspoon Tabasco
½ cup parsley, chopped
1 Tablespoon lemon juice
2 cups cooked rice

1. Make a roux of browned flour and olive oil in a 4-quart heavy pot or Dutch oven.

2. Add chopped vegetables, seasonings; sauté, uncovered, 30 minutes over medium heat until onions are transparent, soft.

3. Add tomato paste; sauté 3 minutes.

4. Add tomatoes with liquid, tomato sauce, stock. Simmer very slowly, partially covered, 1 hour, stirring occasionally.

5. Add shrimp; cook until shrimp are just done, about 10 minutes.

6. Add Tabasco, parsley, lemon juice.

7. Stir; cover; remove from heat.

8. Serve over rice.

Do not boil or overcook the shrimp. Use a food processor to chop vegetables.

This old New Orleans family recipe is wonderful for family or guests because it can be made ahead. Best when allowed to stand several hours or overnight. Cool and refrigerate. Freezes well. Thaw and reheat.

Accompaniments: Hot French bread, tossed green salad, white wine.

ELEGANT SHRIMP, CHICKEN, AND ARTICHOKE CASSEROLE

Preparation time: 20 minutes
Baking time: 40 minutes

Serves: 10

2 8½-ounce jars artichoke hearts, drained
2 pounds large shrimp, cooked, shelled, deveined
4 whole chicken breasts, cooked, cut up (reserve broth)
1½ Tablespoons butter, melted
1½ pounds fresh sliced mushrooms

3 cups thick and creamy white sauce
1 Tablespoon Worcestershire sauce
Salt, pepper to taste
½ cup dry sherry
⅓ cup grated cheese
Paprika
Parsley

1. Arrange artichokes in bottom of buttered 9x12-inch casserole.
2. Add chicken and shrimp.
3. Sauté mushrooms in melted butter in a skillet.
4. Drain; add to casserole.
5. Prepare thick and creamy white sauce
6. Add Worcestershire, seasonings, sherry to white sauce. Pour over casserole.
7. Sprinkle with cheese, paprika, parsley.
8. Bake at 375° on the center oven rack for 40 minutes.

May be prepared 1 day ahead.

Thick and Creamy White Sauce

¾ cup margarine, melted
¾ cup flour

1½ cups half and half
1½ cups chicken broth

1. Stir flour into melted margarine in a small pan. Mixture will be thick, pasty.
2. Gradually add cream, chicken broth, stirring constantly.

Accompaniments: Fruit salad or mixed greens, Chardonnay wine.

GREEK STYLE SHRIMP

Preparation time: 30 -40 minutes   *Serves: 6*

¼ cup virgin olive oil
3 cloves garlic, minced
1 pound (36-40 count) shrimp,
   peeled

¼ cup ouzo (Greek liqueur)
4 cups tomato sauce
½ pound feta cheese, cubed
1 pound spinach, washed,
   stems removed

1. In a large sauté pan over high heat, cook garlic in olive oil until it begins to sizzle but does not brown.

2. Add shrimp; stir, cooking 1-2 minutes.

3. Remove pan from heat; add ouzo.

4. Return pan to heat. Tip pan toward flame to ignite. Burn off alcohol.

5. Remove shrimp.

6. Add remaining ingredients.

7. Cover pan to wilt spinach and melt feta, about 2 minutes.

8. Return shrimp to pan to reheat.

9. Serve shrimp, sauce on hot plates.

Be sure to remove pan from heat before adding ouzo, as it is very flammable.

The Winds Café
Yellow Springs, Ohio

Accompaniments: Rice or rice-shaped pasta, Spanish red wine.

Cooks Incorporated

SHRIMP WITH ORIENTAL VEGETABLES

Preparation time: 20 minutes   *Serves: 4-6*

3 Tablespoons salad oil, heated
1 pound fresh or frozen shrimp, shelled, deveined
2 10-ounce packages frozen Japanese-style vegetables
1 heaping Tablespoon cornstarch

1 ¼-ounce package teriyaki sauce mix
½ cup water
½ head (2 cups) iceberg lettuce, shredded
3 cups hot cooked rice

1. Cook shrimp, vegetables in hot oil over medium heat in a wok or a large, covered skillet, separating with a fork and stirring occasionally. (If vegetables have spice cubes or seasoning packet, do not use water as package directs.)

2. In a small bowl, dissolve cornstarch and teriyaki mix in water.

3. Stir into shrimp mixture.

4. Cook, uncovered, stirring occasionally, about 3 minutes until thickened.

5. Add lettuce; cook 1 minute. Stir.

6. Serve immediately with rice.

Any vegetable combination may be used. If oriental seasonings cannot be found, make your own, using Japanese soy sauce, wine, a little sugar, water. Fresh vegetables, such as broccoli, mushrooms, pea pods, red peppers, onions, green beans, are also good.

Accompaniments: Warm sake, rolls, fruit or sherbert, cookies.

EASY EGG FOO YUNG

Preparation time: 30 minutes   *Serves: 6*

2   medium onions, diced
1   14-ounce can bean sprouts,
    drained
½   pound shrimp, cut into small
    pieces or 2 4½-ounce cans
    tiny shrimp

2   eggs
¼   teaspoon salt
1   Tablespoon (or more) flour
3   Tablespoons hot cooking oil
Soy sauce

1. Mix all ingredients except oil. Mixture should be wet but
   fairly thick.
2. Drop by large spoonfuls into hot oil.
3. Fry until done.
4. Drain onto paper towels.
5. Serve with soy sauce on the side.

An easy dish to prepare. Diced, cooked chicken or pork may be substituted for shrimp.

Accompaniments: Hot, fluffy rice, salad, plum wine.

THAI SHRIMP

Preparation time: 30-45 minutes   *Serves: 4*

1 pound (50-60 count) fresh or frozen shrimp, shelled, deveined
¼ pound fresh or canned small button mushrooms
1 cup unsweetened coconut milk
1 Tablespoon dry sherry
½ teaspoon Chinese hot chili sauce with garlic
1 Tablespoon vegetable oil

1 Tablespoon butter or margarine
4 cloves fresh garlic, finely minced
2 teaspoons dried basil
2 teaspoons dried mint
¼ cup green onion, chopped
1 Tablespoon cornstarch
1 Tablespoon cold water
1 Tablespoon lime juice
1 pound Italian or Chinese noodles

1. Prepare shrimp, mushrooms.
2. Combine coconut milk, sherry, chili sauce; set aside.
3. Heat wok to 350°, or heat sauté pan until very hot. Add oil, butter.
4. When butter melts, begins to bubble, add garlic. Sauté 5 seconds.
5. Add shrimp; sauté 3 minutes until slightly pink.
6. Add mushrooms, basil, mint, onions; stir fry 15 seconds.
7. Add coconut milk mixture. Bring sauce to a very low boil.
8. Mix cornstarch, cold water. Add to thicken sauce.
9. Stir in lime juice.
10. Serve over noodles prepared according to package directions.

Unsweetened coconut milk is a must.

Accompaniment: Salad.

SHEILA'S SHRIMP AND CRABMEAT AU GRATIN

Preparation time: 30 minutes   *Serves: 6*
Baking time: 30 minutes

¼ cup butter, melted, divided
½ pound fresh mushrooms, sliced
1 clove garlic, crushed
2 Tablespoons shallots, minced
¼ cup flour
½ teaspoon salt
½ teaspoon pepper
1 Tablespoon fresh dill, snipped
¾ cup milk
1 8-ounce package sharp
   Cheddar cheese, divided

⅔ cup dry white wine
2 7½-ounce cans king crabmeat or
   15 ounces imitation crabmeat
1 pound shrimp, cooked, shelled,
   deveined
1 9-ounce package frozen artichoke
   hearts, cooked, drained, or 1
   14-ounce can artichoke hearts
2 Tablespoons corn flake crumbs
½ Tablespoon butter

1. Preheat oven to 375°.

2. Sauté mushrooms 5 minutes in a skillet in 2 Tablespoons butter. Remove from heat.

3. Sauté garlic, shallots 5 minutes in a saucepan in 2 Tablespoons butter.

4. Make a sauce by stirring flour, pepper, dill, milk into garlic mixture. Heat to boiling, stirring constantly. Remove from heat.

5. Add ½ of the cheese; stir until melted.

6. Add wine.

7. Drain crabmeat; flake into a buttered 2-quart casserole.

8. Mix lightly sauce, shrimp, artichokes, mushrooms, remaining cheese in a bowl. Pour into casserole.

9. Sprinkle with corn flakes. Dot with butter.

10. Bake on the center oven rack for 30 minutes or more.

11. Let sit 30 minutes before serving to allow sauce to thicken.

Accompaniments: Crusty French bread, tossed green salad.

BAKED SEAFOOD CASSEROLE

Preparation time: 20 minutes   *Serves: 6*
Baking time: 20-25 minutes

1 **pound crabmeat and lobster combined**
1 **pound shrimp, cooked, deveined**
1 **cup mayonnaise**
½ **cup green pepper, finely chopped**
¼ **cup onion, minced**

1½ **cups celery, finely chopped**
½ **teaspoon salt**
1 **Tablespoon Worcestershire sauce**
Potato chips, crushed
Paprika

1. Mix all ingredients except chips, paprika. Place in a casserole.

2. Cover top completely with crushed potato chips.

3. Bake at 400° for 20-25 minutes.

4. Sprinkle with paprika.

Smaller portions make a good appetizer.

CIOPPINO

½ cup olive or salad oil, heated
3 cloves garlic, finely chopped
1¼ cups onion, chopped
¾ cup green onion, chopped
¾ cup green pepper, chopped
1 28-ounce can tomatoes
   with liquid
1 6-ounce can tomato paste
1¾ cups Burgundy wine
⅓ cup parsley, chopped

2 teaspoons dried oregano leaves
½ teaspoon dried basil leaves
2 teaspoons salt
¼ teaspoon pepper
¾ cup water
½ pound raw shrimp, peeled, deveined
1½ pounds heavy white fish, cut
   into chunks
1 pound crabmeat or
   imitation crabmeat

1. Sauté garlic, onions, green pepper until tender in hot oil in a 6-quart kettle.

2. Add remaining ingredients, except seafoods.

3. Bring to a boil; reduce heat; simmer, uncovered, 10 minutes.

4. Add fish, shrimp, crab to tomato mixture.

5. Simmer, covered, 15 minutes.

6. Simmer, uncovered, 15 minutes longer.

Mussels, clams, and scallops may also be added during the last 15 minutes.

This hearty Italian-style bouillabaisse refrigerates well for 2 days and may also be frozen after cooking and cooling.

Accompaniments: Salad, bread, and wine.

PEGGY AND BILL'S CRAB IMPERIAL

Preparation time: 15 minutes   *Serves: 10*
Baking time: 20 minutes

¼ cup butter, melted
⅓ cup onion, finely chopped
⅓ cup green pepper, finely chopped
⅓ cup pimento, chopped
½ cup mayonnaise
2 teaspoons capers
3 Tablespoons parsley, chopped

2 teaspoons Worcestershire sauce
2 teaspoons prepared yellow
   mustard
½ teaspoon salt
Freshly ground pepper to taste
2 pounds backfin crabmeat
Butter
Paprika to taste

1. Sauté onions, green pepper in melted butter until tender.

2. Remove from heat.

3. Combine with remaining ingredients, except crabmeat, butter, paprika. Mix well.

4. Gently fold in crabmeat. Avoid breaking up the large lumps.

5. Place mixture in well-greased crab shells or individual ramekins.

6. Dot with butter. Sprinkle with paprika.

7. Bake at 350° on the center oven rack for 20 minutes.

The flavor suggests just a hint of mustard, and the capers provide an interesting addition.

This recipe comes from South Carolina where crab is king.

CRABCAKES

2   teaspoons margarine, melted
¼   cup onion, finely diced
¼   cup celery, finely diced
¾   cup fine cracker crumbs or
     seasoned bread crumbs
1   egg, beaten, or ½ package egg
     substitute (Egg Beaters suggested)
½   teaspoon Worcestershire sauce

½   teaspoon dry mustard
½   teaspoon pepper (freshly ground)
¼   cup milk or cream
1   Tablespoon light mayonnaise
12 ounces fresh or imitation crabmeat
2   Tablespoons fresh parsley, chopped
2   Tablespoons oil

1. Sauté onion, celery in melted margarine 3 minutes.

2. Transfer to a large bowl. Add crumbs, egg, seasonings, milk, mayonnaise; mix well.

3. If using imitation crabmeat, place in a food processor; chop until fine.

4. Add crabmeat, parsley to crumb mixture. Mix well.

5. Form into 6 patties about ½-inch thick.

6. In a skillet, heat oil until hot.

7. Brown patties on both sides.

This easy recipe refrigerates well for 2 days.

Accompaniments: Snap peas, corn on the cob.

CRAB LOUIS IN AVOCADO HALVES

Preparation time: 30-35 minutes   *Serves: 4*

1 egg yolk
2 teaspoons Dijon mustard
½ teaspoon Worcestershire sauce
2 teaspoons red wine vinegar
½ cup canola oil
1 Tablespoon chili sauce
¼ cup scallions, including green part, finely chopped

4 large black olives, chopped
Salt, pepper
1 pound crabmeat or imitation crabmeat
4 ripe avocados
Lettuce leaves
2 hard cooked eggs for garnish (optional)

1. Using a wire whisk, beat egg yolk, mustard, Worcestershire sauce, vinegar.

2. Add oil gradually, beating rapidly until thickened and smooth.

3. Add chili sauce, scallions, olives.

4. Season with salt, pepper.

5. Place crab in a bowl; add ½ sauce. Mix gently.

6. Split avocados in half; discard pits.

7. Pile equal portions of the crab into avocado halves.

8. Spoon remaining sauce over crab.

9. Serve on a bed of lettuce garnished with egg or other garnish of choice.

An excellent ladies' luncheon, this may be prepared 2 hours ahead of serving.

For a lower calorie dish, eliminate the avocado.

SHRIMP AND SCALLOP PASTA

Preparation time: 30 minutes   *Serves: 4*

2 Tablespoons butter or margarine, melted
1 clove garlic, cut in half lengthwise
½ pound uncooked shrimp, peeled
½ pound bay scallops, rinsed, patted dry
Dash cayenne pepper
Salt to taste
Freshly ground pepper to taste
¼ cup dry vermouth

½ cup green onions, chopped
½ cup fresh parsley, chopped
2 Tablespoons butter or margarine, melted
2 Tablespoons flour
16 ounces half and half
1 egg, beaten
½ cup fresh Parmesan cheese, grated
1 pound fettucine
2 Tablespoons dry vermouth
Fresh parsley, chopped, for garnish

1. Sauté garlic in butter 45 seconds in a large 2-quart pan.

2. Add shrimp; sauté 2 minutes.

3. Add scallops; cook 1 minute.

4. Add seasonings.

5. Stir in vermouth; heat through.

6. Remove seafood with a slotted spoon; set aside.

7. Reserve liquid in pan. (If there is no liquid, add another ¼ cup vermouth.)

8. Add onions to liquid; braise 2 minutes.

9. Add parsley; continue cooking 1 minute.

10. Pour sauce over seafood.

11. In the same pan used to make sauce, melt butter. Add flour; mix thoroughly.

12. Gradually add half and half, stirring with a whisk.

13. Add egg, continuing to mix.

14. Add cheese.

15. Cook pasta as directed on package.

(Continued on facing page)

Cooks Incorporated

16. Just before serving, add seafood mixture, pan liquid to sauce. Mix thoroughly. If required, thin sauce with 2 Tablespoons vermouth.

17. Serve over pasta garnished with parsley.

The seasonings add zip to the seafood.

Accompaniments: Tossed salad, breads.

SAUTÉED SEA SCALLOPS WITH FINES HERBES

Preparation time: 10 minutes   *Serves: 3-4*

½ cup clarified butter
1 pound fresh sea scallops
Flour
Salt, pepper
1 teaspoon fines herbes

1 teaspoon fresh garlic, chopped
¼ cup dry sherry
Juice of 1 lemon
1 teaspoon Worcestershire sauce
½ cup chicken or clam broth

1. Place enough butter to cover the surface into a large sauté pan with a non-stick surface. Heat until hot.

2. Dust scallops with seasoned flour. Shake off excess.

3. Add scallops, fines herbes to pan.

4. Cook 1 minute on one side until just brown.

5. Turn scallops; cook 1 minute.

6. Add garlic; toss 20 seconds.

7. Add remaining ingredients.

8. Cook several seconds, shaking back and forth until sauce is a creamy consistency.

9. Serve immediately.

Di Paolo's Restaurant
Oxford, Ohio

BAKED SCALLOPS

Preparation time: 15 minutes   *Serves: 4*
Baking time: 30 minutes

1   **cup cracker crumbs**   **Salt, pepper to taste**
    (Ritz suggested)   ½ **cup margarine, melted**
1   **pound bay or sea scallops**

1. Grease a 1½-quart casserole.

2. Layer cracker crumbs, scallops. Season.

3. Pour melted margarine over top.

4. Bake at 375°, uncovered, for 30 minutes.

A quick, easy Cape Cod recipe with outstanding flavor and texture.

BROILED SCALLOPS

Preparation time: 35 minutes   *Serves: 3-4*
Broiling time: 5 minutes

1   **Tablespoon butter, melted**   ¼ **teaspoon thyme**
Juice of 1 lemon or lime   ½ **cup dry white wine**
                                        1   **pound scallops**

1. Combine all ingredients except scallops.

2. Pour over scallops.

3. Marinate at room temperature 30 minutes.

4. Broil for 5 minutes.

PERFECT SCALLOPED OYSTERS

Preparation time: 15 minutes   *Serves: 6*
Baking time: 40 minutes

1 **pound oysters**
2 **cups cracker crumbs, medium coarse,**
   divided
½ **cup butter or margarine, melted**
½ **teaspoon salt**

Dash pepper
¾ **cup cream**
½ **cup oyster liquor**
¼ **teaspoon Worcestershire sauce**

1. In a colander, drain oysters well, reserving liquor. Pat dry.

2. Combine crumbs, butter, salt, pepper.

3. Spread half of crumb mixture in a greased 1½-quart casserole.

4. Cover with half the oysters.

5. Using half the remaining crumbs, spread a second layer.

6. Cover with remaining oysters.

7. Combine cream, oyster liquor, Worcestershire sauce. Pour over oysters.

8. Top with remaining crumbs.

9. Bake at 350° on the center oven rack for 40 minutes.

May be prepared 4-6 hours ahead. Refrigerate; bake just before serving.

A wonderful side dish with a holiday meal.

CRANBERRY APPLESAUCE

Preparation time: 40 minutes   *Yield: 6 cups*

3 pounds (about 10) McIntosh apples, quartered
12 ounces (3 ¼ cups) cranberries
1 3-inch cinnamon stick, halved

4 2-inch strips lemon zest
1 cup brown sugar, firmly packed
1 cup water
Ground cinnamon to taste
Nutmeg

1. Combine all ingredients except ground cinnamon, nutmeg in a kettle. Bring to a boil.

2. Cover. Simmer, stirring occasionally, 30-35 minutes until apples are tender.

3. Put mixture through a food mill or large sieve.

4. Cover. Chill.

5. Sprinkle with cinnamon, nutmeg when ready to serve.

Refrigerates and freezes well.
A nice side dish to serve with chicken or turkey.

RHUBARB CONSERVE

Preparation time: 45 minutes   *Serves: 6*

4 cups fresh rhubarb, washed, cut into 1-inch lengths
½ cup water
2 cups sugar

1 orange, peeled, cut into ½-inch sections
Rind of 1 lemon, grated
Juice of 1 lemon

1. Combine all ingredients.

2. Boil ½ hour until rhubarb is tender.

3. Cool. Refrigerate.

Keeps for 1 week in the refrigerator.
A nice accompaniment with poultry or meat dishes. Also good on ice cream.

POULTRY DAYS CHICKEN BARBEQUE SAUCE

Preparation time: 10 minutes   *Yield: 1 quart*

1   **pint vinegar**
1   **pint water**

½   cup butter
¼   cup salt
2   Tablespoons Worcestershire sauce

1. Combine all ingredients.
2. Bring to a boil.
3. Refrigerate until ready to use.
4. Baste chicken while cooking on the grill.

Enough sauce for 5 chickens.

Poultry Days Festival
Versailles, Ohio

MARINADE FOR LONDON BROIL OR CHICKEN

Preparation time: 5 minutes   *Serves: 4*

1   **cup Italian dressing**
1   **teaspoon soy sauce**
1   **teaspoon lemon juice**

½   cup sherry
3   Tablespoons catsup
1   teaspoon Worcestershire sauce

1. Combine all ingredients.
2. Pour over a 2 ½-inch thick London broil roast or 4 chicken breasts.
3. Refrigerate. Marinate 24 hours.

Refrigerates well for 1 week.

MARINADE FOR BEEF OR CHICKEN

Preparation time: 5 minutes   *Serves: 2 - 4*

¼   cup red wine vinegar
2   Tablespoons vegetable oil
2   Tablespoons soy sauce

2   Tablespoons catsup
¼   teaspoon onion salt
Garlic powder to taste (optional)
Black pepper to taste (optional)

1. Combine all ingredients.
2. Refrigerate. Marinate 2 steaks or 4 chicken breasts 6-8 hours.

BARBEQUE SAUCE FOR CHICKEN OR PORK

Preparation time: 15 minutes *Yield: 2 ½ cups*

1   cup onion, finely chopped
1   cup catsup
¼   cup yellow mustard

¼   cup vinegar
¼   cup brown sugar, firmly packed

1.   Mix all ingredients well in a medium-sized bowl. Blend thoroughly.

2.   Spread liberally over pork chops, ribs, or chicken before baking.

May be prepared several days in advance. Refrigerates well.

RED PEPPER COULIS SAUCE

Preparation time: 20 minutes *Serves: 8*

8   ounces roasted red peppers
1   Tablespoon olive oil
1   Tablespoon balsamic vinegar

1   teaspoon garlic
1   Tablespoon sugar
1   teaspoon salt
Pepper to taste

1.   Purée peppers in a blender; place in a saucepan. Cook over medium heat.

2.   Add oil, vinegar; bring to a boil. Reduce heat to simmer.

3.   Add garlic, sugar, seasonings. Simmer to blend well.

4.   Serve sauce over beef tenderloin, chicken or turkey breast, pork loin, or filet of sole. Use 1 ounce of sauce per serving.

The Dayton Marriott, Dayton, Ohio

MARINADE FOR BEEF TENDERLOIN FILLETS

Preparation time: 5 minutes *Serves: 2*

⅓   cup red wine vinegar
¼   cup catsup
2   Tablespoons cooking oil
2   Tablespoons soy sauce

1   Tablespoon Worcestershire sauce
1   teaspoon prepared mustard
1   teaspoon salt
¼   teaspoon pepper
¼   teaspoon garlic powder

1.   Combine all ingredients.

2.   Marinate fillets several hours.

PARMESAN SAUCE FOR FISH

Preparation time: 5 minutes　　　　　　　　　　　　　　　*Serves: 4*

3　Tablespoons light mayonnaise
2　Tablespoons onion, minced
½　cup grated Parmesan cheese
1½ Tablespoons margarine, melted

½　teaspoon dried dill weed
　　(optional)
¼　teaspoon lemon juice
Dash Tabasco

1. Combine all ingredients. Mix well.

2. Spread over broiled fish.

3. Return to broiler for about 2 minutes until cheese bubbles, browns lightly. Watch closely to avoid burning.

4. Serve immediately.

Enough sauce for 1 pound of fish or 4 fillets.
Suitable for use with any white fish.

MUSTARD SAUCE

Preparation time: 25 minutes　　　　　　　　　　　　　*Serves: 20*

1　cup sugar
2　Tablespoons dry mustard
1　egg yolk

1　cup cream
1　Tablespoon flour
½　cup vinegar

1. Mix dry ingredients with a fork.

2. Place egg yolk in a saucepan. Add dry ingredients. Blend.

3. Add cream. Blend.

4. Add vinegar very slowly. Boil until thick, creamy.

5. Serve immediately or refrigerate.

Refrigerates well for months. May be served warm or cold.

This sweet and sour sauce is great with ham.

TIPS ON ENTREES

(From Our Good Cooks!)

To precook chicken pieces before grilling, place them skin side down in a micro-wave-proof dish. Cover with waxed paper. Cook on high 6 minutes per pound, turning, rearranging once. Later, grill on each side 5 minutes.

After flouring chicken, chill 1 hour to allow coating to adhere better during frying.

Measure fish at the thickest point. Allow 10 minutes cooking time for each inch of thickness. Double cooking time for frozen fish. Add an extra 5 minutes for fish cooking in sauce.

Fresh fish in a supermarket may be from 1-21 days old. Fresh-frozen is frozen on the day caught, eliminating the chance of spoilage, so fresh-frozen fish is often better quality than fresh fish. Fresh-frozen fish is usually thawed just before being sold.

Thaw fish in milk to draw out the frozen taste and provide a fresh-caught flavor.

Browning meat is quicker and more effective if the meat is dry and the fat very hot.

Place a slice of bacon in the bottom of the pan to prevent meat loaf from sticking.

Add a cup of water to the bottom of a broiling pan before placing in the oven to absorb smoke, grease.

Marinate meat or poultry by placing it in a plastic bag in a bowl. Turn several times.

When making meatballs, form a square of the meat mixture on a piece of waxed paper. Cut into equal small squares. Roll into balls.

Brown pale gravy by adding a little instant coffee right from the jar.

Brown flour well before adding it to the liquid to eliminate pale or lumpy gravy. Flour placed in a custard cup beside the meat in the oven will be brown when meat is done.

Waynesville, Ohio

Waynesville might aptly paraphrase a well-known literary title and call itself the Village for All Seasons. Beginning in May with *A Touch of Spring*, the calendar of scheduled events carries right on through Christmas.

If one's interests include antiquing, the treasures of Waynesville will provide many occasions of happy discovery! The village features over 30 collections of antique furniture, quilts, jewelry, fine arts, and miscellany. Other collectibles can also be found all along Main Street, one after another. It's a feast day for collectors, dealers, and, of course, browsers.

This unusual concentration of shops represents the largest of its kind in the Midwest. The thousands of visitors who come each year to this treasure trove of antiquities are part of the reason Waynesville has been declared "The Antiques Capital of the Midwest" by USA Today.

A major event of this little village is the annual *Ohio Sauerkraut Festival.* More than a quarter million people are drawn to the entertainment as well as the star of the show – sauerkraut – fixed in more ways than one can count. Known as one of the finest folk-art festivals in the country, this October event is particularly suited to family outings.

Christmas in the Village begins after Thanksgiving. The four weekend revival of old customs will get everyone in the Christmas mood while strolling along Main Street listening to carolers, greeting old friends, and making new ones. Walking tours and carriage rides, ribbons and unusual one-of-a-kind gifts complete the experience of an old fashioned holiday.

Visitors will find that in Waynesville, every season is the season to be jolly!

Vegetables

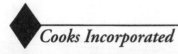
Cooks Incorporated

ARTICHOKES AND TOMATOES

Preparation time: 20 minutes   *Serves: 6*
Baking time: 20 - 30 minutes

1 **28-ounce can plum tomatoes, drained**   ¼ **cup butter, melted**
1 **14-ounce can artichokes, drained**   1½ **teaspoons fresh or ½ teaspoon**
½ **cup onion, finely chopped**   **dried basil**
2 **Tablespoons shallot, finely**   1 **Tablespoon sugar**
   chopped   **Salt, pepper to taste**

1. Cut drained tomatoes, artichokes into quarters. Remove any tough outer layer from artichokes.

2. Drain again.

3. Sauté onion, shallot in butter until tender.

4. Add vegetables, basil. Heat 3-5 minutes. Stir gently.

5. Add sugar, seasonings.

6. Pour into a greased 7 ¼x11-inch glass casserole.

7. Bake at 325° on the center oven rack for 20-30 minutes until heated through.

When increasing the recipe, reduce the amount of sugar.

Accompaniments: Chicken Parmesan, spinach salad.

CREAMY ARTICHOKE AND SPINACH CASSEROLE

Preparation time: 20 minutes   *Serves: 6 - 8*
Baking time: 35 - 40 minutes

1   6½-ounce jar marinated
    artichoke hearts
1   clove garlic, minced
1   small onion, chopped
½   pound mushrooms, sliced
2   10-ounce packages frozen
    spinach, thawed, drained

1   10¾-ounce can cream of
    mushroom soup
½   cup sour cream
2   eggs, beaten
¼   teaspoon dried oregano
¼   teaspoon ground nutmeg
¼   teaspoon ground white pepper
½   teaspoon lemon juice
1   cup seasoned croutons, crushed

1. Drain artichoke hearts, reserving marinade; set aside.

2. Place marinade in a skillet. Add mushrooms, garlic, onion. Cook, stirring until onion is limp.

3. Stir in remaining ingredients, except croutons, until well-blended.

4. Spoon half the spinach mixture into a greased 1 ½-quart shallow casserole.

5. Arrange artichokes on top. Add remaining spinach mixture.

6. Top with croutons.

7. Bake at 325° for 35-40 minutes until crust is set.

8. Let stand 5 minutes before serving.

If making ahead, cover and chill before baking. Bake 50 minutes if chilled.

NUTRIENT ANALYSIS (Per Serving)
Carbohydrate ....27 grams
Protein ....10 grams
Fat ....10 grams
Calories ....226 (40% from fat)
Cholesterol ....82 milligrams
Sodium ....1045 milligrams

Cooks Incorporated

CREAMY ARTICHOKE AND SPINACH CASSEROLE – LIGHT OPTION

Preparation time: 20 minutes   *Serves: 6*
Baking time: 35 - 40 minutes

1   6½-ounce jar marinated artichoke
    hearts
1   clove garlic, minced
1   small onion, chopped
½   pound mushrooms, sliced
2   10-ounce packages frozen spinach,
    thawed, drained
1   10¾-ounce can low fat cream of
    mushroom soup (Healthy Request
    suggested)

½   cup light sour cream
1   egg, beaten
2   egg whites, beaten
¼   teaspoon oregano leaves
¼   teaspoon ground nutmeg
¼   teaspoon ground white pepper
½   teaspoon lemon juice
5   slices toasted bread, cubed

1. Drain artichoke hearts, reserving marinade; set aside.

2. Place marinade in a skillet. Add mushrooms, garlic, onion. Cook, stirring until
    onion is limp.

3. Stir in remaining ingredients, except bread cubes, until well-blended.

4. Spoon half the spinach mixture into a 1½-quart shallow casserole which has been
    sprayed with non-stick cooking spray.

5. Arrange artichokes on top. Add remaining spinach mixture.

6. Top with bread cubes.

7. Bake at 325° for 35-40 minutes until crust is set.

8. Let stand 5 minutes before serving.

NUTRIENT ANALYSIS (Per Serving)
Carbohydrate .... 4 grams
Protein .... 9 grams
Fat .... 4 grams
Calories .... 163 (22% from fat)
Cholesterol .... 41 milligrams
Sodium .... 425 milligrams

ARTICHOKE - SPINACH CASSEROLE

Preparation time: 10 minutes   *Serves: 6 - 8*
Baking time: 40 minutes

1 **14-ounce can artichoke hearts, drained**
3 **packages frozen chopped spinach, thawed, well drained**
1 **8-ounce package cream cheese, softened**

3 **Tablespoons mayonnaise**
6 **Tablespoons milk**
3 to 5 **Tablespoons Parmesan or Romano cheese, freshly grated**

1. Preheat oven to 375°.

2. Cut drained artichoke hearts in half. Spread halves over bottom of a lightly greased 8x10-inch casserole.

3. Place well-drained spinach on top of artichokes.

4. Blend cream cheese, mayonnaise, milk. Spread over spinach.

5. Sprinkle cheese liberally over top.

6. Bake on the center oven rack for 40 minutes.

Important to drain spinach as thoroughly as possible.
Guests will ask for seconds and the recipe!

ASPARAGUS TIMBALES

Preparation time: 25 minutes   *Serves: 6*
Baking time: 20 - 25 minutes

2 **Tablespoons butter or margarine,**
   melted
2 **Tablespoons flour**
⅔ **cup milk**
½ **teaspoon salt**
¼ **teaspoon pepper**
Pinch dried oregano

Pinch dried basil
Pinch dried parsley
1 **cup ham, cubed**
1½ **cups asparagus, cooked,**
   cut up
2 **eggs**
2 **cups carrots, shredded, steamed**

1. Blend flour into melted butter; add milk gradually. Cook, stirring constantly until white sauce is thick, smooth.

2. Place white sauce and other ingredients, except carrots, into food processor container. Whirl 1 minute until well blended.

3. Spoon into well-greased custard cups.

4. Set cups into a pan of hot water.

5. Bake at 350° on the center oven rack for 20-25 minutes until set.

6. Unmold on a bed of seasoned carrots. Garnish with asparagus tips.

A tasty luncheon with fruit or gelatin salad.

ASPARAGUS STRUDEL

Preparation time: 45 minutes

Serves: 6 - 8

Baking time: 40 - 45 minutes

¾ pound asparagus, cut into 1-inch pieces

2 medium leeks, white part only, cut into quarters, thinly sliced

1 Tablespoon shallot, finely chopped

½ cup Gruyère cheese, grated

2 ounces sliced almonds, toasted

3 medium eggs

2 Tablespoons fresh parsley, finely chopped

2 Tablespoons fresh chives, thinly sliced

4 Tablespoons fresh dill, finely chopped

1 teaspoon salt

½ teaspoon black pepper, finely ground

½ teaspoon paprika

Dash cayenne

2 Tablespoons lemon juice

½ pound butter, melted

12 sheets phyllo dough

1. Blanch asparagus until tender, firm.

2. Sauté leeks, shallots 3-4 minutes until soft. Cool.

3. Mix all ingredients in a bowl; set aside.

4. Preheat oven to 350°.

5. Working quickly, brush melted butter on each sheet of phyllo dough. Stack sheets on top of one another. Do not brush final sheet.

6. Place prepared mixture on the lower quarter on long side of dough, leaving enough space on each side to fold sides in.

7. Roll like a jelly roll. Place seam side down on a greased 12x9-inch jelly roll pan. Brush with butter.

8. Bake for 40-45 minutes until golden brown.

9. Slice to serve.

ASPARAGUS PALESTINE

Preparation time: 20 minutes   *Serves: 4*

1 Tablespoon salad oil, heated
½ cup bacon, finely chopped
1 cup chicken bouillon
1 teaspoon soy sauce

1 Tablespoon cornstarch
2 Tablespoons cold water
2 cups cut asparagus, cooked
1 teaspoon Accent (optional)

1. Cook bacon in a skillet in oil, stirring until bacon is golden crisp.
2. Slowly add bouillon, soy sauce; cook 3 minutes.
3. Stir cornstarch into cold water until a smooth paste forms. Add to skillet mixture.
4. Continue cooking until sauce is smooth, thick, clear.
5. Add asparagus, Accent if desired.

Accompaniments: Chicken, noodles.

BROCCOLI RICE CUSTARD

Preparation time: 10 minutes   *Serves: 8*
Baking time: 20 minutes

2 Tablespoons butter
5 ounces wild rice, cooked
3 ounces pecans, chopped
3 Tablespoons green onion, chopped

1½ cups broccoli florets, blanched
1½ cups heavy cream
4 eggs
Salt, pepper to taste

1. Butter 8 3-inch ramekins.
2. Combine rice, pecans, onions, broccoli.
3. Divide mixture into ramekins.
4. Combine remaining ingredients.
5. Pour custard into ramekins. Place in a pan with warm water.
6. Bake at 350° on the center oven rack for 20 minutes until custard is set.
7. Unmold onto plates to serve.

The Dayton Woman's Club
Dayton, Ohio

CAULIFLOWER PARMESAN

Preparation time: 15 minutes
Baking time: 20 minutes

Serves: 6

1 head cauliflower, separated into 12 florets
½ cup bread crumbs

½ cup grated Parmesan cheese
1 egg
1 Tablespoon milk
2 Tablespoons margarine, melted

1. Cook cauliflower in salted water 7 minutes. Drain.

2. Mix bread crumbs, cheese. Beat egg with milk.

3. Dip each floret into egg wash, then crumb mixture.

4. Arrange in a buttered 8x8-inch casserole. Pour margarine over florets. Cover.

5. Bake at 350° on the center oven rack for 20 minutes.

CAULIFLOWER SUPREME

Preparation time: 30 minutes
Baking time: 30 minutes

Serves: 6 - 8

1 large head cauliflower
2 cups frozen peas
¼ cup margarine, melted
¾ cup onion, chopped
3 Tablespoons flour

1¾ cups milk
¼ teaspoon pepper
½ teaspoon nutmeg
1 Tablespoon sugar
½ cup cornflakes, crushed
3 Tablespoons butter

1. Separate cauliflower into small pieces. Cook 12 minutes in salted water. Drain.

2. Cook peas in ½ cup salted water 3-4 minutes. Drain; save liquid.

3. Sauté onion in margarine until soft; blend flour into onion.

4. Add liquid from peas with milk to make 2 cups white sauce. Season with pepper, nutmeg, sugar.

5. Place vegetables in a 2-quart buttered casserole. Pour white sauce over the vegetables; mix slightly. Top with cornflake crumbs; dot with butter.

6. Bake at 325° on the lower oven rack for 30 minutes.

May be prepared ahead and refrigerated. Bake for 1 hour if it has been refrigerated.

MARINATED CAULIFLOWER

Preparation time: 30 minutes   *Serves: 8*

1 **large head cauliflower**
1 **package Italian salad dressing**
   mix (Good Seasons suggested)
2 **Tablespoons gourmet rice**
   vinegar

2 **Tablespoons water**
½ **cup light sour cream**
¼ **teaspoon scallion, chopped**
½ **cup bleu cheese, crumbled**
2 **Tablespoons slivered almonds**

1. Steam cauliflower 20 minutes. Cool.

2. Mix salad dressing mix with vinegar, water. Add remaining ingredients. Mix well.

3. Pour over cooled cauliflower. Chill before serving.

CABBAGE PIE

Preparation time: 15 minutes   *Serves: 6 - 8*
Baking time: 40 minutes

7   **cups cabbage, shredded medium**
16 **soda crackers, coarsely crumbled**
2   **cups milk**
¼   **cup butter**

2   **teaspoons salt**
½   **teaspoon ground black pepper**
½   **teaspoon celery seed**

1. Preheat oven to 350°.

2. Fill a buttered 1½-quart casserole with alternating layers of cabbage and crackers, having 3 layers each with cabbage on bottom, crackers on top.

3. Heat milk with remaining ingredients. Pour over cabbage.

4. Bake for 40 minutes until lightly browned.

CABBAGE AND ONION SAUTÉ

Preparation time: 20 minutes   *Serves: 6 - 8*

1   **Tablespoon butter, melted**
1½   **pounds cabbage, shredded**

1   **medium sweet red onion, chopped**
     Salt, pepper to taste

1. Sauté cabbage, onion in butter until hot, wilted.

2. Season before serving.

TIPSY CARROTS

Preparation time: 5 minutes   *Serves: 6*
Cooking time: 40 minutes

2 **pounds carrots, scraped**   ½ **cup brown sugar, firmly packed**
2 **Tablespoons sugar**   ½ **cup cranberry orange relish**
Water   **(Ocean Spray suggested)**
¼ **cup butter, melted**   2 **Tablespoons brandy**

1. Cook carrots in sugar and water 30 minutes. Drain.

2. Add remaining ingredients to melted butter in a skillet. Stir.

3. Add carrots.

4. Cook 10 minutes until carrots are glazed. Simmer until ready to serve.

CARROTS WITH CRANBERRIES

Preparation time: 20 minutes   *Serves: 6*
Baking time: 40 minutes

1 **apple, peeled, cored, grated**   4 **Tablespoons light brown sugar**
1 **cup washed cranberries**   ½ **teaspoon salt**
4 **cups carrots, grated or**   ½ **cup apple cider**
   thinly sliced   2 **Tablespoons butter**

1. Preheat oven to 350°.

2. Combine all ingredients, except butter. Place in a shallow, buttered casserole.

4. Dot with butter. Cover. Bake for 40 minutes, stirring once.

For best flavor use farm market cider.

JEANNETTE'S CARROTS AND GRAPES

Preparation time: 25 minutes   *Serves: 10 - 12*
Baking time: 5 minutes

2   **pounds carrots, julienned**   **Pinch celery salt**
2   **Tablespoons basil**   3   **cups seedless grapes**
½   **cup butter, melted**   2   **Tablespoons lemon juice**
1   **Tablespoon chervil**   **Dash salt**
⅛   **teaspoon garlic**   **Dash white pepper**

1. Cook carrots with basil in enough water to steam carrots. Drain.

2. Mix together butter, chervil, garlic, celery salt in a 9x12-inch casserole.

3. Add carrots; toss.

4. Just before serving, add grapes, lemon juice. Season.

5. Heat at 350° on the center oven rack for 5 minutes just until grapes are hot.

An unusual color combination and blending of flavors.

SPICED CARROTS AND APPLES

Preparation time: 20 minutes   *Serves: 6-8*
Baking time: 20 minutes

1   **pound carrots, julienned**   ¼   **cup water**
¼   **cup water**   1   **teaspoon lemon juice**
1   **teaspoon paprika**   ¼   **cup brown sugar, firmly packed**
6   **apples, peeled, cored, sliced** 1   **teaspoon cinnamon**
                                      2   **Tablespoons margarine**

1. Place carrots, water, paprika in a small saucepan. Cover; steam 5 minutes. (Paprika will intensify color of carrots.) Drain.

2. Place apples, water, lemon juice in a small saucepan. Cover; steam 3-4 minutes. Drain.

3. Combine carrots, apples in a casserole.

4. Mix brown sugar, cinnamon. Sprinkle over carrots, apples.

5. Dot with margarine. Cover.

6. Bake at 350° for 20 minutes.

FAR EAST CELERY

Preparation time: 15 minutes
Baking time: 25 - 30 minutes

Serves: 4 - 6

4 cups celery, diced, with 1 stalk cut slightly larger
1 8-ounce can sliced water chestnuts
1 2-ounce jar sliced pimentos
¼ cup slivered almonds

1 10¾-ounce can cream of chicken soup
¼ cup milk
1 cup bread crumbs, buttered

1. Crisp cook celery. Drain.

2. Add water chestnuts, pimentos, almonds.

3. Thin soup with milk.

4. Add to celery mixture.

5. Place in casserole.

6. Top with buttered crumbs.

7. Bake at 350° for 25-30 minutes.

For more oriental flavor add 1 teaspoon soy sauce and top with chow mein noodles.

FERN'S CORN PUDDING

Preparation time: 10 minutes
Baking time: 1 hour

Serves: 4 - 6

6 egg yolks, slightly beaten
2¼ cups milk
3 Tablespoons sugar
1½ teaspoons salt

4½ Tablespoons flour
Dash pepper
3 cups whole kernel corn, fresh, frozen, or canned
1½ Tablespoons butter, melted

1. Combine first 6 ingredients.

2. Add corn, butter. Mix well.

3. Pour into a buttered casserole.

4. Bake at 375° on the center oven rack for 1 hour.

SWISS CORN BAKE

Preparation time: 25 minutes
Baking time: 25 minutes

Serves: 6

1 cup boiling water, salted
3 cups fresh corn, cut from cob, or
  2 9-ounce packages frozen corn
6 ounces evaporated milk
1 egg, beaten
2 Tablespoons onion, finely chopped

½ teaspoon salt
Dash pepper
¾ cup shredded Swiss cheese
½ cup soft bread crumbs
1 Tablespoon butter, melted
¼ cup shredded Swiss cheese

1. Cook fresh corn in boiling salted water 2-3 minutes until tender, or cook frozen corn according to package directions. Drain well.

2. Combine corn with milk, egg, onion, seasonings, cheese.

3. Place in a 10x6x1½-inch baking dish.

4. Toss remaining 3 ingredients for topping. Sprinkle over top.

5. Bake at 350° for 25 minutes.

Sweet Corn Festival, Inc.
Millersport, Ohio

EGGPLANT SLICES

Preparation time: 20 minutes
Baking time: 12 - 15 minutes

Serves: 6

1 medium eggplant, peeled
Salted water
½ cup low calorie, low fat
  mayonnaise

1 Tablespoon onion flakes
⅓ cup very fine bread crumbs
⅓ cup grated Parmesan cheese
½ teaspoon Italian seasoning

1. Slice eggplant into ½-inch slices. Soak a few minutes in salted water.

2. Mix mayonnaise, onion flakes.

3. Mix crumbs, cheese, seasoning.

4. Dry eggplant slices.

5. Spread slices on both sides with mayonnaise mixture, then on both sides with crumb mixture.

6. Bake at 400° on the center oven rack for 12-15 minutes. Slices need not be turned.

EGGPLANT CASSEROLE

Preparation time: 15 minutes
Baking time: 30 minutes

Serves: 6 - 8

1 eggplant, peeled
Salted water
Flour
Hot oil
2 cups onions, sliced
2 cups green pepper, sliced

2 cups ripe olives
2½ teaspoons salt
1 8-ounce can tomato sauce
2 cups sharp cheese, shredded
1 cup soft bread crumbs
2 Tablespoons butter, melted

1. Slice eggplant into ¼-inch slices. Soak in salted water a few minutes.

2. Dry eggplant slices.

3. Toss slices in flour, brown in hot oil. Remove from pan.

4. Brown onions, green pepper in same pan.

5. Add olives, salt.

6. Place in a 2-quart casserole in layers, alternating eggplant and onion mixture.

7. Pour tomato sauce over top.

8. Top with cheese.

9. Toss bread crumbs with melted butter; place on top of cheese.

10. Bake at 350° for 30 minutes.

Cooks Incorporated

HERBED GREEN BEANS

Preparation time: 25 minutes   *Serves: 6*

1   **pound green beans or equivalent
    of frozen beans**
¼   **cup butter or margarine, melted**
½   **cup onion, chopped**

¼   **cup celery, chopped**
¼   **cup parsley, minced**
¼   **teaspoon dried rosemary**
¼   **teaspoon dried basil**

1. Cook beans in lightly salted water; drain if necessary.

2. Add onions, celery to melted butter in a small saucepan. Cook over medium heat 5 minutes until transparent, not brown.

3. Add remaining ingredients. Cook over low heat 10 minutes.

4. Pour over cooked beans.

5. For best flavor, let stand 5 minutes before serving.

SAVORY LIMA BEANS

Preparation time: 45 minutes   *Serves: 6*

⅓   **cup onion, diced**
⅓   **cup celery, diced**
1   **cup fresh mushrooms, sliced**
¼   **teaspoon garlic, minced**
2   **cups canned or frozen lima beans**
2   **cups low sodium tomato juice**

1   **cup water**
1   **medium tomato, diced**
½   **cup ham or turkey ham, fat
    removed, diced**
1   **teaspoon dried parsley**
1   **teaspoon dried basil**

1. Sauté onion, celery, mushrooms, garlic over medium heat until tender in a skillet coated with non-stick spray.

2. Add remaining ingredients.

3. Reduce heat. Simmer 30 minutes, stirring occasionally.

To prepare as an entrée, cook until liquid is almost gone. Top with shredded low fat cheese; cook untl cheese melts.

DILLED LIMA BEANS

Preparation time: 25 minutes

Serves: 4 - 6

1 package frozen baby lima beans,
  cooked, drained
½ cup sliced water chestnuts
¼ cup butter

2 Tablespoons red wine vinegar
Pinch sugar
2 teaspoons dill weed
Salt, pepper to taste

1. Combine all ingredients.

2. Heat; serve.

FOUR BEAN CASSEROLE

Preparation time: 15 - 20 minutes
Baking time: 1 hour

Serves: 10

2 16-ounce cans vegetarian
  baked beans
1 17-ounce can lima beans
1 15-ounce can kidney beans
1 15-ounce can butter beans
3 medium onions, chopped

⅓ cup brown sugar
½ cup vinegar
½ cup catsup
½ Tablespoon mustard
1 teaspoon garlic powder
½ teaspoon black pepper

1. Rinse beans in a colander under warm tap water. Place in a large baking dish.

2. Add onions.

3. Combine remaining ingredients in a small bowl. Mix well.

4. Add to beans. Mix thoroughly.

5. Bake at 350° for 1 hour.

A low fat, high fiber dish with no cholesterol.
To reduce sodium, substitute cooked dried beans.

Accompaniments: Ham, crisp salad.

Cooks Incorporated

MUSHROOM PIE

Preparation time: 15 minutes
Baking time: 30 minutes

Serves: 6 - 8

½ cup butter, melted
2 8-ounce cans chopped mushrooms, drained
1 large onion, chopped
2 Tablespoons butter, melted
2 Tablespoons flour

1 cup strong chicken stock
½ cup Madeira wine
Celery salt, salt, pepper
Dash cayenne pepper
1 pastry crust (Pillsbury All-Ready Pie Crust suggested)

1. Sauté onion in melted butter. Mix in mushrooms.

2. Place in a shallow casserole or deep 9-inch pie pan.

3. Brown flour in melted butter. Add chicken stock, wine. Cook until thick.

4. Add seasonings to taste.

5. Pour sauce over mushroom mixture. Cover with pastry crust.

6. Bake at 375° for 30 minutes.

MUSHROOMS AU GRATIN

Preparation time: 20 minutes
Baking time: 10 minutes

Serves: 4

2 Tablespoons butter, melted
1 pound mushrooms, sliced
⅓ cup sour cream
Salt to taste

Dash pepper
1 Tablespoon flour
¼ cup parsley, minced
½ cup Gruyère cheese, shredded

1. Sauté mushrooms in melted butter.

2. Blend sour cream, salt, pepper, flour. Stir into mushrooms.

3. Heat until beginning to boil.

4. Place mixture in a shallow glass baking dish. Sprinkle with parsley, cheese.

6. Bake uncovered at 450° on the center oven rack for 10 minutes until heated through, cheese melted.

May be refrigerated for 1 day before baking.

MUSHROOM STRATA

Preparation time: mixing, 25 minutes; standing, 4 hours   *Serves: 6*
Baking time: 1 hour

12 slices white bread, crusts
    removed
Butter
1 pound fresh mushrooms
3 to 4 green onions, thinly sliced

½ cup mayonnaise
2 eggs, beaten
Milk
1 10¾-ounce can cream of
   mushroom soup

1. Butter, cube bread.

2. Place half of bread on bottom of a buttered casserole.

3. Quickly sauté mushrooms. Drain. Reserve liquid.

4. Add onions, mayonnaise to mushrooms. Place over bread cubes in casserole.

5. To beaten eggs add juice from mushrooms and enough milk to make 1 cup liquid.

6. Top casserole with remaining bread cubes.

7. Pour egg mixture over bread.

8. Cover with soup. Let stand at least 4 hours.

9. Bake at 325° on the center oven rack for 1 hour.

QUICKIE MUSHROOMS AND ONIONS

Preparation time: 10 minutes   *Serves: 4*
Baking time: 10 minutes

2 cups whole fresh mushrooms,
   ends trimmed
½ cup red onion, julienned

Dash dill weed
Dash garlic powder
Dash black pepper, freshly ground
1 teaspoon margarine

1. Place mushrooms, onion on a 12x12-inch foil sheet.

2. Top with spices, then margarine.

3. Fold foil in a seam; fold edges.

4. Bake at 350° on the center oven rack for 10 minutes or grill for 10 minutes.

Cooks Incorporated

DUTCH ONION PIE

Preparation time: 20 minutes   *Serves: 6*
Baking time: 45 minutes

Crust

1½ cups flour
2 teaspoons baking powder
¼ teaspoon salt

½ cup solid shortening
  (Crisco suggested)
¾ cup milk

1. Sift together first 3 ingredients.
2. Cut in shortening.
3. Add milk to make a soft dough.
4. Press into a 9-inch pie pan.

Filling

4 Tablespoons butter, melted
4 large Vidalia onions, sliced
1 egg, well-beaten

2 Tablespoons parsley, minced
½ teaspoon salt
1 cup sour cream

1. Sauté onions until soft in melted butter.
2. Combine remaining ingredients. Add to onions.
3. Pour filling into prepared crust.
4. Bake at 375° for 45 minutes.

A prepared pie crust may be used.

Accompaniment: Roast beef or lamb.

SPINACH IN ONION SHELLS

Preparation time: 20 minutes   *Serves: 6*
Baking time: 35 - 40 minutes

1 **10-ounce package frozen chopped**   ¼ **cup grated Parmesan cheese**
   spinach, cooked, well-drained   ¼ **cup milk**
2 **eggs**   ¼ **teaspoon salt**
1 **3-ounce package cream cheese,**   **Dash pepper**
   softened   1 **large flat white onion or several**
½ **cup soft bread crumbs**   **small onions, peeled**

1. Beat together cream cheese, eggs.

2. Stir in crumbs, cheese, milk, seasonings. Mix well.

3. Stir in spinach.

4. Cut onion in half crosswise. Carefully separate layers to form shells. Place in a casserole.

5. Fill shells with spinach mixture. If necessary, piece bottoms of shells with onion pieces. Cover with foil.

6. Bake at 350° on the center oven rack for 35-40 minutes.

May be prepared and refrigerated 8 hours before baking.
Individual servings nice for a buffet.

FRED'S SPINACH

Preparation time: 10 minutes   *Serves: 6*
Baking time: 25 minutes; Microwave time: 12½ minutes

2 **10-ounce packages frozen spinach**   1 **Tablespoon horseradish**
1 **small onion, finely chopped**   3 **Tablespoons cream or sour cream**
3 **Tablespoons butter or margarine,**   1½ **teaspoons seasoned salt**
   melted   **(Lawry's suggested)**

1. Cook spinach according to package directions.

2. Sauté onion in melted butter in a small pan.

3. Combine remaining ingredients. Add spinach, onions.

4. Place in a glass casserole. Bake at 300° for 25 minutes.

(Continued on facing page)

Fred's Spinach Microwave Instructions

1. Microwave each package of spinach separately on high 5 minutes.
2. In an oven-proof dish, melt butter on high 30 seconds.
3. Sauté onion in melted butter on high 1¼ minutes.
4. After spinach cools, squeeze dry with hands.
5. Mix spinach with onions. Mix in remaining ingredients.
7. Microwave on high 1 minute.

May be prepared 6 hours ahead of serving. Heat 3 minutes in microwave.

SPINACH PIE LE GRAND FROMAGE

Preparation time: 25 minutes　　　　　　　　　　　　　　*Serves: 8*
Baking time: 30 - 40 minutes

2　10-ounce packages frozen
　　chopped spinach, drained
1　large onion, minced
¼ cup butter, melted
½ teaspoon salt
¼ teaspoon pepper

1　clove garlic, chopped
1　cup shredded sharp
　　Cheddar cheese
1　egg, well beaten
½ pound shredded Swiss cheese

1. Sauté onion in melted butter. Add spinach, seasonings, garlic.
2. Spoon half the spinach mixture into a buttered 8 or 9-inch pie pan.
3. Cover with Cheddar cheese. Add remaining spinach.
4. Spoon egg evenly over top. Cover with Swiss cheese.
5. Bake at 350° on the center oven rack for 30-40 minutes.
6. Let stand 10 minutes before cutting into wedges.

Accompaniment: Standing rib roast or beef tenderloin.

BAKED STUFFED TOMATOES

Preparation time: 30 minutes   *Serves: 6*
Baking time: 20 - 25 mimutes

6 medium tomatoes
⅓ cup green pepper, finely chopped
⅓ cup green onion, finely chopped
⅓ cup celery, finely chopped
2 Tablespoons margarine, melted

16 soda crackers, rolled into fine crumbs
Salt, pepper to taste
Grated Parmesan cheese
Paprika
Margarine

1. Scald tomatoes. Peel. Leaving a thick shell, scoop out inside, reserving pulp.

2. Turn shells upside down; drain.

3. Chop pulp; set aside.

4. Sauté pepper, onion, celery in margarine until tender, not brown.

5. Add tomato pulp, cracker crumbs. Season to taste.

6. Place tomato shells in a baking dish. Fill shells with mixture.

7. Sprinkle with Parmesan, paprika. Dot with margarine.

8. Bake at 400° on the center oven rack for 20-25 minutes.

MARINATED SLICED TOMATOES

Preparation time: 10 minutes + chilling   *Serves: 8*

6 large tomatoes, peeled
⅓ cup vegetable oil
1 Tablespoon + 1 teaspoon fresh
   lemon juice
½ teaspoon minced garlic

½ teaspoon salt
½ teaspoon finely rubbed dried
   oregano
2 Tablespoons fresh parsley,
   minced

1. Slice peeled tomatoes into fairly thick slices.

2. Combine remaining ingredeients, except parsley. Mix well.

3. Pour over tomato slices.

4. Cover. Refrigerate for 3-4 hours until thoroughly chilled.

5. Sprinkle with parsley just before serving.

Cooks Incorporated

BAKED TOMATO SLICES

Preparation time: 15 minutes
Baking time: 15 minutes

Serves: 6

3 ripe tomatoes
3 Tablespoons mayonnaise
1 teaspoon Dijon mustard
3 Tablespoons fresh parsley, chopped
2 Tablespoons onion, chopped

¼ teaspoon salt
¼ teaspoon pepper
3 Tablespoons Parmesan cheese, freshly grated
Chopped parsley

1. Cut tomatoes into ¾-inch slices.

2. Combine all ingredients except cheese. Spread over tomatoes.

3. Sprinkle with cheese.

4. Bake at 400° for 15 minutes.

5. Broil several minutes until lightly browned.

6. Sprinkle with chopped parsley.

FRESH TOMATO PIE

Preparation time: 30 minutes
Baking time: 30 minutes

Serves: 6

1½ cups soft bread crumbs, divided
1 medium onion, sliced
4 or 5 fresh tomatoes, peeled, sliced
¼ pound shredded sharp Cheddar cheese

½ teaspoon salt
Pepper
2 eggs, lightly beaten
3 strips bacon, halved

1. Butter a 9-inch pie pan. Cover bottom with 1 cup crumbs.

2. Alternate layers of tomatoes, onions, cheese.

3. Add salt, pepper to beaten eggs. Pour over layers. Sprinkle with remaining crumbs.

4. Arrange bacon strips on top in spoke fashion.

5. Bake at 350° on the center oven rack for 30 minutes until bacon is crisp, crumbs are browned.

Increase baking time by 20-30 minutes if made ahead and refrigerated.

BAKED ACORN SQUASH

Preparation time: 15 minutes
Baking time: 45 minutes

Serves: 6

3   acorn squash
6   cloves garlic, peeled

½ cup butter
Salt, pepper

1. Preheat oven to 350°.
2. Cover a baking sheet with foil; rub with butter.
3. Cut squash in halves, removing seeds.
4. Place on baking sheet cut side down. Squash halves must be flush against pan to insure proper baking.
5. Place one peeled garlic clove under each dome.
6. Bake on the center oven rack for 45 minutes until soft.
7. Remove from oven; pick up squash with oven mitt. Remove pulp into a bowl.
9. Add baked garlic, butter; mash. Season to taste.

Butternut squash may be substituted. Add rosemary, sage, thyme with butter for variation. Refrigerates well for 2 days. May be frozen after mashing.

The Winds Café
Yellow Springs, Ohio

Accompaniment: Turkey breast sliced around squash.

ZUCCHINI AND ONION SAUTÉ

Preparation time: 15 - 20 minutes

Serves: 6 - 8

3   zucchini, coarsely shredded, drained
1   sweet onion, shredded
1½ Tablespoons butter, melted

1. Sauté zucchini, onion in melted butter.

A delicious quickie!

Cooks Incorporated

ZUCCHINI FRITTERS

Preparation time: 30 minutes

Serves: 4

1 large zucchini, grated
1 small onion, grated
2 eggs, beaten

Salt, pepper to taste
⅓ cup biscuit mix (Bisquick suggested)
¼ cup Parmesan cheese
Oil

1. Combine all ingredients.

2. Heat oil to 375° in a large skillet with a non-stick surface.

3. Drop batter into oil by heaping Tablespoons.

4. Flatten fritters slightly.

5. Brown on both sides.

6. Serve hot.

SPAGHETTI - ZUCCHINI FRITTERS

Preparation time: 30 minutes

Serves: 12

1 cup flour
¾ teaspoon salt
Pepper to taste
1 large egg
1 cup water

4 ounces spaghetti, cooked,
   coarsely chopped
2 green onions, chopped
1 medium (8 ounce) zucchini, shredded
⅓ cup salad oil

1. Mix flour, seasonings, egg, water.

2. Fold in spaghetti, onions, zucchini.

3. Drop batter into hot oil in a skillet, using about ½ cup batter per fritter,

4. Flatten fritters slightly.

5. Brown on both sides.

Also a good way to use 2 cups of leftover spaghetti.

SWEET-SOUR ZUCCHINI

Preparation time: 45 - 60 minutes   *Serves: 6*

2   Tablespoons vegetable oil
4   teaspoons cornstarch
1   Tablespoon sugar
1   Tablespoon instant golden onion
2   teaspoons prepared mustard
¾   teaspoon salt
½   teaspoon garlic salt

Pepper to taste
½   cup water
¼   cup vinegar
4   cups zucchini, sliced on bias
1   cup celery, sliced on bias
1   sweet onion, sliced
2   fresh tomatoes, peeled, diced, or 1
    can tomato wedges, drained

1. Mix together first 8 ingredients in a large saucepan.

2. Add water, vinegar; cook until thick.

3. Add zucchini, celery, onion; cook 7-8 minutes.

4. Add tomatoes; cook until liquid is reduced.

MARINATED VEGETABLE MEDLEY

Preparation time: 40 minutes + refrigeration   *Serves: 8*

1½ cups light salad oil
⅔ cup champagne wine vinegar
1   teaspoon salt
1   teaspoon pepper
2 to 3 garlic cloves, crushed
2   Tablespoons sugar, or more
    to taste
4   carrots, peeled, thinly sliced

4   celery stalks, sliced
1   4-ounce jar pitted black olives,
    drained
1   4-ounce jar pitted green olives,
    drained
1 to 2 14-ounce cans artichoke hearts,
    drained, halved
½ pound fresh mushrooms or 1 can
    button mushrooms
Cherry tomatoes

1. Combine first 5 ingredients in a blender.

2. Add sugar to taste until dressing is still slightly bitter, not sweet.

3. Pour over vegetables. Refrigerate at least 6 hours to blend. Stir occasionally.

Substitute any vegetables you have.

Cooks Incorporated

SOPHISTICATED SUCCOTASH

Preparation time: 45 minutes   *Serves: 10*

12 ounces broccoli, cut into florets
6 Tablespoons unsalted butter, melted
1 pound carrots, peeled, cut into ¼-inch slices
2 medium red bell peppers, seeded, cut into ¼-inch strips

2 medium yellow crookneck squash, cut into ¼-inch slices
1 10-ounce package frozen baby lima beans, thawed, cooked, drained
Salt, freshly ground pepper
Parmesan cheese

1. Blanch broccoli in salted boiling water in a large pot for 2 minutes. Drain.

2. Place immediately in a bowl of ice water; let stand until cold. Drain; pat dry.

3. Add carrots to melted butter in a large heavy skillet. Cover. Cook 15 minutes over medium low heat, stirring occasionally.

4. Increase heat to medium high. Add peppers; stir 5 minutes.

5. Add squash; stir 1 minute.

6. Add lima beans, broccoli, salt. Cover. Cook 4 minutes until heated through, stirring occasionally.

7. Season generously. Sprinkle generously with Parmesan.

8. Serve immediately.

Broccoli may be prepared a day ahead. Wrap tightly; refrigerate.

Carrots may be cooked 6 hours ahead. Cover; let stand at room temperature.

An excellent holiday vegetable.

Accompaniment: Turkey or beef.

HONEY PEA PODS, CARROTS, AND WATER CHESTNUTS

Preparation time: 30 minutes
Microwave time: 12 - 16 minutes

Serves: 4 - 6

¾ cup water
2 cups carrots, scraped sliced
 ¼-inch thick (4 medium carrots)
4 ounces fresh or 6 ounces frozen
 pea pods

1 8-ounce can sliced water chestnuts
3 Tablespoons butter or margarine
½ teaspoon cornstarch
2 Tablespoons honey

1. Bring water to a boil in a 2-quart saucepan.

2. Add carrots. Cover. Cook over medium heat 10-12 minutes until crisp, tender.

3. Add pea pods, water chestnuts. Continue cooking 1-2 minutes until crisp, tender. Drain; set aside.

4. In same pan, melt margarine.

5. Stir in cornstarch. Add honey, vegetables.

6. Cook over medium heat 2-3 minutes stirring occasionally until heated through.

Microwave Instructions

1. Place carrots and ¼ cup water in a 1¼-quart casserole. Cover. Microwave on high 4 minutes.

2. Stir. Continue cooking on high 4-6 minutes until crisp, tender.

3. Add pea pods, water chestnuts. Cover. Microwave on high 1-2 minutes. Drain; set aside.

4. In same dish, melt margarine on high (50-60 seconds).

5. Stir in cornstarch. Microwave on high 1 minute.

6. Stir in honey, vegetables. Cover. Microwave on high 1-2 minutes.

Accompaniment: Ham.

PARTY POTATOES

Preparation time: 40 minutes
Baking time: 25 minutes

Serves: 8 - 10

8 to 10 medium potatoes, peeled, cut into quarters
8 ounces cream cheese
1 cup sour cream

4 Tablespoons butter
⅓ cup chives, chopped
Salt, pepper to taste
Butter
Paprika

1. Boil potatoes until tender; drain.

2. Beat together cream cheese, sour cream.

3. Add hot potatoes; beat until smooth.

4. Add butter, chives, salt, pepper.

5. Place in a well-greased 2-quart casserole.

6. Dot with butter. Sprinkle with paprika.

7. Bake at 350° on the center oven rack for 25 minutes.

May be prepared 1 to 2 days before baking.

CRUNCHY POTATOES

Preparation time: 15 minutes
Baking time: 30 minutes

Serves: 6

⅓ cup butter or margarine
3 to 4 large Idaho potatoes, peeled
¾ cup cornflakes, crushed

1½ cups shredded sharp Cheddar cheese
2 teaspoons salt
1½ teaspoons paprika

1. Melt butter in a jelly roll pan in a 375° oven.

2. Slice potatoes crosswise into ¼-inch slices.

3. Place in a pan in a single layer, turning each slice in butter to coat.

4. Mix remaining ingredients; sprinkle over potatoes.

5. Bake at 375° on the center oven rack for 30 minutes until tops are crispy.

May be prepared ahead.

CYNTHIA'S CYNFUL SCALLOPED POTATOES

Preparation time: 30 minutes
Baking time: 75 minutes

Serves: 6

4 cups Idaho potatoes, thinly sliced
1½ cups Gruyère cheese, grated
¼ cup Parmesan cheese,
   freshly grated
½ cup butter or margarine

1 teaspoon salt
Ground pepper to taste
Garlic powder to taste
1 cup whipping cream
2 eggs, lightly beaten

1. Preheat oven to 375°.

2. Layer half of potatoes, half of cheeses, half of butter in a greased casserole or soufflé dish. Sprinkle with half the seasonings.

3. Repeat layers except cheeses.

4. Combine cream, eggs. Pour over casserole.

5. Top with remaining half of cheeses.

6. Cover with foil.

7. Bake for 45 minutes. Uncover; bake for 30 minutes.

Accompaniment: Roast beef.

NUTRIENT ANALYSIS (Per Serving)
Carbohydrate .... 22 grams
Protein .... 16 grams
Fat .... 35 grams
Calories .... 456 (69% from fat)
Cholesterol .... 159 milligrams
Sodium .... 727 milligrams

CYNTHIA'S CYNFUL SCALLOPED POTATOES - LIGHT OPTION

Preparation time: 30 minutes   *Serves: 6*
Baking time: 75 minutes

1¼ cups low fat (1%) cottage cheese
4 cups Idaho potatoes, thinly sliced
½ cup Parmesan cheese, freshly grated
¼ teaspoon salt

¼ teaspoon ground pepper
1 teaspoon garlic powder
1 cup evaporated skim milk
1 egg, lightly beaten
2 egg whites, lightly beaten

1. Preheat oven to 375°.

2. Place cottage cheese in a blender. Process until smooth.

3. Spray a casserole or soufflé dish with non-stick cooking spray.

4. Layer half of potatoes, half of cheese in casserole. Sprinkle with half the seasonings.

5. Repeat layers except cheese.

6. Combine milk, egg, egg whites. Blend well. Pour over casserole.

7. Top with remaining half of cheeses.

8. Cover with foil.

9. Bake for 45 minutes. Uncover; bake for 30 minutes.

NUTRIENT ANALYSIS (Per Serving)
Carbohydrate .... 27 grams
Protein .... 0 grams
Fat .... 4 grams
Calories .... 213 (17% from fat)
Cholesterol .... 45 milligrams
Sodium .... 525 milligrams

SCALLOPED POTATOES WITH BLEU CHEESE

Preparation time: 30 minutes   *Serves: 6*
Baking time: 30 minutes

5   medium potatoes, boiled,   1   cup milk or evaporated milk
    peeled, sliced   2   Tablespoons parsley, chopped
2   Tablespoons butter, melted   ¼   cup onion, grated
2   Tablespoons flour   2   cups creamed cottage cheese
½   teaspoon salt   3   ounces bleu cheese, crumbled
Dash pepper   Dash paprika

1. Add flour to melted butter. Cook 2 minutes.

2. Add salt, pepper.

3. Add milk slowly, stirring constantly. Cook until white sauce begins to thicken.
   Remove from heat.

4. Add parsley, onion.

5. Grease a 9x12-inch casserole.

6. Alternate layers of potatoes, cottage cheese, bleu cheese, sauce.

7. Repeat layers, ending with sauce.

8. Sprinkle with paprika.

9. Bake at 350° on the center oven rack for 30 minutes.

May be prepared ahead and refrigerated or frozen. Bake 1 hour if frozen.

Accompaniments: Steak or ham.

PIKE'S PEAK POTATOES

Preparation time: 10 minutes   *Serves: 6*
Baking time: 1 hour

1½ pounds new potatoes, unpeeled   **½ cup chicken broth**
Salt, pepper to taste   **1 to 1½ cups shredded Swiss cheese**
¾ cup heavy cream   **Paprika**

1. Slice potatoes. Work rapidly; place potatoes in water until ready to cook to prevent discoloration. Drain.

2. Place potatoes in a greased 9x9-inch baking dish. Sprinkle with salt, pepper.

3. Mix cream, broth; pour over potatoes.

4. Cover; bake at 350° on the center oven rack for 30 minutes.

5. Uncover; bake another 30 minutes.

6. Sprinkle with cheese; bake until cheese is melted.

7. Sprinkle with paprika.

BAKED POTATO SALAD

Preparation time: 30 - 45 minutes   *Serves: 8*
Baking time: 1½ hours

8 potatoes, unpeeled   **1 cup mayonnaise**
1 pound process cheese product,   **   (Hellmann's suggested)**
**   cubed (Velveeta suggested)**   **¼ cup black olives, sliced**
½ cup onion, diced   **½ pound bacon, cooked and**
                                              **   crumbled**

1. Cook potatoes until tender, about ½ hour.

2. When cooled, cut potatoes into cubes.

3. Mix potatoes with cheese, onion, mayonnaise.

4. Place in a 3-quart casserole. Top with olives, bacon.

5. Bake at 325° on the middle oven rack for 1½ hours.

Accompaniments: Picnic foods.

YAM AND APPLE CASSEROLE

Preparation time: 30 minutes *Serves: 6 - 8*
Baking time: 25 - 30 minutes

2　pounds fresh or canned sweet
　　potatoes, peeled, sliced
1¼ pounds cooking apples, peeled,
　　sliced
⅔　cup dark brown sugar
6　Tablespoons butter

¼　cup apple cider
3　Tablespoons maple syrup
1　Tablespoon lemon juice
1　teaspoon cinnamon
¼　teaspoon ginger

1. Arrange potato and apple slices alternately in a shallow baking dish.

2. Combine remaining ingredients in a small saucepan.

3. Bring to a boil. Simmer 10 minutes.

4. Pour over potatoes and apples.

5. Bake at 325° for 25-30 minutes until apples tender.

Children especially like the apple flavor.

SWEET POTATO CASSEROLE

Preparation time: 5 minutes *Serves: 6 - 8*
Baking time: 45 minutes

2　18-ounce cans vacuum
　　packed sweet potatoes
¼　cup orange juice

2　Tablespoons brown sugar
1　Tablespoon margarine, melted
1　16-ounce can whole cranberry
　　sauce, cubed

1. Place potatoes in a 10-inch casserole.

2. Pour juice, sugar, margarine over potatoes.

3. Bake at 350° for 30 minutes.

4. Add cranberry sauce.

5. Bake 15 minutes.

6. Serve immediately.

Cooks Incorporated

HORSERADISH SAUCE FOR VEGETABLES

Preparation time: 15 minutes   *Serves: 8*

1 cup mayonnaise
2 hard cooked eggs, chopped
1 heaping Tablespoon horseradish
1 teaspoon Worcestershire sauce

Garlic, celery or onion salt to taste
Pepper to taste
1½ teaspoons parsley flakes
Juice of 1 lemon

1. Blend all ingredients.

2. Serve at room temperature on green vegetables.

GREEN CHILI PESTO FOR VEGETABLES

Preparation time: 20 minutes   *Serves: 6*

2 cloves garlic, peeled
5 ounces Parmesan cheese,
   cut into chunks
2 4-ounce cans mild green chilies,
   drained, seeded
¾ cup walnuts

½ cup fresh parsley, large
   stems removed
5 to 6 Tablespoons vegetable oil
Salt to taste
Chicken stock
Vegetables

1. Using metal blade, drop garlic, cheese through feed tube of a food processor with motor running. Process until cheese is finely grated.

2. Add seeded chilies to work bowl.

3. Add nuts, parsley, oil. Process to make paste.

4. Add salt.

5. Refrigerate up to 1 week or freeze until ready to serve.

6. When ready to serve, mix 3 Tablespoons pesto to 2 Tablespoons chicken stock.

7. Toss with lightly cooked green beans, corn, red pepper to coat.

Sauce may be used with any combination of vegetables. Adjust amount for degree of spiciness desired.

TIPS ON VEGETABLES

(From Our Good Cooks!)

To shed fewer tears, cut off the root end of the onion last.

To remove every strand of corn silk, brush downward on a cob of corn with a dampened paper towel or terry cloth.

To remove kernels of sweet corn from the cob, use a clean metal shoe horn. The shape is just right for shearing off the kernels quickly.

Remove the green shoot from a garlic clove. It is bitter if it has started to sprout.

To hasten ripening of tomatoes or avocados, place them in a closed brown paper bag at room temperature for several days.

To roast bell peppers, place them on a baking sheet in a 500° oven for 20 minutes until skin is blackened, charred. Place in a paper bag; seal top. Refrigerate 10 minutes until cool. Peel away skin with fingers; discard seeds. To roast and peel in a microwave, coat peppers lightly with vegetable oil. Pierce on 2 sides with a knife. Place stem side out on a microwave-safe plate. Working with 1/2 pound at a time, cover with a paper towel; cook on high 4 minutes; turn; rotate plate. Cook 4-6 minutes until peppers blister at stem end. Remove; cover tightly with a cloth towel. Let rest 10 minutes. Peel under cold running water.

To hasten potato baking, boil potatoes in salted water 10 minutes before placing in a very hot oven. Or, cut a thin slice from each end of a potato.

Rebake a leftover baked potato by dipping it in water and baking at 350° for about 20 minutes.

Add a few drops of lemon juice to simmering rice to keep the grains separate.

If vegetables or entrées are too sweet, add a teaspoon of cider vinegar.

Some vegetables do not store well together: Carrots turn bitter beside apples. Potatoes rot more quickly when stored with onions. Leafy greens spoil faster when stored with tomatoes or eggplants.

Troy, Ohio

In the spirit of this book, 20,000 Trojans have found a recipe for successful living. They combine and blend the love of neighbors, the opportunity to work, the time to play, the courage to dream, and the spirit to create.

Troy provides the comfort of country living with the vitality of a major industrial and commercial complex. Employment opportunities at huge international enterprises and a host of successful local professional and commercial businesses nourish the Trojan economy.

Woven into the fabric of recreational, artistic, and educational facilities are Troy's special events, the largest being the *Strawberry Festival.* This magnificent event, held at the time of the June harvest, attracts thousands to a fulsome schedule of parades, dances, athletic events, entertainments and band concerts. Of course, the featured attraction of the festival is the Strawberry itself – the prima donna of Troy's agricultural community. One can sample a multitude of wonderful, rich strawberry dishes, or simply enjoy the red, ripe, juicy fruit dipped in sugar.

The flavor of America emanates from the public square where outstanding examples of the architecture of the 19th Century can be found. The Miami County Courthouse, together with handsome residential buildings on Main Street, Market Street, and other streets running like spokes from the public square offer fine examples of period homes.

Troy's remarkable growth and prosperity is grounded in the spirit of its people and the vision of its leaders. Indeed, it is a community of people working aggressively toward the future while nurturing their roots.

Cooks Incorporated

PENNSYLVANIA DUTCH APPLE CAKE

Preparation time: 30 minutes
Baking time: 1 hour

Serves: 12

4   cups apples, peeled, chopped
2   eggs, beaten
¼   cup oil
2   cups sugar
½   cup nuts, chopped

½   cup raisins
2   cups flour
2   teaspoons baking soda
½   teaspoon salt
2   teaspoons cinnamon
1   teaspoon vanilla

Sauce

¾   cup brown sugar
⅓   cup cornstarch

3   cups boiling water
1   teaspoon butter or margarine
1   teaspoon vanilla

1.   Combine apples, eggs. Stir to coat apples.

2.   Add oil, sugar, nuts, raisins. Mix well.

3.   Add remaining cake ingredients. Mix well.

4.   Pour into a greased, floured 9x13-inch pan.

5.   Bake at 325° for 1 hour. Cool.

6.   Combine brown sugar, cornstarch in a saucepan.

7.   Slowly add boiling water. Stir until dissolved; cook until thick.

8.   Add butter, vanilla.

9.   Pour sauce over cake squares when served.

Variation: Use cream cheese frosting instead of sauce.

RHUBARB CAKE

Preparation time: 30 minutes
Baking time: 35-45 minutes

Serves: 20-24

1½ cups brown sugar
½ cup margarine
1 egg
1 teaspoon vanilla
2 cups flour
1 teaspoon baking soda

½ teaspoon salt
1 cup buttermilk or sour milk
1½ cups fresh rhubarb, diced, or
  unthawed frozen rhubarb
½ cup brown sugar
1 teaspoon cinnamon
Ice cream or whipped cream

1. Preheat oven to 350°.

2. Cream together sugar, margarine. Beat in egg, vanilla.

3. Combine flour, soda, salt; add alternately with milk to creamed mixture.

4. Fold in rhubarb. Pour into a lightly greased 8x12-inch baking dish.

5. Mix together sugar, cinnamon; sprinkle over batter.

6. Bake on the center oven rack for 35-45 minutes.

7. Serve warm or cold with ice cream or whipped cream.

SPICE CAKE

Preparation time: 25 minutes
Baking time: 30-35 minutes

Serves: 10-12

¾ cup shortening
2¼ cups cake flour, sifted
1 cup sugar
1 teaspoon baking powder
1 teaspoon salt

¾ teaspoon baking soda
¾ teaspoon cinnamon
½ teaspoon cloves
¾ cup brown sugar
1 cup buttermilk or sour milk
3 eggs

1. Stir shortening just to soften.

2. Sift dry ingredients, except brown sugar, into shortening.

3. Add brown sugar, buttermilk. Mix well until all flour is dampened.

4. Beat vigorously 2 minutes. Add eggs; beat 2 minutes.

5. Pour batter into 2 paper-lined 9-inch round cake pans.

6. Bake at 350° for 30-35 minutes.

Mrs. Frances Sroufe, 1970 Ohio State Fair

PINEAPPLE CRUNCH CAKE

Preparation time: 25 minutes
Baking time: 35 minutes

Serves: 8-10

1 8-ounce can crushed pineapple with liquid
⅓ cup shortening
½ cup sugar
1 teaspoon vanilla
1 egg
1¼ cups flour

1½ teaspoons baking powder
¼ teaspoon salt
½ cup flaked coconut
⅓ cup brown sugar, firmly packed
⅓ cup walnuts, chopped
3 Tablespoons margarine, melted
Whipped topping (optional)

1. Drain pineapple well, reserving ½ cup syrup. (Add water if necessary to make ½ cup.)

2. Cream shortening, sugar, vanilla.

3. Add egg; beat well.

4. Sift together dry ingredients.

5. Add to creamed mixture alternately with pineapple syrup, beating after each addition.

6. Pour half of batter into a greased, floured 8¼ or 9-inch ovenware dish.

7. Spoon pineapple over.

8. Cover with remaining batter.

9. Combine coconut, brown sugar, walnuts. Place over batter.

10. Drizzle margarine over all.

11. Bake at 350° on the center oven rack for 35 minutes.

12. Serve warm with whipped topping, if desired.

Also good as a coffee cake.

PORTUGUESE ALMOND CAKE WITH RASPBERRIES

Preparation time: 25 minutes   *Serves: 8*
Baking time: 40-50 minutes

¾ cup sugar
½ cup unsalted butter, softened
1 7 or 8-ounce can almond paste
3 eggs
1 Tablespoon Grand Marnier, triple sec, or kirsch
¼ teaspoon almond extract

¼ cup all-purpose flour
⅓ teaspoon baking powder
Powdered sugar
2 cups fresh raspberries or 12 ounces frozen unsweetened raspberries, thawed
2 Tablespoons sugar to taste

1. Preheat oven to 350°.

2. Generously grease, flour an 8-inch round cake pan.

3. Combine sugar, butter, almond paste in a medium bowl. Blend well.

4. Beat in eggs, liqueur, almond extract.

5. Add flour, baking powder; beat until just mixed.

6. Bake 40-50 minutes on the center oven rack. Cool.

7. Invert onto a serving platter.

8. Dust lightly with powdered sugar.

9. Combine raspberries, sugar in a blender; puree.

10. Gently press through a fine sieve to remove seeds.

11. Serve raspberry sauce as an accompaniment to cake.

Cake keeps for 1-2 days at room temperature.
A light, elegant, unusual dessert.

GINGERBREAD CAKE

Preparation time: 15-20 minutes
Baking time: 1¼ hours

Serves: 10-12

1 16-ounce can applesauce
1 cup dark molasses
2 teaspoons baking soda
3 cups all-purpose flour
½ teaspoon salt
2 teaspoons ginger

1½ teaspoons cinnamon
½ teaspoon ground cloves
4 large eggs
1⅓ cups sugar
⅔ cup vegetable oil
Whipped cream or lemon whipped
    cream

1. Preheat oven to 325°.

2. Place applesauce in a medium saucepan. Bring to a boil.

3. Stir in molasses, soda. Set aside to cool.

4. Combine flour, salt, spices. Set aside.

5. Beat eggs until light in color in a large bowl with an electric mixer.

6. Gradually beat in sugar until thick.

7. Gradually beat in oil.

8. Mix in flour mixture alternately with applesauce mixture.

9. Pour into a greased 10-inch Bundt pan.

10. Bake on the center oven rack for 1¼ hours. Check after 1 hour, as some ovens bake this cake faster.

11. Cool 15 minutes before removing from pan.

12. Serve warm with whipped cream or lemon whipped cream.

Freezes well.
A great alternative to pumpkin pie.

IMPERIAL CROWN CAKE

Preparation time: 30 minutes   *Serves: 10-12*
Baking time: 30-35 minutes

⅔ cup butter or margarine, softened
1¾ cups sugar
2 eggs, at room temperature
1 teaspoon vanilla
2½ squares unsweetened chocolate,
  melted, cooled

2½ cups cake flour, sifted
½ teaspoon salt
1¼ teaspoons baking soda
1¼ cups ice water
Chocolate Buttercream Pecan Filling
Buttercream Frosting

1. Cream butter, sugar until light, fluffy.

2. Add eggs, vanilla; beat well. Blend in cooled chocolate.

3. Sift together flour, salt, soda.

4. Add sifted ingredients to creamed mixture alternately with ice water, beginning and ending with flour mixture. Beat well after each addition.

5. Pour batter into 2 paper-lined 9-inch round pans.

6. Bake at 350° for 30-35 minutes. Cool thoroughly.

7. Frost between layers with Chocolate Buttercream Pecan Filling. Frost sides, top with Buttercream Frosting.

CHOCOLATE BUTTERCREAM PECAN FILLING

Preparation time: 15 minutes   *Yield: Frosting for 1 9-inch layer*

1 Tablespoon butter or margarine,
  melted

½ cup pecans, chopped
⅓ cup semi-sweet chocolate pieces

1. Add pecans to melted butter in a small skillet. Toast 5 minutes, stirring frequently. Remove from heat.

2. Add chocolate. Let stand several minutes to soften. Stir to combine.

3. Cool completely.

4. Add to ½ cup Buttercream Frosting.

BUTTERCREAM FROSTING

Preparation time: 15 minutes   *Yield: Frosting for 9-inch cake*

5 Tablespoons milk
2 Tablespoons butter or margarine,
   softened
¾ cup + 2 Tablespoons solid shortening

1 pound confectioners' sugar, sifted
¾ teaspoon salt
1 teaspoon vanilla or ½ teaspoon
   almond extract

1. Combine all ingredients. Beat well.

2. Thin down a small quantity to coat crumbs on side of cake before frosting
    the cake.

*Variation: For a more yellow frosting, substitute ⅔ cup butter for shortening; use a
pinch of salt.*

FOURTH OF JULY FUDGE CAKE

Preparation time: 25 minutes   *Serves: 8-12*
Baking time: 30 minutes

4 Tablespoons butter, melted
2 cups sugar
2 egg yolks
4 squares unsweetened chocolate,
   melted, cooled
1 teaspoon vanilla
2 cups flour

2 teaspoons baking powder
1½ cups whole milk
1 cup English walnuts or pecans,
   coarsely chopped
2 egg whites, stiffly beaten
Stemmed strawberries or cherries,
   chocolate curls (optional)

1. Cream butter, sugar.

2. Add egg yolks; beat well. Stir in chocolate, vanilla.

3. Sift together flour, baking powder.

4. Add to chocolate mixture alternately with milk, mixing well.

5. Add nuts. Fold in egg whites.

6. Pour batter into 2 greased, floured 9-inch or 3 8-inch cake pans.

7. Bake at 350° for 30 minutes.

8. Cool. Frost with a vanilla frosting.

9. Garnish with fruit, chocolate curls if desired.

CAPPUCCINO CHEESECAKE

Preparation time: 45 minutes   *Serves: 13*
Baking time: 1¼ hours

16 chocolate wafers, broken into pieces
2   Tablespoons sugar
3   Tablespoons butter, melted
2¼ pounds cream cheese, cut into 1-
    inch pieces
1   cup sugar
¼ cup heavy cream
1½ teaspoons vanilla

5   eggs
1   ounce semi-sweet chocolate, cut
    into ½-inch pieces
¼ cup boiling water
2   teaspoons instant espresso powder
3   Tablespoons creme de cacao
½ teaspoon lemon juice
Grated chocolate (optional)

1. Preheat oven to 350°.

2. Coat a 9-inch springform pan with butter. Cover outside of pan with foil to prevent leakage.

3. Use metal blade of a food processor to process wafers, sugar for 30 seconds until in fine crumbs.

4. Add butter; process 5 seconds just to combine.

5. Press mixture into bottom and sides of pan.

6. Refrigerate 10 minutes.

7. Bake 8 minutes. Cool on a rack.

8. Process cream cheese 1½ minutes until smooth, scraping bowl when necessary.

9. Add sugar, cream, vanilla; process 15 seconds to combine.

10. With motor running, add eggs, one at a time, through feed tube.

11. Scrape down bowl; process 10 seconds to mix well; reserve.

12. Remove, clean metal blade; rinse, wipe bowl dry.

13. Process chocolate 30 seconds until finely chopped.

14. With motor runnung, slowly pour boiling water through feed tube.

15. Process 15 seconds until chocolate is melted.

16. Add espresso powder, liqueur; process 5 seconds to combine. Leave in bowl.

(Continued on facing page)

17. Pour all but about 2¼ cups of cream cheese mixture into bowl; process 10 seconds to combine. Scrape down bowl.

18. Pour into prepared crust.

19. Bake on the center oven rack 40 minutes just until rim is set. (Center will be soft.) Carefully remove from oven.

20. Reduce oven temperature to 325°.

21. Stir lemon juice into reserved 2¼ cups cream cheese mixture.

22. Carefully pour mixture around rim of pan where cake is set, allowing filling to flow into center.

23. Return to oven; bake 35 minutes until sides rise, center is just set.

24. Cool on a wire rack until bottom and sides are completely cool.

25. Remove rim; continue to cool at room temperature.

26. Cover loosely with plastic wrap; refrigerate until firm, at least 4 hours, preferably overnight.

27. Sprinkle grated chocolate over top before serving if desired.

Must be made with a food processor.
Be careful not to pour the cream cheese mixture into the center of the cake, as it will collapse.
A great dessert for coffee drinkers.

PARTY AMARETTO CHEESECAKE

Preparation time: 2 hours 　　　　　　　　　　　　*Serves: 30-40*
Baking time: 1½ hours

Crust

6　cups graham cracker crumbs
¾　cup blanched almonds, toasted, cooled, finely chopped by hand

¼　teaspoon cinnamon
1　cup butter or margarine, melted

Filling

3　pounds cream cheese, softened to room temperature
3　cups sugar
9　eggs, at room temperature

3　cups sour cream, at room temperature
1½　cups heavy cream
¾　cup amaretto liqueur

Almond Garnish

1½ cups sugar
¾ cup water
1　Tablespoon amaretto

1　teaspoon almond extract
3　cups sliced almonds with brown outer layer

1. Combine all crust ingredients in a medium bowl.

2. Mix until butter is evenly distributed.

3. Place in a very large 12 or 14-inch ungreased springform pan.

4. Press mixture in bottom and 2 inches up sides of pan.

5. Refrigerate to set crust.

6. Preheat oven to 350°.

7. Using a food processor, make filling in 3 batches, using ⅓ of ingredients for each batch. (Only a very large or commercial food processor will handle all filling ingredients at once.)

8. Beat cream cheese, sugar until light, creamy.

9. Add eggs, 1 at a time, mixing thoroughly after each addition.

10. Add remaining ingredients. Mix thoroughly.

(Continued on facing page)

11. Carefully pour mixture into cold crust.

12. Bake for at least 1½ hours, according to pan size.

13. While cake is baking, prepare almond garnish.

14. Combine sugar, water in a small saucepan. Bring to a boil; boil 2 minutes until mixture becomes a thin syrup. (Watch carefully to avoid foaming over.)

15. Stir in amaretto, almond extract.

16. Cover a baking sheet with waxed paper.

17. Using a large fork or slotted spoon, add small amounts of sliced almonds to sugar mixture.

18. Remove coated almonds to the waxed paper; separate with a fork.

19. Repeat with remaining almonds.

20. Cool.

21. 15 minutes before end of baking, test filling by inserting a wooden skewer. Some filling should adhere to skewer.

22. Carefully arrange almonds in a several-inch wide circle around outer edge of cake. Almonds should not touch pan sides.

23. Continue to bake 15 minutes. If cake browns too fast, cover top with foil.

24. Cool cake 15-25 minutes before removing sides of pan. Cool completely.

25. Refrigerate overnight before serving on a large, flat plate.

Place a shallow pan half full of hot water on the lower oven rack to prevent cheesecake from cracking.
Wonderful texture, great flavor.

CHEWY PEANUT BROWNIE BARS

Preparation time: 40 minutes   *Yield: 50*
Baking time: 15-18 minutes

Crust

1   20½-ounce package fudge brownie mix   ½ cup butter or margarine, melted
                                            1   egg

Filling

1   cup corn syrup   1   Tablespoon butter or margarine,
¾ cup peanut butter   melted
1   cup unsalted peanuts   ½ teaspoon vanilla

Glaze

1   Tablespoon butter or margarine   7½ teaspoons water
1   ounce unsweetened chocolate   1   cup powdered sugar
                                            ½ teaspoon vanilla

1. Preheat oven to 350°.

2. Combine all crust ingredients in a large bowl. Mix well.

3. Press mixture evenly over bottom of an ungreased 15x10x1-inch pan.

4. Combine corn syrup, peanut butter in a small bowl.

5. Beat until well blended at low speed of an electric mixer.

6. Stir in remaining filling ingredients.

7. Spread filling evenly over crust to within ½ inch of edges.

8. Bake for 15-18 minutes until edges are firm, center just firm to touch. Cool
   completely.

9. Combine butter, chocolate, water in a small saucepan.

10. Melt, stirring constantly until smooth.

11. Whisk in powdered sugar, vanilla; blend until smooth.

12. Drizzle glaze over cooled brownies. Allow glaze to set. Cut into bars.

*Variations: Use crunchy peanut butter; omit peanuts. Use premelted baking chocolate
instead of bar chocolate.*

APRICOT BARS

Preparation time: 25 minutes
Baking time: 20-25 minutes

Yield: 48

⅓ cup butter, softened
1½ cups brown sugar, firmly packed
½ cup honey
3 eggs, beaten
1¾ cups all-purpose flour
1 teaspoon baking powder

1 teaspoon salt
1 6-ounce package dried apricots, finely chopped
1 cup pecans, chopped
¾ cup powdered sugar
1 Tablespoon lemon juice

1. Cream butter. Gradually add sugar. Beat well.

2. Add honey, eggs. Mix.

3. Combine flour, baking powder, salt; add to butter mixture. Mix well.

4. Add apricots, pecans. Spread batter in a greased, floured 15x10x1-inch pan.

5. Bake at 350° for 20-25 minutes. Cool in pan 15 minutes.

6. Combine powdered sugar, lemon juice for glaze. Brush mixture in pan with glaze.

7. Cool completely. Cut into bars.

Variation: Add golden raisins to batter.

RICH LEMON BARS

Preparation time: 20 minutes
Baking time: 45 minutes

Yield: 30-36

1 cup butter or margarine or ½ cup each, melted
½ cup powdered sugar
2 cups sifted flour
¼ teaspoon salt
4 eggs

2 cups granulated sugar
¼ cup flour
¼ cup lemon juice
Grated rind of 1 lemon
¼ teaspoon salt
Powdered sugar

1. Blend first 4 ingredients for crust. Press into an ungreased 12x8-inch pan.

2. Bake at 350° on the center oven rack for 20 minutes. Cool 10 minutes.

3. Meanwhile, blend remaining ingredients, except powdered sugar, for filling.

4. Pour over crust. Bake for 25 minutes.

5. Sprinkle powdered sugar on top. Cut into 2-inch squares.

Freeze very well.

OATMEAL-RAISIN COOKIES

Preparation time: 15-20 minutes *Yield: 60*
Baking time: 7-10 minutes

2 cups oatmeal	1½ cups sugar
1 cup raisins	1 teaspoon baking soda
2 cups sifted flour	2½ Tablespoons hot water
1 heaping teaspoon cinnamon	1 cup vegetable oil
1 heaping teaspoon nutmeg	2 eggs
Pinch salt	1 cup black walnuts, chopped (optional)

1. Preheat oven to 375°.

2. Grind oatmeal in a food processor.

3. Grind raisins in food processor.

4. Combine flour, spices, salt, sugar. Set aside.

5. Dissolve baking soda in hot water.

6. Combine all ingredients except walnuts. Mix thoroughly.

7. Fold in walnuts if desired.

8. Drop by rounded teaspoonfuls onto ungreased baking sheets.

9. Bake on the center oven rack for 7-10 minutes.

An old German recipe.

NUTRIENT ANALYSIS (Per Cookie)

Carbohydrate .... 10 grams
Protein .... 1 gram
Fat .... 4 grams
Calories .... 90 (42% from fat)
Cholesterol .... 7 milligrams
Sodium .... 13 milligrams

OATMEAL-RAISIN COOKIES – LIGHT OPTION

Preparation time: 5-10 minutes
Baking time: 8-10 minutes

Yield: 36

1 cup sifted flour
½ teaspoon baking soda
½ teaspoon cinnamon
½ teaspoon nutmeg
1½ cups oatmeal
1 cup brown sugar, firmly packed

⅓ cup canola oil
2 egg whites
2 Tablespoons skim milk
1 teaspoon vanilla
1 cup raisins

1. Preheat oven to 375°.

2. Combine flour, soda, spices. Stir in oatmeal.

3. Combine all remaining ingredients in a separate bowl.

4. Add to flour mixture. Mix well.

5. Drop by rounded teaspoonfuls onto baking sheets sprayed with no-stick cooking spray.

6. Bake on the center oven rack for 8-10 minutes.

An excellent low-fat, high-fiber cookie.

NUTRIENT ANALYSIS (Per Cookie)

Carbohydrate .... 12 grams
Protein .... 1 gram
Fat .... 2 grams
Calories .... 73 (29% from fat)
Cholesterol .... 0 milligram
Sodium .... 10 milligrams

BROWN SUGAR OATMEAL COOKIES

Preparation time: 30 minutes   *Yield: 36*
Baking time: 8-10 minutes

1 cup butter or margarine, softened	1 teaspoon baking soda
2 eggs	½ teaspoon salt
2 cups brown sugar, firmly packed	1 teaspoon vanilla
1½ cups flour	3 cups quick-cooking oatmeal
1 teaspoon baking powder	Powdered sugar

1. Blend butter, eggs, brown sugar 5 minutes until creamy.

2. Add dry ingredients. Mix well.

3. Add vanilla. Mix well. Stir in oatmeal.

4. Shape into walnut-sized balls. (Add more flour or oatmeal if a stiffer dough is needed.) Roll in powdered sugar. Place on an ungreased baking sheet.

5. Bake at 375° on the center oven rack for 8-10 minutes.

Recipe does not double well. Dough may be refrigerated overnight before baking. Powdered sugar adds a nice touch.

DREAM PECAN SQUARES

Preparation time: 10 minutes   *Serves: 12*
Baking time: 30 minutes

1 cup flour	1 teaspoon vanilla
½ cup brown sugar, firmly packed	1 cup pecans, chopped
½ cup butter, melted	2 Tablespoons flour
2 eggs, beaten	½ teaspoon salt
1 cup brown sugar, firmly packed	Whipped cream or vanilla ice cream

1. Combine first 3 ingredients. Blend well.

2. Spread in a lightly greased 11x7-inch pan.

3. Bake at 375° on the center oven rack for 10 minutes.

4. Meanwhile, combine remaining ingredients. Mix well.

5. Reduce oven temperature to 325°.

6. Spread pecan mixture over baked crust. Bake for 20 minutes.

7. Top with whipped cream or ice cream if desired.

PUMPKIN-WALNUT COOKIES

Preparation time: 20 minutes
Baking time: 12-14 minutes

Yield: 48

½ cup butter, softened
1½ cups brown sugar, firmly packed
2 large eggs
1 cup cooked or canned pumpkin
1 teaspoon vanilla
1 teaspoon lemon peel, grated
1 teaspoon fresh lemon juice
2½ cups sifted flour

3 teaspoons baking powder
1 teaspoon salt
1½ teaspoons pumpkin pie spice
¼ teaspoon ginger
1 cup black or English walnuts, chopped
Sour cream or buttercream frosting (optional)

1. Cream butter, sugar together until fluffy. Beat in eggs 1 at a time.

2. Stir in vanilla, pumpkin, lemon peel, juice.

3. Sift together flour, baking powder, salt, spices. Blend into butter mixture.

4. Stir in walnuts. Drop by Tablespoons 2 inches apart onto greased baking sheets.

5. Bake at 375° on the center oven rack for 12-14 minutes.

6. Decorate with sour cream or buttercream frosting if desired.

CHERRY DATE-NUT COOKIES

Preparation time: 30 minutes + chilling
Baking time: 8-10 minutes

Yield: 48

1 cup solid shortening
2 cups brown sugar, firmly packed
2 eggs, beaten
½ cup sour milk or ½ cup water
3½ cups sifted flour

1 teaspoon baking soda
1 teaspoon salt
1½ cups pecans, chopped
2 cups candied cherries
2 cups dates, chopped

1. Combine shortening, brown sugar, eggs. Mix well.

2. Stir in sour milk or water.

3. Sift together flour, soda, salt. Stir into mixed ingredients.

4. Fold remaining ingredients into batter. Chill 1 hour.

5. Drop by teaspoonfuls onto lightly greased baking sheets.

6. Bake at 400° on the center oven rack for 8-10 minutes.

OLD-FASHIONED GERMAN COOKIES

Preparation time: 10 minutes
Baking time: 15 minutes

Yield: 48

1 **pound salted Spanish peanuts**	3 **Tablespoons flour**
3 **egg whites, very stiffly beaten**	1 **cup sugar**

1. Grind peanuts in a food chopper.

2. Add remaining ingredients to peanuts. Stir to mix well.

3. Drop by teaspoonfuls onto greased, floured baking sheets.

4. Bake at 400° for 15 minutes.

5. Cool before storing indefinately in cardboard boxes. Do not store in a canister or cookie jar.

Accompaniment: Fruit or ice cream.

CHOCOLATE LOVER'S ULTRA CHOCOLATE COOKIES

Preparation time: 30 minutes
Baking time: 15 minutes

Yield: 36

8 **ounces semi-sweet chocolate**	1 **cup sugar**
3 **ounces unsweetened chocolate**	2 **teaspoons vanilla**
6 **Tablespoons butter**	1½ **cups semi-sweet chocolate chips**
⅓ **cup all-purpose flour**	**or ¾ cup chocolate chips,**
¼ **teaspoon baking powder**	**¾ cup white chocolate pieces**
¼ **teaspoon salt**	1 **cup walnuts, chopped**
3 **eggs**	1 **cup pecans, chopped**

1. Melt chocolates with butter in microwave (90 seconds). Cool.

2. Sift together flour, baking powder, salt. Set aside.

3. Combine eggs, sugar, vanilla in a large bowl. Beat until fluffy.

4. Add chocolate, then flour mixture to egg mixture. Beat until blended.

5. Stir in nuts, chocolate chips or chips and pieces

6. Drop by Tablespoons onto lightly greased baking sheets.

7. Bake at 350° on the center oven rack for 15 minutes.

SWEDISH CHRISTMAS COOKIES

Preparation time; 15 minutes
Baking time: 12-15 minutes

Yield: 60

2 cups butter, softened
2 cups sugar
2 egg yolks

3½ cups flour
1 teaspoon salt
2 teaspoons almond extract
Walnut or pecan halves

1. Cream butter, sugar.

2. Add egg yolks. Mix. Gradually add flour, salt, almond extract.

3. Roll into small balls, using a teaspoon of dough for each.

4. Place on ungreased baking sheets. Press a nut onto top of each ball.

5. Bake at 350° for 12-15 minutes until golden brown.

Variation: Top each with a cherry. Freeze well after baking.

SUGAR-FREE COOKIES

Preparation time: 15 minutes
Baking time: 10-12 minutes

Yield: 100

2 cups flour
2 teaspoons baking soda
1 teaspoon salt
2 cups quick oats
3 teaspoons pumpkin pie spice
2 teaspoons vanilla

2 teaspoons liquid sweetener
1 cup cooking oil
1 20-ounce can crushed pineapple, drained
4 eggs, beaten
2 cups raisins

1. Mix all together. Drop by teaspoonfuls onto cookie sheets sprayed with no-stick cooking spray.

2. Bake at 375° for 10-12 minutes.

NUTRIENT ANALYSIS (Per Cookie)
Carbohydrate ....6 grams
Protein ....1 gram
Fat ....3 grams
Calories ....51 (46% from fat)
Cholesterol ....8 milligrams
Sodium ....33 milligrams

TURTLE COOKIES

Preparation time: 45 minutes
Baking time: 20 minutes

Yield: 36

¾ cup butter or margarine, softened
⅔ cup confectioners' sugar
1 teaspoon vanilla
1¼ cups all-purpose flour
¾ cup oatmeal (quick or
  old-fashioned), uncooked
¾ cup pecans, finely chopped

¼ teaspoon salt
25 caramels
2 Tablespoons water
6 ounces or 1 cup semi-sweet
  chocolate pieces
1 Tablespoon vegetable oil

1. Beat together butter, sugar until light, fluffy.

2. Blend in vanilla.

3. Combine flour, oats, pecans, salt.

4. Add to butter mixture; mix well.

5. Shape to form 1-inch balls.

6. Bake on an ungreased cookie sheet at 325° on the center oven rack for
   20 minutes until edges are light golden brown.

7. Cool completely on a wire rack.

8. Combine caramels, water in a small, heavy saucepan. Melt over low heat, stirring
   frequently.

9. Spread or drizzle 1 teaspoon caramel sauce over each cookie.

10. Combine chocolate, oil in a small, heavy saucepan. Melt over low heat.

11. Spoon or drizzle 1 teaspoon chocolate over each cookie.

12. Refrigerate to set chocolate.

13. Store in a tightly covered container at room temperature.

Exceptional flavor, nice presentation. A great addition to a dessert table.

NEVER-FAIL PIE CRUST

Preparation time: 15 minutes   *Yield: Double crust for a 9-inch pie*

2½ cups flour
½ teaspoon salt
1 cup solid shortening (Crisco
   suggested)

1 egg, slightly beaten
½ teaspoon vinegar
3 Tablespoons cold water
Flour

1. Mix flour, salt, shortening until crumbly with a long-tined fork.

2. Add egg, vinegar, water. Mix thoroughly.

3. Use a little more flour to roll out pastry.

A first prize winner, Apple Fest 1990
Aullwood Audubon Center and Farm
Dayton, Ohio

PAT GILBERT'S APPLE PIE

Preparation time: 20 minutes   *Serves: 6-8*
Baking time: 55 minutes

1 Never-Fail Pie Crust
½ cup granulated sugar
¼ cup light brown sugar
½ teaspoon cinnamon
1 teaspoon lemon juice

4 cups McIntosh apples, peeled,
   sliced
2 Tablespoons butter or margarine
Milk
Sugar

1. Place pastry in a 9-inch pie pan.

2. Mix sugars, cinnamon, lemon juice. Sprinkle over apples. Dot with butter.

3. Let stand until sugar makes syrup. Stir well. Pour into crust.

4. Moisten edges of crust with ice water. Cover with top crust; make slits. Seal; flute edge.

5. Brush top crust lightly with milk. Sprinkle lightly with sugar.

6. Bake at 400° for 15 minutes.

7. Reduce heat to 350°. Bake for 40 minutes until brown, bubbly.

A first prize winner, Apple Fest 1990
Aullwood Audubon Center and Farm
Dayton, Ohio

ALL-AMERICAN APPLE PIE

Preparation time: 20 minutes　　　　　　　　　　　　　　*Serves: 8*
Baking time: 55 minutes

2　unbaked 10-inch pie crusts
4　cups tart apples, peeled, sliced
Ascorbic acid water
¾ cup white sugar
2　Tablespoons brown sugar
2　Tablespoons cornstarch
¼ teaspoon salt

½ teaspoon cinnamon
¼ teaspoon nutmeg
2　Tablespoons walnuts, chopped
¼ cup shredded American cheese
¼ cup corn syrup
2　Tablespoons butter
Evaporated milk
White sugar

1. Preheat oven to 400°.

2. Place sliced apples in ascorbic acid water.

3. Mix dry ingredients in a large bowl.

4. Drain apples.

5. Add apples, walnuts, cheese, corn syrup to dry ingredients.

6. Pour into pie shell. Dot with butter.

7. Moisten edge of lower crust.

8. Make several slits or a design on top crust to allow steam to escape.

9. Place top crust over apples. Seal; flute edge.

10. Brush top crust with evaporated milk. Sprinkle lightly with sugar.

11. Bake for 15 minutes.

12. Reduce heat to 350°. Bake for 40 minutes.

13. Serve warm.

As American as apple pie and cheese.

Jyl Kerr-Boné
1970 Ohio State Fair

SOUR CREAM APPLE PIE

Preparation time: 1 hour
Baking time: 40 minutes

Serves: 8

1 unbaked 9-inch pie shell
2 cups apples, peeled, finely chopped
¾ cup sugar
2 Tablespoons flour
1 egg, slightly beaten

½ teaspoon vanilla
1 cup sour cream
½ cup butter, softened
1 teaspoon cinnamon
½ cup sugar
¾ cup flour

1. Mix apples, sugar, flour; set aside.

2. Mix egg, vanilla, sour cream; add to apple mixture; mix well. Pour into pie shell.

3. Bake at 350° on the center oven rack for 30 minutes.

4. Cream together remaining ingredients for topping, using enough flour to make mixture crumbly. Cover pie with topping.

5. Bake an additional 10 minutes.

6. Serve warm or cold.

FINGER SUGAR PIE

Preparation time: 15 minutes
Baking time: 1 hour

Serves: 6-8

1 unbaked 9-inch pie shell
1¼ cups sugar
5 Tablespoons flour

1¾ cups milk
2 Tablespoons margarine
1 teaspoon cinnamon
1 teaspoon nutmeg

1. Mix sugar, flour with fingers in a pie shell taking care not to break the shell.

2. Gradually add milk; stir with fingers.

3. Dot with margarine. Sprinkle with cinnamon, nutmeg.

4. Bake at 400° on the center oven rack for 10 minutes.

5. Reduce heat to 350°. Bake for 50 minutes until pie filling just begins to bubble in middle.

A good old-fashioned pie.

STRAWBERRY LOVER'S PIE

Preparation time: 20 minutes   *Serves: 6*

1 8-inch pie shell, baked, cooled
2 ounces semi-sweet chocolate
1 Tablespoon butter
3 ounces cream cheese, softened
⅓ cup sour cream

½ teaspoon vanilla
1 quart fresh strawberries, hulled
2 Tablespoons sugar
¼ cup strawberry jam
2 Tablespoons water

1. Melt together chocolate, butter.
2. While still warm, spread evenly over bottom, sides of pie shell.
3. Refrigerate.
4. Combine cream cheese, sour cream, vanilla. Beat until smooth.
5. Spread evenly in pie shell.
6. Combine strawberries, sugar.
7. Arrange berries hulled side down over creamed filling.
8. Warm jam with enough water to make a thick syrup.
9. Spoon over berries.
10. Chill before serving.

Fruit glaze may be used instead of jam.

Strawberry Festival
Troy, Ohio

SUGAR-FREE STRAWBERRY PIE

Preparation time: 30 minutes   *Serves: 6-8*

1 9-inch pie shell, baked, cooled   2½ cups cold water
1 small box sugar-free vanilla pudding   4 cups sliced or whole fresh strawber-
   (not instant)   ries, washed, hulled
1 small box sugar-free strawberry jello   Whipped topping (optional)

1. Mix pudding, jello, water in a saucepan. Stir over medium heat until mixture comes to a full boil.

2. Cool in refrigerator until slightly thickened.

3. Arrange strawberries in pie shell.

4. Pour cooled mixture over berries.

5. Chill until set.

NUTRIENT ANALYSIS (Per Serving)

Carbohydrate .... 19 grams
Protein .... 3 grams
Fat .... 8 grams
Calories .... 154 (46% from fat)
Cholesterol .... 0 milligrams
Sodium .... 87 milligrams

STRAWBERRY-RHUBARB CREAM PIE

Preparation time: 45 minutes   *Serves: 8*
Baking time: 50-55 minutes

1   9-inch unbaked pie shell
1½ cups sugar
¼ cup flour
¾ teaspoon ground nutmeg
3   eggs, slightly beaten

2   cups fresh strawberries, sliced
2   cups fresh or frozen rhubarb, sliced
½ cup flour
¼ cup sugar
⅓ cup butter or margarine, softened

1. Stir together sugar, flour, nutmeg in a large bowl. Add eggs; blend well.

2. Gently add strawberries, rhubarb. Place mixture into pie shell.

3. Stir together remaining flour, sugar in a small bowl. Cut in butter until mixture is crumbly. Sprinkle over top of pie.

4. Wrap edges of pie with foil.

5. Bake at 400° on the center oven rack for 30 minutes.

6. Remove foil. Bake for 25 minutes.

Refrigerates well for 2 days.

PEACH PRALINE PIE

Preparation time: 30 minutes   *Serves: 6-8*
Baking time: 30 minutes

1   unbaked 9-inch pie shell
4   cups fresh peaches, sliced
¼ to ½ cup sugar
2   Tablespoons quick tapioca
1   teaspoon lemon juice

¼ cup flour
¼ cup brown sugar
½ cup pecan halves
¼ cup butter, softened

1. Combine peaches, sugar, tapioca, lemon juice. Let stand 15 minutes.

2. Combine flour, brown sugar, nuts. Cut in butter with a pastry blender.

3. Sprinkle ⅓ of flour mixture into peach mixture. Mix.

4. Pour into pie shell. Sprinkle remaining flour mixture on top.

5. Bake at 450° on the center oven rack for 10 minutes.

6. Reduce heat to 350°. Bake for 20 minutes until brown.

The amount of sugar mixed with peaches depends upon the ripeness of the fruit.

KEY LIME PIE

Preparation time: 10 minutes   *Serves: 10*
Baking time: 10 minutes

1   prepared graham cracker crust   4   ounces Key lime juice
1   can sweetened condensed milk   Dash orange bitters
4   egg yolks   1   Tablespoon dark rum
½   scant teaspoon cream of tartar   Whipped cream or sliced fruits
1   Tablespoon Grand Marnier

1.   Combine all ingredients in a blender.

2.   Blend on high until smooth. Pour into crust.

3.   Bake at 300° for 10 minutes until just set. Do not overbake.

4.   Cool slightly. Refrigerate until ready to serve.

5.   Garnish with whipped cream or fruits (kiwi, bananas) if desired.

A purchased graham cracker crust is more easily removed from the pan. If making the crust, use margarine that is soft at refrigerator temperature.

Traditional Key Lime pie is served without topping, but fruits give an interesting balance.

SOUTHERN TEXAS PECAN PIE

Preparation time: 15 minutes   *Yield: 1 pie*
Baking time: 40-50 minutes

1   unbaked 8-inch pastry shell   2   Tablespoons milk
1   cup brown sugar, firmly packed   1   teaspoon vanilla
½   cup sugar   ½   cup butter, melted
1   Tablespoon flour   1½ cups pecans, halved or chopped
2   eggs   Whipped cream or ice cream

1.   Mix both sugars, flour.

2.   Add eggs, milk, vanilla, butter. Beat well.

3.   Fold in pecans. Pour mixture into pastry shell.

4.   Bake at 375° on the center oven rack for 40-50 minutes.

5.   Serve slightly warm. Top with whipped cream or ice cream if desired.

Use only real butter.

CHOCOLATE CREAM PIE

Preparation time: 1 hour   *Serves: 6-8*

1 9-inch pie shell, baked, cooled
⅓ cup sugar
2 Tablespoons cornstarch
1 envelope unflavored gelatin
¼ teaspoon salt
2 cups milk

2 1-ounce squares baking chocolate
   or 2 ounces pre-melted chocolate
3 egg yolks, slightly beaten
3 unbeaten egg whites
1 teaspoon vanilla
⅓ cup sugar
   Whipped cream, shaved chocolate
   (optional)

1. Combine sugar, cornstarch, gelatin, salt in a saucepan. Mix thoroughly.

2. Blend in milk.

3. Add chocolate. Heat, stirring constantly until mixture thickens, comes to a boil. Remove from heat.

4. Stir a small amount of hot mixture into beaten egg yolks. Blend egg yolk mixture into hot mixture.

5. Return to heat. Bring to a boil; cook, stir 1 minute.

6. Cool 15 minutes.

7. Beat egg whites, vanilla until soft peaks form.

8. Slowly add sugar; beat until stiff peaks form.

9. Gradually fold in chocolate mixture; blend well.

10. Chill until mixture mounds slightly when spooned.

11. Pile into pastry shell.

12. Chill until firm.

13. Top with whipped cream, shaved chocolate if desired.

FUDGE PIE

Preparation time: 15 minutes   *Serves: 6-8*
Baking time: 30 minutes

1 **cup sugar**	⅓ **cup flour**
½ **cup butter, softened**	1 **teaspoon vanilla**
2 **egg yolks**	2 **egg whites**
2 **ounces unsweetened chocolate baking squares**	⅛ **teaspoon salt**
	Ice cream

1. Sift sugar.

2. Beat butter until soft.

3. Gradually add sugar to butter; blend until creamy.

4. Beat in egg yolks. Set aside.

5. Melt chocolate squares over hot water in a double boiler.

6. Cool slightly; beat into other mixture.

7. Sift flour before measuring; beat into other ingredients.

8. Add vanilla.

9. Beat egg whites, salt until stiff. Fold into batter.

10. Place batter in a greased 8½-inch glass pie plate.

11. Bake at 325° for 30 minutes.

12. Serve topped with ice cream.

Refrigerates well for 2-3 days.

REAL MEAT MINCEMEAT PIE

Preparation time: 45 minutes   *Yield: 2 pies*
Baking time: 55 minutes

2   cups ground chuck or shank beef,   1   Tablespoon cider vinegar
    cooked until tender   ½   teaspoon ground cinnamon
4   cups (3 pounds) Jonathan apples,   ¼   teaspoon ground cloves
    peeled, cored   ¼   teaspoon ground nutmeg
1   cup brown sugar   2   8-inch pie shells, tops, unbaked
2   cups apple cider   Brandy, rum, or orange juice for flavor
1   cup raisins or ½ cup raisins,   (optional)
    ½ cup currants

1. Coursely grind enough meat in a grinder to make 2 cups.

2. Grind or finely chop apples to make 4 cups.

3. Combine brown sugar, cider in a saucepan.

4. Cook raisins in brown sugar mixture until tender.

5. Add vinegar; simmer several minutes.

6. Combine raisin mixture with meat, apples, spices.

7. Refrigerate. Let stand about 1 week to allow adequate seasoning.

8. Pour into 2 8-inch pie shells.

9. If desired, add flavoring.

10. Cover with top crust, cutting slits for steam. Seal; crimp edges.

11. Bake at 400° for 10 minutes; reduce heat to 350°; bake for 45 minutes.

*Do not use hamburger. Use a grinder instead of a food processor to cut meat,
apples more evenly.*

*Refrigerates well for several weeks. May also be frozen ahead before baking. Add ½ hour
to baking time for frozen pies.*

Accompaniment: Hard sauce.

PEAR TORTE

Preparation time: 15 minutes
Baking time: 35 minutes

Serves: 10-12

Crust

½ cup butter, softened
⅓ cup sugar

½ teaspoon vanilla
⅔ cup nuts, finely chopped
¾ cup flour

Filling

8 ounces cream cheese, softened
1 egg
¼ cup sugar

½ teaspoon vanilla
2 to 3 ripe fresh pears, pared, thinly sliced, or canned pears, drained

Topping

1 teaspoon sugar

½ teaspoon cinnamon

1. Blend butter, sugar, vanilla.
2. Combine nuts, flour. Add to butter mixture.
3. Press into an 11-inch tart pan.
4. Bake at 350° for 10 minutes. Cool.
5. Blend all filling ingredients, except pears. Spread on cooled crust.
6. Arrange pears over cream cheese mixture.
7. Combine topping ingredients. Sprinkle over top.
8. Bake at 375° for 25 minutes.
9. Chill before serving.

SPICED PEACHES WITH NUTTY DUMPLINGS

Preparation time: 15-20 minutes   *Serves: 4*

½ cup flour
1 teaspoon baking powder
¼ teaspoon salt
¼ cup sugar, divided
2 Tablespoons pecans toasted, chopped

¼ cup skim milk
⅛ teaspoon butter flavoring
2 cups fresh peaches, sliced
⅔ cup unsweetened white grape juice
¼ teaspoon apple pie spice

1. Combine flour, baking powder, salt, 2 Tablespoons sugar, pecans.

2. Stir in milk, butter flavoring. Set aside.

3. Combine remaining ingredients with 2 Tablespoons sugar in a saucepan. Stir well; bring to a boil.

4. Drop ¼ of the batter at a time into the boiling peach mixture.

5. Cover; cook over medium heat 10-12 minutes.

A low-fat, no cholesterol dessert.

ESCALLOPED FRESH RHUBARB

Preparation time: 15 minutes   *Serves: 6*
Baking time: 1 hour

4 cups fresh rhubarb, washed, trimmed, cut into 1-inch pieces
1 cup sugar, divided

3 cups day-old white bread, cut into ½-inch cubes
2 Tablespoons butter
2 Tablespoons water

1. Mix rhubarb with ½ cup sugar. Place in a well-greased 8x8-inch baking dish.

2. Mix bread cubes with remaining sugar; place over rhubarb.

3. Dot with butter; sprinkle water over all.

4. Bake at 325° on the center oven rack for 1 hour.

5. Serve at room tempoerature or slightly warm.

Use a firm white bread (Pepperidge Farm suggested) for best results.

Served 40 years ago in The Rike-Kumler Company dining room as a main dish accompaniment and also on the vegetable plate.

FRUIT TRIFLE

Preparation time: 1 hour
Cooking time: 6-7 minutes

Serves: 10-12

2 cups milk
4 egg yolks
½ cup sugar
3 Tablespoons cornstarch
¼ teaspoon salt
2 Tablespoons butter
1 teaspoon vanilla
1 16-ounce pound cake, cut into ½-inch slices
½ cup cream sherry or rum

1 pound fresh strawberries, sliced
2 bananas (2 cups), peeled, sliced
1 11-ounce can mandarin orange sections, drained
2 kiwis, peeled, sliced
1 cup heavy cream, whipped to soft peak stage
2 Tablespoons powdered sugar
Whole strawberries, mint sprigs for garnish

1. Combine first 5 ingredients in a food processor or blender; mix well.

2. Pour into a medium-sized glass bowl.

3. Microwave on high 6-7 minutes until thick, stirring halfway through cooking time.

4. Whisk in butter, vanilla.

5. Cover. Refrigerate until softly set.

6. Brush cake slices generously with sherry or rum.

7. Arrange half of slices in a single layer in trifle or other deep bowl.

8. Layer half of fruits. Spoon half of custard over fruits.

9. Repeat layering with remaining cake, fruits, custard.

10. Gradually beat powdered sugar into whipped cream; beat until stiff.

11. Spoon or pipe whipped cream mixture over top of trifle.

12. Garnish with strawberries, mint sprigs. Chill until ready to serve.

Variation: Substitute instant vanilla pudding and whipped topping for custard and whipped cream if in a hurry.

PAVLOVA

Preparation time: 20 minutes   *Serves: 8*
Baking time: 1½ hours

4 **egg whites, at room temperature**   1 **teaspoon vinegar**
Pinch salt   1 **Tablespoon cornstarch, sifted**
1 **cup sugar**   1 **cup heavy cream, whipped**
½ **teaspoon vanilla**   2 **cups fresh fruit – kiwis,**
                                              strawberries, blueberries

1. Preheat oven to 400°.

2. Beat egg whites with salt until almost stiff.

3. Gradually add sugar, vanilla, vinegar. Beat until stiff.

4. Lightly fold in cornstarch.

5. Place evenly in a dampened 9-inch ovenware pie plate.

6. Using a spatula, make sides slightly higher than center.

7. Place in oven.

8. Immediately reduce heat to 250°. Bake undisturbed for 1½ hours.

9. Cool.

10. Cover with whipped cream. Decorate with fruit.

A variation of the New Zealand national dessert.

FRUIT DIP

Preparation time: 5 minutes   *Yield: 1½ cups*

7 ounces marshmallow creme   2 **Tablespoons orange juice**
8 ounces cream cheese, softened   2 **Tablespoons orange rind, grated**

1. Mix all ingredients.

2. Serve at room temperature.

May be made ahead and refrigerated.

Very attractive placed in a cup and surrounded with assorted fresh fruits on a platter.

PUMPKIN AND CREAM CHEESE ROLL-UP

Preparation time: 45 minutes   *Serves: 12*
Baking time: 15 minutes

¾ cup sifted all-purpose flour
1 teaspoon baking powder
2 teaspoons cinnamon
1 teaspoon pumpkin pie spice
½ teaspoon nutmeg

½ teaspoon salt
3 eggs
1 cup sugar
⅔ cup canned solid-pack pumpkin
1 cup black walnuts, chopped
1 cup confectioners' sugar, sifted

Cream Cheese Filling

8 ounces cream cheese, softened
6 Tablespoons butter or margarine, softened

1 teaspoon vanilla

1. Preheat oven to 375°.

2. Grease a 15x10x1-inch jelly roll pan. Line with waxed paper. Grease, flour the waxed paper.

3. Sift together first 6 ingredients.

4. Beat eggs with sugar in a large bowl until thick, fluffy.

5. Beat in pumpkin.

6. Stir sifted ingredients into pumpkin mixture.

7. Spread evenly in prepared pan. Sprinkle with walnuts.

8. Bake for 15 minutes until center springs back when lightly touched.

9. Loosen cake edges with a knife. Invert onto a clean, damp towel dusted with confectioners' sugar. Peel off waxed paper.

10. Using the towel, roll up cake from short side.

11. Place cake seam side down. Cool completely.

12. While cake cools, combine filling ingredients. Beat until smooth.

13. Unroll cake. Spread with filling. Roll up cake again.

14. Refrigerate until ready to serve.

Refrigerates and freezes well.

Black Walnut Festival
Camden, Ohio

BOCCONE DOLCE (SWEET MOUTHFUL)

Preparation time: 30 minutes   *Serves: 8*
Baking time: 20-25 minutes

Meringue

4 egg whites   ¼ teaspoon cream of tartar
Pinch salt   1 cup sugar

Filling

6 ounces semi-sweet chocolate   3 cups heavy cream, whipped until
3 Tablespoons water   stiff
⅓ cup sugar   1 pint fresh strawberries, sliced

1. Preheat oven to 250°.

2. Beat egg whites, salt, cream of tartar until stiff.

3. Gradually beat in sugar; beat until stiff, glossy.

4. Line baking sheets with waxed paper. Trace 3 circles, each 8 inches in diameter, on the paper.

5. Spread meringue ¼ inch thick evenly over each circle.

6. Bake for 20-25 minutes until pale gold, still pliable.

7. Remove from oven; carefully peel paper from bottoms.

8. Place meringues on cake racks to dry.

9. Melt chocolate with water.

10. Gradually add sugar to whipped cream. Beat until very stiff.

11. Place 1 meringue layer on a serving plate.

12. Spread with a thin coating of melted chocolate.

13. Spread with a ¾-inch layer of whipped cream.

14. Top with sliced strawberries.

15. Place a second meringue layer over berries.

16. Repeat chocolate, whipped cream, strawberry layers.

17. Top with third layer of meringue.

18. Frost sides, top with whipped cream. Top with strawberries.

19. Refrigerate 2 hours before cutting into wedges to serve.

ITALIAN MERINGUE TORTE WITH AMARETTO CREAM SAUCE

Preparation time: 30 minutes + refrigeration   *Serves: 8*
Baking time: 1½ hours

Torte

4 egg whites, at room temperature
½ teaspoon cream of tartar

1 cup sugar
1 teaspoon vanilla extract

Filling

1 teaspoon instant coffee
4 Tablespoons coffee liqueur

2 cups heavy cream, whipped,
   slightly sweetened with sugar
1 10-ounce semi-sweet chocolate
   bar, coarsely chopped

Amaretto Cream Sauce

1½ cups vanilla ice cream

4 Tablespoons amaretto

1. Preheat oven to 250°.
2. Beat egg whites with cream of tartar until frothy.
3. Continue beating, adding 1 Tablespoon sugar every minute until all sugar is incorporated. Add vanilla; beat 2 minutes until egg whites hold very stiff peaks.
4. Butter, flour 2 baking sheets. Trace an 8-inch circle on each sheet.
5. Spoon meringue evenly onto circles.
6. Using a spatula, make decorative swirls on top of 1 circle. Bake for 1½ hours.
7. Turn off heat. Leave meringues in closed oven 3-4 hours to dry.
8. Remove from oven. Flex bottoms of baking sheets to loosen meringues. Leave on pans until cooled to room temperature.
9. Blend coffee, coffee liqueur. Add to whipped cream. Fold in chocolate.
10. Place plain meringue on a serving platter.
11. Spread whipped cream mixture evenly over top. Top with decorative meringue.
12. Refrigerate 8 hours or overnight.
13. Soften ice cream. Add amaretto. Serve sauce in a small pitcher.

Torte and filling keep well if prepared a day ahead.

RUM BISQUE

Preparation time: 20 minutes   *Serves: 8*

1   cup milk
1   teaspoon gelatin
2   Tablespoons cold milk
2   egg yolks, beaten

½   cup sugar
½   pint heavy cream, whipped
3   Tablespoons rum to taste
    Crumbled macaroons or
        shaved chocolate

1. Scald milk in a double boiler.

2. Dissolve gelatin in cold milk.

3. Combine beaten egg yolks, sugar.

4. Place gelatin, egg yolk mixtures in scalded milk. Cook until thickened. Cool.

5. Fold whipped cream into mixture.

6. Flavor with rum. Serve in stemmed dessert glasses.

8. Garnish with crumbled macaroons or shaved chocolate.

ZESTY BLUEBERRY-ORANGE SAUCE

Preparation time: 40 minutes   *Yield: 1¾ cups*

1½ cups fresh or frozen (thawed)
       blueberries
⅛   cup sugar
1   Tablespoon orange juice concentrate

½   teaspoon lemon peel, grated
2   Tablespoons orange marmalade
⅓   cup blueberries

1. In a food processor, add together blueberries, sugar, juice concentrate. Process 45 seconds.

2. Transfer mixture to a saucepan; bring to a boil.

3. Reduce heat; simmer 10 minutes, stirring occasionally. Remove from heat.

4. Stir in lemon peel, marmalade. Cool.

5. Gently stir in blueberries.

May be prepared 3 days ahead.

Accompaniments: Ice cream, berries, shortcake, or white chocolate mousse. Also delicious on waffles or pancakes for weekend breakfasts.

DELICIOUS HOT OR COLD FUDGE SAUCE

Preparation time: 20 minutes   *Yield: 2 cups*

5   squares unsweetened chocolate   3   cups confectioners' sugar
½   cup butter   1   12-ounce can evaporated milk
                                           1¼ teaspoons vanilla

1.   Combine chocolate, butter in a saucepan. Melt over low heat. Remove from heat.
2.   Mix in sugar alternately with milk.
3.   Return to medium heat. Bring to a boil, stirring constantly.
4.   Cook, stir at least 10 minutes until thick, creamy. Remove from heat.
5.   Stir in vanilla.
6.   Serve warm as a creamy, smooth sauce or cold as a creamy solid.

Do not use margarine as a substitute for butter.
Accompaniment: Vanilla ice cream rolled in chopped pecans.

PECAN-CARAMEL TOPPING

Preparation time: 15 minutes   *Yield: 1¾ cups*

¼   cup margarine   1   cup brown sugar, firmly packed
½   cup pecans, chopped   1   cup heavy cream

1.   Combine margarine, pecans in a medium saucepan.
2.   Cook, stir 5 minutes over medium heat until pecans are toasted, margarine is light brown.
3.   Stir in sugar, heavy cream.
4.   Bring just to a boil over low heat, stirring constantly.
5.   Simmer uncovered 2 minutes.
6.   Cool slightly. Serve over ice cream or warm coffee cake.

TIPS ON SWEETS

(From Our Good Cooks!)

To prevent pastry from absorbing any liquid, bake pie immediately after assembling.

Shake salt into spillovers from juicy fruit pies. Spills will burn to a crisp and are easily scraped up with a spatula.

To help prevent cracks in cheesecakes, avoid overbeating batter after adding eggs and do not open oven door during the first 30 minutes of baking. After removing from oven, carefully loosen cake from sides of spring form pan to allow it to contract freely when cooling. Cool away from drafts.

For a perfect meringue, add a teaspoonful of cornstarch to the sugar before beating it into the egg whites.

Cut a meringue cleanly by using a knife coated with butter.

To eliminate sticking, cover a meringue pie with waxed paper or plastic wrap which has been coated with margarine.

A sliced apple placed in the container will keep brown sugar soft.

If brown sugar hardens, use a grater to obtain the amount needed.

A slice of soft bread placed in a package of hardened brown sugar will soften it in a couple of hours.

A dip of the spoon or measuring cup into hot water before measuring shortening, butter, or margarine will cause it to slip out easily without sticking.

Grate a stick of butter for quick softening.

Save soupy whipped cream by adding an egg white, then chilling thoroughly. Rebeat.

Add a few drops of lemon juice to whipping cream for faster, better whipping.

Add ¼ teaspoonful gelatin per cup of cream to prevent cream whipped ahead of time from separating.

Sugar may be reduced at least ⅓ in baked goods without affecting the final product.

Middletown, Ohio

For three days each October, Middletown, Ohio takes on an exotic look and feel as the City Centre Plaza is transformed into a microcosm of a single foreign country. The event is *Middfest International*, the culmination of a year-long educational program. The aura, excitement, and dignity of Middfest distinguish it as a unique exchange of ideas and cultural pursuits. This is not an event to merely witness. This is an event to experience!

Middfest International, sponsored by the Middfest International Foundation, was first held in 1981 when Luxembourg was the featured country. Its mission to promote world understanding, friendship, and peace – one country at a time – is accomplished by allowing the guest country to tell its own story through art, dance, music, food, crafts, and cultural exhibits.

Government officials, artisans, and dignitaries of the guest country present programs, conduct workshops, and hold lectures. They share insights regarding business, industry, and trade at the Middfest business conference. Schools and universities in the Middletown area and beyond participate in various educational projects and benefit from the teaching materials developed by *Middfest International*.

Area gourmands have delighted in the changes in local cuisine. Since its earliest days, Middfest has prompted a noticeable addition of ethnic foods to the menus of area restaurants. Esoteric spices and exotic vegetables and fruits are now readily available in many local groceries.

Attracting well over 100,000 visitors each year, *Middfest International* has featured neighboring countries such as Mexico, and Canada; European countries such as Italy, Switzerland and Ireland; and ancient cultures such as Egypt and Japan.

Lagniappe

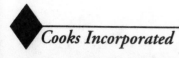

Cooks Incorporated

MODIFYING RECIPES FOR FLAVOR AND GOOD HEALTH

A healthy diet consists of a healthful balance of foods. The usual notion that all great tasting foods are not good for one is just not true. Achieving a healthful balance is as simple as making wise, lower fat, higher nutrition choices. Preparation tips will help with these choices.

Broiling and steaming are two methods for low-fat, low-calorie cooking. For sautéing, use small amounts of broth instead of oil. A minimum of oil or butter or, better still, a non-stick vegetable spray works well for stir-frying. Roast meat on a rack so that fats can drip away. Fish and chicken are delicious when poached in broth, tomato juice or water. Microwave with a minimum of fat.

Low-fat taste enhancers include flavored extracts, vinegars and salsas, as well as grated orange and lemon rind. Sugar-free fruit spreads are flavorful toppings for waffles and pancakes. The new oil-free salad dressings make wonderful meat marinades. Use whipped instead of stick margarine, except in baking.

The following chart is a guide to modifying recipes for decreased cholesterol and saturated fat:

If recipe ingredient is:	Then Substitute:
1 egg yolk	1 egg white (batters, entrées) or 1 egg white + 2 tsp. oil (baking)
1 whole egg	¼ cup commercial egg substitute or 2 egg whites
1 cup butter or hydrogenated shortening	1 cup margarine
1 cup butter	1 cup soft margarine
1 cup buttermilk	1 Tbsp. lemon juice or vinegar and skim milk to make 1 cup
1 cup light cream	1 cup evaporated skim milk
1 cup sour cream	1 cup low fat or non-fat cottage cheese or 1 cup non-fat plain yogurt
1 oz. (1 square) baking chocolate	3 Tbsp. powdered cocoa & 1 Tbsp. allowed oil
1 cup thin white sauce	½ Tbsp. allowed oil, 1 Tbsp. flour, 1 cup skim milk, ½ tsp. salt, dash white pepper
1 cup medium white sauce	1 Tbsp. allowed oil, 2 Tbsp. flour, 1 cup skim milk, ½ tsp. salt, dash white pepper

Nutritional information was supplied by Miami Valley Hospital's Nutritional Services Department through the efforts of Natalie Fuller, a registered, licensed clinical dietician.

SHAKE THE SALT HABIT

Sodium is needed by the body in small amounts, but most people consume too much. This can be harmful. Reducing the amount of sodium in your diet does not mean sacrificing flavor. Use spices instead of salt in your shaker. Seasoning with herbs and spices will enhance your favorite recipes. Use your imagination, experiment, have fun. The following is a seasoning guide for various foods. Begin with small amounts.

BREADS .... caraway, cardamom, cinnamon, dill, garlic, marjoram, poppy seed, saffron, sesame

ENTREES

Poultry: .... bay leaves, curry, ginger, marjoram, oregano, paprika, rosemary, sage, saffron, savory, tarragon, thyme

Fish: .... allspice, bay leaves, curry, marjoram, dry mustard, oregano, paprika, sage, savory, tarragon, thyme

Beef: .... allspice, basil, bay leaves, caraway seed, chili powder, cumin, ginger, mace, marjoram, oregano, paprika, rosemary, savory, tarragon, thyme

Pork: .... bay leaves, caraway seed, chili powder, cloves, curry, marjoram, oregano, rosemary, sage, thyme

Lamb: .... allspice, basil, bay leaves, curry, dill, ginger, marjoram, mint, oregano, rosemary, savory, thyme

Veal: .... bay leaves, ginger, mace, marjoram, mint, oregano, rosemary, savory, thyme

Eggs: .... basil, chervil, chili powder, cumin, curry, dill, dry mustard, marjoram, paprika, pepper, rosemary, savory, tarragon, thyme

Pasta & Rice .... caraway, cumin, dry mustard, oregano, poppy seed, saffron, savory, sesame

SALADS & DRESSINGS

Potato Salads: .... caraway, celery seed, cumin, curry, dill, dry mustard, paprika

Fruit Salads: .... anise, mint

Dressings: .... celery seed, dill, garlic, ginger, paprika, turmeric

SOUPS .... bay leaves, sage

VEGETABLES

Artichokes: .... bay leaves, thyme

Asparagus: .... caraway seed, dry mustard, sesame seed, tarragon

Green Beans: .... basil, bay leaves, curry, dill, dry mustard, marjoram, oregano, savory, sesame seed, tarragon, thyme

Lima Beans: .... chili powder, curry, oregano, sage

Baked Beans: .... cloves, ginger, oregano

Beets: .... allspice, bay leaves, caraway seed, cloves, ginger, nutmeg, savory, tarragon, thyme

Broccoli: .... caraway seed, dry mustard, oregano

Brussel Sprouts: ..... caraway seed, dry mustard, nutmeg, sage

Cabbage: .... allspice, basil, caraway seed, dill, dry mustard, fennel, nutmeg, oregano, savory, tarragon

Carrots: .... allspice, bay leaves, caraway seed, chives, curry, dill, ginger, mace, marjoram, mint, nutmeg, savory, tarragon, thyme

Cauliflower: .... caraway seed, chili powder, curry, dill, dry mustard, fennel, nutmeg, oregano, savory, tarragon

Corn: .... chili powder, chives

Eggplant: .... allspice, basil, bay leaves, chili powder, marjoram, sage, thyme

Mushrooms: .... rosemary, tarragon, thyme

Onions: .... basil, bay leaves, caraway seed, chili powder, curry, ginger, dry mustard, nutmeg, oregano, sage, thyme

Peas: .... basil, chili powder, dill, marjoram, mint, dry mustard, oregano, rosemary, sage

Potatoes, White: .... basil, bay leaves, caraway seed, chives, dill, mace, mustard, oregano, rosemary, savory, sesame seed, thyme

Potatoes, Sweet: ..... allspice, cardamom, cinnamon, cloves, ginger, nutmeg

Spinach: .... allspice, basil, cinnamon, dill, mace, marjoram, nutmeg, oregano, rosemary, sesame seed

Squash, Summer: ... basil, bay leaves, mace, marjoram, mustard, rosemary

Squash, Winter: ..... allspice, basil, cinnamon, cloves, ginger, nutmeg

Tomatoes: .... basil, bay leaves, caraway seed, curry, dill, oregano, rosemary, sage, sesame seed, thyme

Turnips: .... allspice, caraway seed, dill, oregano

SWEETS

Baked Goods: .... cardamom, cinnamon, fennel, flavored extract, mace, mint, nutmeg, saffron, sesame

Fruit Desserts: .... cardamom, cinnamon, mint, nutmeg

ALL ABOUT WINES

Morley Safer and CBS' *Sixty Minutes* made an interesting observation in a 1991 television piece titled "The French Paradox". The feature compared the French male's diet with his American counterpart's, and hypothesized that alcohol in moderation (in this particular example, red wine) has a positive medical result. Who knows? Those of us in the wine trade have believed for years that wine adds something very special to any meal. It makes almost any meal an occasion and creates a mood and an ambiance that is lacking when absent.

Traditions of red wine with red meat and white wines with fish or fowl are sound—the results of centuries of experiment. Delicate, dry white wine will be overwhelmed by a beef stew or roast just as heavier, more robust Bordeaux would overpower the delicate flavor of a lemon sole dish. When more than one type of wine is to be served with a meal, serve the lighter wines: Sauvignon Blanc with the appetizer, Cabernet Sauvignon with the filet mignon.

Use of correct glassware for the wine is an important element. A good all-purpose wine glass is a clear-stemmed six to nine ounce glass. (For sparkling white wines, a taller, tapered bowl glass is best. Champagne is served in flute glasses to confine the bubbles so that they last longer.) All wines should be served in three to five-ounce servings, except for dessert and áperitif wines which should have two to three ounces per glass. If more than one wine is to be served, the glass for the first wine is placed farthest to the right. No more than three wine glasses should be in front of each guest at any one time.

Just as you care for your other investments, you must be alert to the needs of wine. All bottles of wine should be laid down to keep the corks moist and prohibit air from coming in contact with the wine. The temperature must remain as constant as possible, the ideal range being between 50-55 degrees F. Guard against frequent disturbances. Store your sparkling wines nearest the floor, next the still whites, and on top, the reds.

All wines have optimum life expectancy. White wines should be consumed young; two to three years is ideal, although the great wines last longer. Red wines remain sound up to ten years or longer, depending upon many factors. In some cases, older red wines may throw some sediment. Should this occur, the wine can be decanted through a fine cheesecloth, leaving the sediment behind and the wine available for consumption.

SERVING TEMPERATURES

Champagne and Asti Spumante	35 Degrees F.	One hour in cracked ice water or in refrigerator
White and Blush Wines	50 Degrees F.	One-half hour in cracked ice water or one hour in refrigerator
Red Wines	70 Degrees F.	Stand bottle up 1 to 2 hours before serving

Below is a limited list of wines and the foods they marry most successfully:

Food	American Wines	Imported Wines
		France
Steaks, Roasts,	Cabernet Sauvignon	Bordeaux:
Stews, Game, Pasta,	Zinfandel	St. Emilion
Casseroles	Merlot	Medoc
	Pinot Noir	Chateau - Lafite
	Gamay Beaujolais	Rothschild
		Meyney
		Talbot
		Petrus
		Burgundy:
		Beaujolais
		Pommard
		Spain
		Rioja
		Chile
		Cabernet Sauvignon
		Italy
		Barolo
		Australia
		Shiraz
		France
Ham, Pork, Lamb,	White Zinfandel	Tavel Rosé
Veal, Poultry	Pinot Noir Blanc	Cabernet Blanc
	Rosé	
	Rosé of Cabernet	
	White Grenache	
		France
Poultry, Soups,	Chardonnay	Pouilly Fusse
Fish, Shellfish,	Sauvignon Blanc	Vouvray
Fruit	Fume Blanc	Muscadet
	Chenin Blanc	Pouilly Fume
	French Colombard	Bordeaux Blanc
	Gewürztraminer	Groves
	Chablis	

Food	American Wines	Imported Wines
Poultry, Soups Fish, Shellfish, Fruit		**German** Rieslings
		Alsace Pinot Blanc Gewürztraminer
		Italy Chardonnay Pinot Grigio
		Portugal Vintage Port
Fruits, Nuts, Cheese, Cake, Cookies	Dessert Wines Port Cream Sherry	**Spain** Amontillado Sherry Cream Sherry

COOKING WITH WINE

Just as a bottle of wine lends elegance and festivity to a meal, cooking with wine adds a flavor and character to certain dishes that couldn't be achieved otherwise. Seasonings provide flavors that may overpower the flavor of the food; wine, on the other hand, brings out the basic food flavors and blends them with its own flavor. In cooking, as in drinking, whites go better with fish and chicken and reds with meats and game.

Information on wines was supplied by Heidelberg Distributing Company through the efforts of Vail K. Miller.

A CALENDAR OF FUN

Menus for a Festive Year – All recipes are included in the book.

January – A Tex-Mex Super Bowl Party

Cowboy Caviar
Tortilla Chips and Crackers,
Quesadillas
Mexican Cheese Dip

Fajitas

Make-Your-Own Sundaes with
Pecan Caramel Topping
Delicious Hot or Cold Fudge Sauce

February – Just for Fun Supper

Dayton's Best Black Bean Soup
Beau Monde Bread

Spinach-Pine Nut Salad

Rich Lemon Bars

March – Shamrocks and Shanks

Cabbage Soup

Easy Lamb Shanks
Party Potatoes
Jeannette's Carrots and Grapes
Old World Bread

Spiced Peaches

April – April Shower

Salute to Asparagus
Parmesan Bread Sticks

Cobb Salad
Luncheon Dinner Rolls

Imperial Crown Cake

May – Derby Day

Bleu Cheese-Vidalia Sandwiches

Elegant Shrimp, Chicken, and Artichoke
Casserole
Wild Rice Casserole
Balsamic Fruit and Avocado Salad
Dill Rye Bread

Pear Torte

June – Goin' Fishin'

Shrimp in Foil
Cashew and Green Pea Salad
Busy Day Biscuits

Turtle Cookies

July – 4th of July Pool Party

Jim's Popcorn
Roquefort Cheese Ball & Crackers

Pork Barbeque with buns
Old Fashioned Potato Salad
Smoked Mozzarella and Tomato Salad

4th of July Fudge Cake

August – Block Party

Golden Chicken Nuggets
Salsa, The Real Thing & Taco Chips

Nick's Greek Salad Supreme
Couscous Salad

Young Mother's Chicken
Best Lasagna, Basil Pesto with Pasta

Fruit Dip with Fresh Apples
Apricot Bars
Dream Pecan Squares
Brown Sugar Oatmeal Cookies

September – Get Well Dinner

Get Well Soup
Honey of a Whole Wheat Bread

7-Up or Tea

October – Spook Dinner

Pizza Party
Carrot and Celery Sticks

Chewy Peanut Butter Brownies

November - Tailgate Party

Cheddar Cheese Chowder
First-Prize Cornbread
Marinated Vegetable Medley

Pumpkin Walnut Cookies

December - Christmas Breakfast

Christmas Quiche
Overnight Cinnamon Rolls
Fresh Fruit

THE BEST OF THE BEST
TASTERS' CHOICES

Cowboy Caviar
Salsa, The Real Thing
Warm Brie With Winter Fruit
Carrot and Orange Soup
Dayton's Best Black Bean Soup
Gazpacho Soup
Peking Hot and Sour Soup
Baked Goat Cheese and Salad
Broccoli Salad with Raisins and Pine Nuts
Celebration Muffins
Cranberry Sour Cream Coffee Cake
Old World Bread
Michelle's Stuffed Shells
Asparagus Quiche
Beer Duck
Elegant Shrimp, Chicken, and Artichoke
Casserole

Herb Roasted Salmon
Shrimp In Foil
Brisket With Vegetables
Cranberry Meat Balls
Celestial Roast Loin of Pork
Veal Scaloppine With Asparagus
Asparagus Timbales
Cynthia's Cynful Scalloped Potatoes
Fred's Spinach
Delicious Hot or Cold Fudge Sauce
Escalloped Fresh Rhubarb
Key Lime Pie
Pear Torte
Real Meat Mincement Pie
Rich Lemon Bars
Strawberry-Rhubarb Pie

SPECIAL PEOPLE

Projects such as *Cooks Incorporated* always tap the talents and generosity of special people. On these next few pages, we salute everyone who gave time, talents, or treasures.

Dayton Emergency Specialists, Inc.
Heidelberg Distributing Company, Vail K. Miller, President
Miami Valley Hospital Department of Nutritional Services

"Civilized man can not live without cooks" –
So said a poet named Lytton.
But even cooks have to study in books,
Lest the one who dines be smitten.

So if it's a cook you would aim to be
I suggest you get on the ball;
As a devotee go to library,
Before entering dining hall.

There you will find, in a splendid array,
The volumes given to eating;
Needless to say they will show you the way
To do the mixing and beating.

Now all that you need to master the art
Is to get into the notion
That there is one part, which only the heart
Can set into proper motion:

And that is your love for the ones who eat
Your culinary invention,
So that as they eat you give them a treat
Far beyond all comprehension.

by William C. Zimmann
Former Board Member
Miami Valley Hospital

COOKS INCORPORATED COMMITTEE

Sara Rich, Co-Chair
Wendy Scholl, Co-Chair
Marjorie Adler, Marketing Co-Chair
Carol Dickerson, Testing Committee Chair
  and Marketing Co-Chair
Lynne Irwin, Co-Treasurer

Jane Porter, Editor
Georgie Woessner, Co-Treasurer
Martha Bastian, Miami Valley Health
  Foundation Staff Liason
Jeanne Eickman, Miami Valley Health
  Foundation President

Maurine Britt	Jeanie Henry	Fern Perrett	Linda Snyder
Sharon Cook	Trish Herbert	Emile Pittman	Virgina Stacy
Jane Corbly	Marge Hicks	Alberta Richardson	Alloweese
Susan Craig	Macy Janney	Alice	Theobald
Mrs. Ernest Fox	Lou Mason	Roedersheimer	Nicoletta Thompson
Mary Kay Feller	Betty Meininger	Chris Saunders	Dawn Treadwell
Annie Garretson	Suzanne Millard	Billi Schmidt	Gwen Troha
Julia Garretson	Terri Miller	Suzanne	Evan Valassiades
Virginia Grice	Ruth Newton	Schneiderman	Mary VanderKaay
Joan Hardy	Nancy Pacenta	Betty Schroeder	Barbara Winslow

OUR GOOD COOKS

Our thanks go to the following people who submitted or tested recipes (or both!) for *Cooks Incorporated*. Over 1000 recipes were submitted for consideration. Each recipe selected for this volume was tested and tasted by dedicated volunteers. They enjoyed a lot of good eating!

Melissa Adams
Peggy Adams
Marti Adler
Georgia Afendoules
Helen Allen
Jean Allen
Sue Allenson
Christine Alley
Mary Lou Amendt
Cathy Anderson
Nancy Anderson
Appalachian Festival,
 Elizabeth Herald
Aullwood Audubon Center
 and Farm's Apple Fest
Mrs. Margaret Atwater
Peggy Babcock
Sarah Burnap Bahner
Marilyn M. Baker
Patti Ballard
Saralynn Barnes
Jean Barre
Charlotte Bastian
Martha Bastian
Suzanne Batista
Nancy Bauman
Pat Beals
Mrs. W.E. Beavers
Mary Becker
Emily Becraft
Benham's Catering,
 Becky Howser
Sue Bennington
Jon F. Berges
Pat Berges
Elizabeth Bertschy
Terry Bevis

Sandy Bicker
Susan Black
Mrs. Charles D. Boehme
Sara B. Bohner
Patty Bonanno
Denise Borns
Kathy Bossong
R. Bowman
Hazel A. Boyd
Mrs. Frederick Brady
Carol Breitenbach
Doris Brennan
Amy Brereton
Helen Brickley
Maurine Britt
Corrine Broad
Olive Brubaker
Sally Bruggeman
Oleta Bruner
Ann Buck
Betty Buchsieb
Helen Buckley
Louann Buquor
Cindy Burt
Barbara Bush
Mary Buttino
Mary Bystrek
Caesar's Creek Pioneer
 Village
Mr. & Mrs. Gordon
 Callihan
Marlene Carlile
Connie Carmichael
Marlene S. Carne
Helen Carrell
Jeanne Carroll
Marilyn Casebere

Cedar Ridge, Linda L.
 Colby
Ruth Chandler
Karen Chelle
Dedra L. Chinn
Helen Clemens
Karen S. Clemens
Susan Clift
Betty Cobb
Phyllis Cochran
Linda L. Colby
Marti Cole
Phyllis Colglazier
Helen Colley
Joan Collins
Leslie Collins
Jane Conrad
Judy Cook
Sharon Cook
Jane Corbly
Linda Coyne
Susan Craig
Priscilla Craine
Betty Cunningham
Current Cuisine
Marge Daher
Dam Fest
Dayton Marriot, John
 Hausdorf/Dorothy
 Yarbrough
Dayton Racquet Club,
 Jason Layman
Dayton Woman's Club
Jeri Deaton
Joan DeLon
Peggy Demar
Pam Denka

Heather Denlinger
Rosemarie Dennehy
Carol Dickerson
Pat Diefenderfer
Kathy Dimlich
A. Louise Dinsley
George DiPaolo,
 DiPaolo's Restaurant
Shirley Docken
Betty Doench
Diana Doench
Mrs. James H. Doench
Mary Donnelly
Dorothy Lane Market
Loretta Dreyer
Adele Driskell
Sonja Durkee
Mrs. Daniel Duval
Mrs. Harry (Martha) Ebeling
Edgewick's Catering, Lou
 Ann Henry
Jeanne Eickman
Dottie Eisenhauer
Chef Katherine Emmenegger
Mary Lou Eppers
Sandra Ettmueller
Dorothy Evans
Fairborn Sweet Corn
 Festival, Mildred Stansbury
Evelyn Fallon
Mary Kay Feller
Gerri Finlan
Bonnie Fischer
Sue Fitzsimons
Anne W. Fosnaught
Helen Fox

Ft. Hamilton-Hughes
Hospital, Karen Kuhn
Doris Gaffney
Gahanna Herb Days, Marian
Harris, Director
Galactic Baking Co., Barbara
Taylor
Paula Gambill
Gloria Gaylor
Patsy Gerlinger
German Picnic in the Park,
Wanda Wiedman
Cindy Gesme
Pat Gilbert
Sandy Gillen
Julie Gilvary
Irene Glass
Anne Marie Goode
Cindy W. Gore
Judy Gottman
Cindy Goubeaux
Barbara Graeff
Dorothy Gray
Greek Festival, Evan
Valassiades
Mrs. John B. Greene
Virginia Grice
Marcia Ann Grimmer
Susan Groen
Sandy Gurnick
Ms. K. Guthrie
Paulie Hadlock
Hafle Vineyards Winery, Scott
Hailey
Mary Ellen Hagan
Scott Hailey
Jane Hall
Joan Hardy
Donna Harte
Marcia Hartmann
Cheryl Ross Hartshorn
Jan Haslar
Diana Hausfeld
Andrew C. Hawk, M.D.
Sandi Heffley
Care Heller-Pittman
Sue Hendricks

Trish Herbert
Virginia Hering
Mrs. Fred Hess
Marge Hicks
Evelyn L. Hill
Nancy Hines
Mrs. Ernest T. Hix
Lois Hoffman
Pat Holbrook
Carol J. Holm
Millie Homan
Mary Houpis
Millie Howard
Jan Hunn
Jean Hunsaker
Bobbi Hutchins
Mary Hutchison
Lynne Irwin
Betty Jackson
Charma Jackson
Jackson Co. Apple Festival
Sara Louise Jacobs, R.N.
Susan Jaeger
Sally James
Chandra Jarboe
Charlene Jaros
Doug Jones
Mary Jones
Jean Judge
Ligita Kalnins
Ann C. Karter
Sonnie Kasch
Jan Kauffman
Janet Kelly
Amy P. Kerr
Jyl Kerr
Pat Kerth
Shan Kilian
Dorothy Kiracafe
Kitty's Restaurant, Eric
French
Mrs. Alan Klein
JoAnn Klein
Roz Klein
Pat Koenig
Sara Kosel
Katy Mahaffey Kramer

Cindy Kress
Kimberly Krug
Kristine Kunesh-Part, M.D.
Mr. & Mrs. Ken Kuntz
Sandy Laubenthal
Kim Lemmon
Charlotte G. Leonard
Lillian Lewis
Nick Lira
Julie Liss-Katz
Becky Lochner
Marijane B. Long, R.N.
Niel Lorenz
Imogene Louk
Sarah Lutton
Pam Lytle
Tom Magoto, Jr.
Mrs. George Mahfouz
Susan Malone
Cindy Marohl
Janet Marstall
Faye Martin
Mary Jo's Cuisine
Lou Mason
Marjorie McCarthy
Molly McCoy
Armonde McElligott
Kathi McKay
Ruthie Mehlberth McKee
James V. McMonagle
Marilyn McWain
Karen B. Medford
Betty Meininger
Kym Mellman
Mrs. H.C. Messenger
Middfest International
Middletown Firefighters
Suzanne Millard
Grace Miller
Terri Miller
Darrell Mindell
Cindy Minton
George Ann Mirre
Janet Moland
Carol Monnier
Donna Moon
Barbara Moore

Manja Moore
Cindy Morton
Debbie Sheridan Moss
Mamie L. Mullen
Miami Valley Hospital
Emergency & Trauma
Center Staff
Miami Valley Hospital
Nutrition Services:
Peggy Bishop
Natalie Fuller
Yolanda Jefferies
Chef Lysne
Marilyn K. Myers
Dorothy Neer
Nancy Neer
New Neighbors' League
Laverne Newton
Pat Nezi
Mrs. Frederick W. Nichols
Mrs. C.C. Norwalk
Virginia O'Connell
Mrs. Michael O'Rourke
Mary Huck Olsen
Cherie L. Orwig
Mrs. Henry Otto
Dottie Overman
Kitty Owen-Sachs
Joy Oxley
Nancy Pacenta
Caroline Palmer
Julia Palmert
Mrs. Paul Palumbo
Mary Pancoast
Cathy Patton
Peasant Stock Restaurant
Kathie Peoples
Fern Perrett
Persimmon Festival
Betty Person
Diane Phillips
Emile Pittman
Jon Pittman
Alice Plybon
Helen Poelking
Jeanne Ponziani
Dave Porter

Jane Porter
Marilyn Portune
Anna Poska
Preble County Pork Festival
Donna Price
Pam Pry
Mrs. Edward Puff
Susan W. Putnam
Dee Quinn
Carol Quinonis
Nan Rauh
Jean Redder
Ruth Reece
Liz Reiling
Lynn Reinke
Julia Rettig
Lu Ann Rhodes
Ann Rich
Sara Rich
Angie Richards
Lou Richardson
Gloria Richardson
Marianne Richter
Sandy Ricker
Chris Robertson
Alice Roedersheimer
Cindy Romano
Lois Ross
Helen Rossmiller
Marion Rothgery
Darlene Ruetschle
Karen Rundlett
Dorothea S. Rye
Mrs. Richard Sachs
Dorothy Sammons
Sauerkraut Festival
Millie Schaeffer
Kathy Schillreff
Mel Schlachter
Billi Schmidt
John Schmidt
Suzanne Schneiderman
Norman Schneiderman, M.D.

Inez Scholl
Wendy Scholl
Dee Schrimpf
Betty Schroeder
Joanne Schroll
Jane Schwartz
Mickey C. Schwartz
Debi Seibert
Betsy Sergent
Martha Shaker
Angie Shaw
Mrs. William Shelton
Stormy Sheridan
Theresa Sherow
Meridel Sherk
Celia Shulman
Ellie Shulman
Joseph Simmons
Ann Simms
Angie Smith
Grayce Smith
Joanne Smith
Mrs. Charles Smith
Linda Snyder
Mrs. Andrew Spiegel
Kathryn Spillman
Spring Valley Potato
   Festival
Frances Sroufe
Virginia Stacy
Bonnie Stalter
Georgia Stamper
Mary Beth Steinkamp
Mrs. Peter L. Stephens
Cherie Stickrath
Dorothy Stickrath
Denise Stickrath
Frances Stillwagon
Charlene Stoeckicht
Tricia Stone
Mrs. William Straughen
Fran Strawsburg
Kathy Strickler

Beth Striebel
Wanda Stumpo
Jane Sussman
Charles R. Sutton
Judy Swabby
Sweet Corn Festival
Gladys Sykes
Margarite Tang
Kitty Tangeman
Mrs. Ralph W. Tapper
Beth Taylor
Shirley Teel
Anna Lee Teets
Bonnie Temple
Dianne Tharp
Alloweese Q. Theobald
Susan Thiele
Mary Kay Thierer
Mise Thompson
Nicoletta Thompson
Susan Thompson
Debbie Thornton
Pam Timmermans
Shirley Tipton
Debbie Tompkins
Doris L. Tompkins
Dawn Treadwell
Rachel Trevethan
Gwen Troha
Troy Strawberry Festival
Truffles Cafe & Catering,
   Harriet Argue
Angela Trupp
Lois Tufts
Jewell Turner
Mary Helen Tuuri
Barbara Unruh
Evanthia Valassiades
Maria VanderKaay
Mary VanderKaay
Mildred Veneyard
Victoria Verity
Dorothy Wagner

Mr. & Mrs. Jim Wahl
Kathy Walker
Sharon Walker
Rob Wasmuth
Karen Wasmuth
Marcia Watts
Judith Weber
Bette Weinheimer
Mrs. Fred W. Weir
Janice Welty
Ann Whittridge
Ina Whitworth-Allen
Janet Wickham
Susan Wild
Sue Wildasinn
Gerald H. Wilkie
Robin E. Williams
Mrs. Jack Williams
Claire Williams
Betty Williamson
Carol Willis
Maureen Willits
Agnes M. Wilson
Anne W. Wilson
Winnie Jo Wilson
Winds Cafe
Barbara Winslow
Beverly Winslow
Gwen Winslow
Jayne Winslow
Dr. J. H. Wittoesch
Janie Wittoesch
Georgie Woessner
Eleanor Wokasien
John Wolf
Joan Wolf
Phyllis Worthman
Veda Younce
Helen Young
Mrs. Fred Young
Norma Young
Maggie Zimmer

INDEX

B

Cooks Incorporated

Miami Valley Health Foundation
31 Wyoming Street • Dayton, Ohio 45409-2753
513-220-2700

Please send ___ copies of Cooks Incorporated @ $19.95 _____
Add postage and handling (1st book) @ $3.50 _____
  (Postage and handling each additional book) @ $2.00 _____
Ohio residents add 6.5% sales tax each book @ $1.30 _____

_____ Total enclosed (Checks payable to: Miami Valley Health Foundation)
_____ Charge to Mastercard # _____ Visa # _____
Cardholder name _____ Expiration date _____
Cardholder signature _____
Name _____ Phone _____
Street _____
City/State/Zip _____

- -

Cooks Incorporated

Miami Valley Health Foundation
31 Wyoming Street • Dayton, Ohio 45409-2753
513-220-2700

Please send ___ copies of Cooks Incorporated @ $19.95 _____
Add postage and handling (1st book) @ $3.50 _____
  (Postage and handling each additional book) @ $2.00 _____
Ohio residents add 6.5 % sales tax each book @ $1.30 _____

_____ Total enclosed (Checks payable to: Miami Valley Health Foundation)
_____ Charge to Mastercard # _____ Visa # _____
Cardholder name _____ Expiration date _____
Cardholder signature _____
Name _____ Phone _____
Street _____
City/State/Zip _____